Children Reading Pictures

Children Reading Pictures: New Contexts and Approaches to Picturebooks offers up-to-date research evidence on the responses of the primary audience for picturebooks – children. The new edition has retained the best of the original while expanding its scope in several directions, including the role of the art museum in helping children and their teachers to broaden and deepen their appreciation of the visual, and the significance of understanding diversity and inclusion while looking at illustrations in picturebooks, in digital form and in the art museum. In particular, the third edition:

- uses new case studies to bring to life exciting initiatives from teachers and art museum educators in the UK and beyond, examining the potential of picturebooks for overcoming cultural, educational, linguistic and other barriers in the classroom and in other settings;
- continues to draw readers' attention to significant international theoretical work in the field and provides structured advice for teachers and graduate students who wish to carry out their own research;
- focuses on new research with pupils, teachers, art educators and researchers working on young people's responses to a variety of visual texts, including digital forms and fine art, and through children's own artistic creations, to develop a more nuanced understanding of visual literacy;
- celebrates the glorious variety of outstanding picturebooks and their makers who offer rich challenge, amusement, pleasure and consolation to young readers in a changing, often troubling world.

Children Reading Pictures is essential reading for undergraduate and postgraduate students of education, art and children's literature, as well as providing important information for primary and early years teachers, literacy coordinators and for all those interested in picturebooks and visual literacy.

Evelyn Arizpe is Professor of Children's Literature at the School of Education, University of Glasgow.

Kate Noble is a Senior Research Associate: Museum Learning at the Fitzwilliam Museum, University of Cambridge.

Morag Styles is Emeritus Professor of Children's Poetry and an Emeritus Fellow of Homerton College, Cambridge.

Children Reading Pictures
New Contexts and Approaches to Picturebooks

THIRD EDITION

Evelyn Arizpe, Kate Noble
and Morag Styles

LONDON AND NEW YORK

Designed cover image: Credit to Rose Noble for the cover image of the book

Third edition published 2023
by Routledge

4 Park Square, Milton Park, Abingdon, Oxon OX14 4RN

and by Routledge
605 Third Avenue, New York, NY 10158

Routledge is an imprint of the Taylor & Francis Group, an informa business

© 2023 Evelyn Arizpe, Kate Noble and Morag Styles

The right of Evelyn Arizpe, Kate Noble and Morag Styles to be identified as authors of this work has been asserted in accordance with sections 77 and 78 of the Copyright, Designs and Patents Act 1988.

All rights reserved. No part of this book may be reprinted or reproduced or utilised in any form or by any electronic, mechanical, or other means, now known or hereafter invented, including photocopying and recording, or in any information storage or retrieval system, without permission in writing from the publishers.

Trademark notice: Product or corporate names may be trademarks or registered trademarks, and are used only for identification and explanation without intent to infringe.

First edition published by Routledge 2002

Second edition published by Routledge 2016

British Library Cataloguing-in-Publication Data
A catalogue record for this book is available from the British Library

Library of Congress Cataloging-in-Publication Data
Names: Arizpe, Evelyn, 1965- author. | Noble, Kate, author. | Styles, Morag, author.
Title: Children reading pictures: new contexts and approaches to picturebooks / Evelyn Arizpe, Kate Noble, Morag Styles.
Other titles: Children reading picturebooks
Description: Third Edition. | New York: Routledge, 2023. | Second edition: 2016. |
Includes bibliographical references and index. |
Identifiers: LCCN 2022037637 (print) | LCCN 2022037638 (ebook) |
ISBN 9780367617431 (Hardback) | ISBN 9780367617424 (Paperback) |
ISBN 9781003106326 (eBook)
Subjects: LCSH: Visual learning. | Pictures in education. | Children—Books and reading.
Classification: LCC LB1067.5 .A75 2023 (print) |
LCC LB1067.5 (ebook) | DDC 371.33/5—dc23/eng/20220825
LC record available at https://lccn.loc.gov/2022037637
LC ebook record available at https://lccn.loc.gov/2022037638

ISBN: 9780367617431 (hbk)
ISBN: 9780367617424 (pbk)
ISBN: 9781003106326 (ebk)

DOI: 10.4324/9781003106326

Typeset in Bembo
by codeMantra

This book is dedicated to the memory of our dear friend and mentor, Margaret Meek Spencer. She was an inspirational and influential scholar, teacher and writer on all things to do with children's literature and reading. Margaret was an original theorist, an intellectual of great capacity and a person of warmth, kindness and generosity. Her students loved as well as admired her. Her willingness to take children seriously and to spend considerable time observing and talking to them in order to understand their thinking was remarkable. She was an expert on a wide range of topics within the fields of literacy and literature, but she has a special place in the hearts of those of us who specialise in picturebooks as her insights were ground-breaking and profound. Her impact on this discipline will never be forgotten.

Contents

List of figures ix
Acknowledgements xi
Notes on authors and contributors xii

Introduction: How texts teach what readers learn: Reasons for a third edition of *Children Reading Pictures* 1
MORAG STYLES

PART I
The original study on children responding to picturebooks 7

1 The original research and guidelines for emerging researchers 9
   MORAG STYLES, EVELYN ARIZPE AND KATE NOBLE

2 On a walk with Lily and Kitamura: How children link words and pictures along the way 22
   EVELYN ARIZPE

3 A gorilla with 'grandpa's eyes': How children interpret ironic visual texts – a case study of Anthony Browne's *Zoo* 37
   MORAG STYLES

4 Picturebooks and metaliteracy: Children talking about how they read pictures 50
   EVELYN ARIZPE

5 Thinking aloud: Looking at children drawing in response to picturebooks 59
   KATE NOBLE

viii *Contents*

PART II
New developments in research on children responding to visual texts   83

  6 **Young learners looking and making in the art museum and classroom**   85
     KATE NOBLE, EVELYN ARIZPE AND MORAG STYLES

  7 **Psyche, picnics and penguin: Case studies of children responding to visual texts**   98
     KATE NOBLE, MARCELA ESCOVAR, LUISA NARANJO AND
     KIM DEAKIN WITH MORAG STYLES

     Case Study 1: 'Inspire' at The Fitzwilliam Museum: Narrative Art and Storytelling – Kate Noble 98
     Case Study 2: Picnic at the MAMBO – Marcela Escovar & Luisa Naranjo 108
     Case Study 3: Danny learning more than reading from Polly Dunbar's Penguin – Kim Deakin 114

  8 **Children reading literary apps**   124
     ALINE FREDERICO

  9 **Diverse readers, diverse picturebooks, diverse responses**   136
     EVELYN ARIZPE

PART III
Research and theory for a better future   149

10 **Understanding children's responses to picturebooks through theory and research**   151
     EVELYN ARIZPE

11 **Epilogue: What children have taught us about reading pictures**   164
     MORAG STYLES, EVELYN ARIZPE AND KATE NOBLE

     Afterword: Reading is marvellous anywhere   168
     JORGE TETL ARGUETA

     Bibliography   169
     Index   183

Figures

2.1	From *Lily Takes a Walk* by Satoshi Kitamura. (Text and illustration copyright © Satoshi Kitamura, 1987, by permission of Scallywag Press Ltd., London)	26
2.2	From *Lily Takes a Walk* by Satoshi Kitamura. (Text and illustration copyright © Satoshi Kitamura, 1987, by permission of Scallywag Press Ltd., London)	26
2.3	From *Lily Takes a Walk* by Satoshi Kitamura. (Text and illustration copyright © Satoshi Kitamura, 1987, by permission of Scallywag Press Ltd., London)	27
2.4	By Charlie (9)	34
5.1	By Amy (4)	61
5.2	By Seamus (7)	61
5.3	By Will (9)	62
5.4	By Sara (4)	63
5.5	By Christina (8)	64
5.6	By Bobby (8)	65
5.7	By Ashok (4)	66
5.8	By Anne (9)	66
5.9	By Erin (7)	68
5.10	By Sally (10)	70
5.11	By Belinda (10)	71
5.12	Unsigned drawing	71
5.13	By Louis (4)	74
5.14	Drawing 1 By Jane (5)	75
5.15	Drawing 2 By Jane (5)	75
5.16	Drawing 1 By Yu (4)	77
5.17	Drawing 2 By Yu (4)	79
5.18	Drawing 3 By Yu (4)	79
6.1	A village festival in Honour of St Hubert and St Anthony by Pieter Brueghel the Younger © The Fitzwilliam Museum	86
6.2	Sharing The Gruffalo in the gallery	94
6.3, 6.4, 6.5	Drawing together in the gallery, Drawing with a friend, Drawing with pencils and string	95
7.1	Cupid and Psyche by Jacopo del Sellaio © The Fitzwilliam Museum, Cambridge	98
7.2	Detail of Psyche's dress designed and made by children from St Peter's School, Wisbech	101

x Figures

7.3	Cupid's arrows made from string, wood, denim and buttons	102
7.4	Design for Psyche's dress with idea of arrow necklace	102
7.5	Children and teachers from Linton Heights leading a public talk	103
7.6	Collaborative making with paint, leaves and pencil	104
7.7	Children entangled, arms crossed and working in tandem as they add final details and texture to mixed media collage	105
7.8	Experimenting with materials and story	105
7.9	Detail of doorway from the collaborative frieze showing the use of mixed media including paint, oil pastel, petals and grass seed	106
7.10	Detail from collaborative frieze showing the use of mixed media including paint, oil pastel, paper, seeds, lollipop sticks and cut grass	106
7.11	Detail from the collaborative frieze showing Psyche meeting Cupid and entering the palace showing the use of mixed media	107
7.12	Mixing palettes, paint brushes, and collage materials	107
7.13	"Joaquín loves Picnic, he was happy today (and he even coloured in the drawing, something which he never does)". Zully Pardo, Colombia	111
7.14	Face to face reading in the MAMBO with Joaquín (Dec 2020)	113
7.15	Joaquín examines an exhibit inside the MAMBO	113
7.16	Zully and Joaquín looking at an exhibit inside the MAMBO	114
7.17	Penguin and Ben	115
7.18	Penguin and lion	116
7.19	'And Penguin said…'	117
7.20	Danny's response to Ben's tantrum	117
7.21	Danny puts himself in the story	118
7.22	Lion licks his lips after eating Danny!	119
7.23	Danny's drawing of himself and Penguin	120
7.24	Lion eat Danny	120
7.25	Danny with Lion	121
7.26	Danny bites Lion's nose	122
8.1	Vignette 1 — Part 1 of the scene – reading the instructions	130
8.2	Vignette 2 — First call from Monkey	130
8.3	Vignette 3 — Third call from Monkey and the end of the scene	132

Acknowledgements

The authors wish to thank Polly Dunbar and Walker Books for generously allowing us to reproduce a number of pages from *Penguin*, including those with Danny Wilkinson's drawn and written responses to the book. Copyright 2007 Polly Dunbar, reproduced by permission of Walker Books Ltd, London SE115HJ www.walker.co.uk. The authors are also grateful to the following for permission to reproduce material: illustrations and text from *Lily Takes a Walk* by Satoshi Kitamura, reprinted by permission of Scallywag Press Ltd., London. We are grateful to Marcela Escovar, Kim Deakin and Luisa Naranjo for their contributions to this book. Special thanks are due to Aline Frederico for Chapter 8, Jorge Argueta for his Afterword and Rose Noble for her drawing for the front cover. We would also like to thank Katja Schreiber for the excellent work she did in proofreading and compiling the Bibliography. Finally, we are indebted to our editors at Routledge for commissioning this third edition and for all their careful work on our book.

Notes on authors and contributors

Evelyn Arizpe is Professor of Children's Literature at the School of Education, University of Glasgow, and is co-founder of the Erasmus Mundus Joint Master's Degree programme, 'Children's Literature, Media and Culture'. She has taught and published widely both nationally and internationally and has co-authored *Children Reading Picturebooks: Interpreting visual texts* (2003/2016) and *Visual Journeys through Wordless Narratives* (2014). She has also co-edited *Children as Readers in Children's Literature: The power of text and the importance of reading* (2016) and *Young people reading: Empirical research across international contexts* (2018). Her current research involves children's literature and the arts in projects on migration, conflict and peacebuilding. Evelyn is a judge for the Han C Andersen Award for 2022 and 2024.

Kate Noble is a Senior Research Associate: Museum Learning at the Fitzwilliam Museum, University of Cambridge, where she leads a teacher training programme which encourages creative teaching and learning using objects and images. Her research interests include visual literacy, young children in museums and participatory research which she has been exploring through a number of museum residencies. Kate worked as a Primary and Early Childhood Teacher before moving into museum education. Her PhD explored the development of visual literacy in young children, and she has contributed articles to the European Early Childhood Education Research Journal, the *International Journal of Art and Design Education* and chapters to *Working with Young Children in Museums: Weaving Theory and Practice* (Hackett et al. 2020), *Talking Beyond the Page: Reading and Responding to Picturebooks* (Evans, 2009) and *Teaching Through Texts* (Anderson and Styles, 2001). She also worked as a Researcher for Tate's Young Cultural Creators Project, and more recently she has led research and evaluation projects on behalf of the National Gallery, London and University of Cambridge Museums. Kate sits on the council for the National Society for Education in Art and Design (NSEAD).

Morag Styles is Emeritus Professor of Children's Poetry and an Emeritus Fellow of Homerton College, Cambridge. She has taught and published widely, including *From the Garden to the Street: 300 Years of Poetry for Children* (1998), and is co-author with Evelyn Arizpe of 2 editions of *Children Reading Picturebooks: Interpreting Visual Texts* (2003, 2016) and *Reading Lessons from the Eighteenth Century: Mothers, Children & Texts* (2006). She is a co-author with Martin Salisbury of 2 editions of *Children's Picturebooks: The Art of Visual Storytelling* (2012, 2020). She was Director of the Caribbean Poetry Project, a collaboration between Cambridge Faculty of Education and The University of the West Indies (2010–15), and she co-edited *Teaching Caribbean Poetry* (2013) with Beverley Bryan. She co-curated an exhibition for the Fitzwilliam Museum on children's picturebooks (2000), and the British Library with Michael Rosen on the history of children's poetry (2009). Morag is a judge for the BolognaRagazzi Award for Poetry and Illustration 2021 and 2022. She is currently finishing a childhood memoir set in Scotland and India.

Jorge Tetl Argueta is an award-winning Salvadoran Poet and Writer of highly acclaimed bilingual children's books, short stories and poems. A native Salvadoran and Pipil Nahua Indian, he spent much of his childhood in rural El Salvador. His children's books are written in poetry form in English and Spanish and reflect the Latino experience and heritage, as well as the immigrant experience; he also writes about the Nahuatl Indians and their deep appreciation and respect for nature. Jorge has spent over 15 years as a Workshop and Classroom Presenter, speaking about the power of poetry in children's lives.

Kim Deakin gained an MEd from Cambridge University in 2014, when she was Literacy Coordinator at Richmond Hill Special School in Luton. Her Headteacher, Jill Miller, encouraged her to work in the creative way that is evident in her contribution to Chapter 7. Kim has since retired and moved to Somerset.

Marcela Escovar studied literature at Los Andes University, and has an MEd in Education and Children's Literature and Literacies from the University of Glasgow. She has worked as an Editor, Writer, Reader, Creator of digital content and Cultural Manager. She is the Director of the reading project, *Picnic de Palabras*, from where she facilitates reading experiences for families around picturebooks in unconventional spaces. This project has been replicated in more than 10 countries and 20 cities around the world. In 2020, in alliance with the Bogotá Art Museum, they carried out the project *Picnic en el Mambo*. Currently, she is an Advisor and works as a Literature Coordinator in the government of Cundinamarca in Colombia.

Aline Frederico (@aline_frederico) is an Adjunct Professor at the School of Communication of the Federal University of Rio de Janeiro, Brazil. She obtained her PhD in children's literature and education from the University of Cambridge with the thesis *Embodiment and Agency in Digital Reading: Preschoolers Making Meaning with Literary Apps*. Her research focuses on digital literature for children and works at the intersection of children's literature, digital literature and media, multimodality and education. Since she returned to Brazil, she coordinated the research project *Read for a Child –Digital Bookshelf* for the Itaú Social Foundation (Brazil), which promotes quality digital literary reading for children, and published guidelines for the selection and mediation of children's digital literature; she also collaborated with the Unesco Chair in Reading (PUC-Rio) in the research project *Brazil who Reads*, which mapped reading promotion initiatives across the country. Aline is an Editorial Assistant for the journal *International Research in Children's Literature* and a Jury Member for the awards Selo Cátedra 10 for Brazilian children's literature and ComKids Interactive – Digital Books for Iberoamerican digital media for children. For further information, please check www.alinefrederico.com.

Luisa Naranjo studied politics at the University of the Andes along with history and theory of art. She worked for six years in the public sector in the Minister's Office and the Directorate of Arts and Crafts of Colombia within the Ministry of Culture. From 2010 to 2020, she was a Researcher in cultural and gastronomic themes. Currently, she has completed a course of studies in Education and she is Subdirector of the Modern Art Museum of Bogota.

Introduction

How texts teach what readers learn: Reasons for a third edition of *Children Reading Pictures*

Morag Styles

The Introduction draws on Margaret Meek Spencer's influential *How Texts Teach What Readers Learn* (1998) in showing how challenging picturebooks teach young readers how 'to derive true meaning from pictures', a quote by Anthony Browne from the first edition of *Children Reading Pictures* (2003). He believes this to be innate ability of children though we also emphasise how important it is to nurture that skill. The current educational climate in the UK (and most other countries) is focused on a narrow range of skills where reading for pleasure and visual literacy take a back seat. One of the reasons for a new edition is to give space to how the art museum has stepped into the breach and to consider work they have been doing with children and teachers to promote art education and appreciation. It also provided the opportunity to foreground diversity and inclusion and to take a more international view of children responding to picturebooks. Their popularity during the recent pandemic and the role picturebooks play in making young readers aware of environmental issues has also been highlighted.

Beginnings

Anthony Browne had this to say in his afterword to the first edition of *Children Reading Picturebooks*:

> When I first read *Children Reading Pictures* I found it intensely moving. I was deeply touched by the children's response to *Zoo* and *The Tunnel*, and equally impressed by the gentle and subtle questions of the interviewers. The children's sophisticated reactions didn't surprise me as I've known for some time how we often undervalue the abilities of children to see and understand. They were able to pick up on themes and ideas that I hadn't expressed in the text, only in the pictures, and proved wonderful readers of visual metaphors. *This book, I think, proves beyond doubt children's innate ability to derive true meaning from pictures.*
>
> (our emphasis)

It is more than twenty years since Evelyn Arizpe and Morag Styles started work on *Children Reading Pictures*. If we were going to realise our aim of finding out how children responded to picturebooks, we needed to work with a large enough cohort to make our findings viable. This required working with a group of researchers and several colleagues immediately came to mind: Kathy Coulthard, then Adviser for ethnic minority achievement in Enfield; the late Helen Bromley (to whom the second edition is dedicated) was a tutor for the Centre for Language in Primary Education; and Kate

Noble, a local infant teacher, who had gained a first class degree at Homerton College, Cambridge in Art and Education and shown herself to be an outstanding student on our undergraduate course, Children and Literature. What a team and how excited we were in 1999 to be on the threshold of investigating what happens when children read picturebooks.

What the children had to say about picturebooks

Our inspiration came from the many wonderful picturebook authors and illustrators we admired and from two main scholarly sources at that point – Louise Rosenblatt's work on meaning being created in the transaction between the text and what the reader brings to it at the moment of reading (Rosenblatt 1978); and Margaret Meek Spencer's *How Texts Teach What Readers Learn* (1988). This small pamphlet-size volume with huge ambition, whose title is explanatory, took the education world by storm, and her ideas have influenced teachers, researchers and academics ever since. Drawing on Rosenblatt, Meek's focus was both on how the reader interacted with the visual and verbal text and how the perfect alchemy was achieved by gifted illustrators creating picturebooks that all but taught children how to read these challenging texts. Margaret Meek died in 2020 and we have dedicated this volume to her seminal work on children's reading, literature and visual literacy.

Despite the popularity of picturebooks and the growing scholarly interest in the topic, little attention had been given to what children could tell us about how they read, understood and valued picturebooks. To find this out we recorded one to one interviews with a cohort of about a hundred children, held discussions with interviewees and invited them to draw in response to the picturebooks.[1] As for the books themselves, we had to find examples which would appeal to children aged 4–11 as the whole primary age range was our scope. We are enormously grateful to Anthony Browne and Satoshi Kitamura for not only allowing us to use their books at the heart of the research project but for taking an interest in the outcomes from the children and being interviewed for the first edition. 'Making complex ideas simple' was the subtitle of a recent article about Satoshi Kitamura's picturebooks (Kosaka 2020); this would equally apply to Anthony Browne's work. However, this quote does not begin to cover the fervent devotion and sheer delight we witnessed in young readers' responses to their books.

The popularity of picturebooks

In the second edition, we were grateful for the generosity of Polly Dunbar and Walker Books for allowing us to use many pages from *Penguin* free of charge, and to Danny Wilkinson, his parents and school for giving us permission to use his inspiring drawn and verbal responses to *Penguin*. We were honoured that the distinguished scholar, Margaret Mackey, agreed to write a chapter on the then burgeoning digital revolution. At that point there was widespread anxiety about the death of the book, including the threat of picturebook apps to printed material. That concern now seems less pressing from the vantage point of 2022, where picturebook sales have increased rather than declined and we can now also look back on how picturebooks were widely used and celebrated during the coronavirus lockdowns. We also wanted to take a fresh look at how the digital revolution with its slick electronic gadgets impacted on picturebooks, both positively and negatively. For this edition, drawing on Margaret's valuable insights about picturebook apps, Aline Frederico has conducted her own case study and updated research in this area.

Another set of people we need to thank for their contributions to all the editions of *Children Reading Pictures* are our students, not only those featured in our books, but masters and doctoral students in Glasgow and Cambridge who have taught us such a lot about visual literacy. And we offer a huge vote of thanks to all the teachers sharing picturebooks with the children we have studied over the years, and to those who have written to us with words of encouragement from many parts of the world, including a large number from Latin America as there is a Spanish edition of our book.

A new focus for third edition

Having produced a second edition in 2016, why should we want to do another only five years later? First of all, Evelyn and Morag have found that in all the books they have written or edited, separately or together, this is the volume that has received the most affection and approval from its readers. Indeed, that is one of the reasons why Routledge invited us to submit a proposal for a further edition. (This is a good moment to thank Alison Foyle and successive editors of the Taylor & Francis group for their belief in us and in the book.) Evelyn's recent work on diversity in general, and refugees in particular, and its topicality today, made us aware that these were issues we wanted to focus on and bring up to date in our new edition which is also more international in perspective than the others.

Another important reason for an update was that primary education in UK and beyond had been changing with increasing focus on a narrow range of skills which has led to a climate where there was less space, time and value given to literature and art education. Despite living in a world dominated by image, successive governments have pursued a reading curriculum dominated by the teaching of phonics and an art curriculum squeezed to the margins. Now is the time more than ever to explore how visual texts teach what it is that readers and viewers learn. This is why we got in touch with Kate Noble who had written a fine-grained doctorate on children talking and drawing in response to picturebooks after contributing to the first edition. What we learned from children *drawing* in response to the picturebooks they were reading had been one of the most exciting outcomes of the first edition and, as an art educator, Kate had led our thinking at the time.

Since then art museum education has taken off, partly to fill the gaps in the school curriculum, but also in developing creative projects to extend children's appreciation of art and to encourage their own art and craft making. Interestingly, for some time there has been a large crop of picturebooks whose subject matter is museums and art galleries. Many readers will be familiar with the popular Katie picturebooks, set in an art gallery, by James Mayhew. Other illustrators make reference to particular artists in stories likely to appeal to young children – from *Babar's Museum of Art* and *Linnea in Monet's Garden* to Scieszka and Smith's *Seen Art?* and Anthony Browne's frequent references to paintings in many of his picturebooks, especially *Willy's Pictures* and *The Shape Game*.

Now that Kate Noble is an experienced art museum educator and researcher, working primarily at the Fitzwilliam Museum, Cambridge, but also on special projects with the National Gallery and Tate Modern in London, she seemed the perfect person to expand the scope of our book to include new approaches in art museum education with particular reference to children's responses to reading paintings. We are very pleased she accepted our invitation to become a co-author of this edition.

What the future holds

The world has changed enormously since we began to research how children responded to challenging picturebooks. The digital revolution with its instant communication, access to information and photographic sophistication, contained within a small hand-held device, has transformed most people's lives – and children are adept at accessing its potential. The enormous challenges faced by all nations, such as climate change, loss of bird and animal species and habitats, the extremes of weather, rising sea levels and heating up of the planet is likely to exacerbate the refugee crisis which is already perilous. And it is our children who have this uncertain future to face. More than ever they need a first class educational system which offers emotional engagement, intellectual challenge, opportunities for discussion, new ways of thinking, aesthetic appreciation and the drive to communicate, all things which challenging picturebooks offer even the youngest reader.

We have been experiencing a world-wide pandemic which has killed millions of people, made economies slump, led to long months of shut-down and the need to isolate. But through these painful times, there have also been positive signs of hope, growth and change. One is a renewal in our appreciation of the natural world; another is the realisation of the importance of the arts in our lives. We have applauded the creative ways artistic institutions have opened up their treasures to a wide audience, and how musicians, actors, dancers, singers have found inventive ways to work together and reach audiences.

Although the picturebook market in the UK and other countries was buoyant pre-pandemic, sales of children's books have fallen over the last 18 months. However, in this same period picturebooks have continued to be published and translated with independent publishers flourishing, such as Tiny Owl and Book Island in the UK, Ekaré in Latinamerica and Spain, and Tulika Books and Pratham Books in India.

More optimistically, David Shelley,[2] the CEO of Hachette (the second largest trade publisher), wrote about the state of the publishing market in December 2021. He reminded those in the publishing industry that 'reading experienced a boom whenever the country locked down' and this was especially true of picturebooks among other genres. He also noted the vital role of independent bookshops and the recent rise in their sales, the fact that issues of diversity and inclusion were now high profile, and that Hachette national offices had moved out of London to Manchester, Sheffield, Newcastle, Bristol and Edinburgh. In keeping with the emphasis on environmental issues, they have employed climate change consultants and were committed to 'science based targets for reducing carbon emissions.'

How this edition works

We have divided this edition into three sections. The first will be familiar to readers of earlier editions as we concentrate on what was most significant in our original research and offer guidance for new researchers in this field.

The middle section is longest and fullest, focusing on new developments in children's responses to visual texts. Here we open with a chapter devoted to research on visual literacy, what we are learning from approaches to reading pictures in the art museum, and where picturebooks fit in. This is followed by two new case studies, one of which is situated in the Museum of Modern Art in Bogota (MAMBO) where reading and art feature strongly and where contacts between illustrators and young readers are explored. The other features an exciting project developed at the Fitzwilliam Museum, Cambridge, with dozens of schools taking part. It shows rich results after children both learn how to look at and interpret a classical painting and are given the opportunity to engage in connected art and craft work. We have also retained the engaging case study of a young autistic person's powerful reactions to *Penguin* and Kim Deacon's sensitive interpretation and documentation of his comments and actions. New for this edition, and a chapter on its own, is Aline Frederico's case study of a child and her mother responding to a picturebook or 'literary' app. It also includes an update of research in this area. The section concludes with an extensive examination of diversity and inclusion in picturebook research, a field that has become highly sensitive and is rapidly changing.

The final section of the book is the shortest but it includes a wide-ranging update of research evidence on children's responses to picturebooks. We conclude with an upbeat appraisal of what children learn from picturebooks, fiction and non-fiction alike, as well as art, design, paintings and all kinds of visual literature. We see huge value in children as artists and makers, using paintings and picturebooks as inspiration. We look more closely at the outcomes of the Power of Picturebooks evidence (CLPE 2021) about how drawing and working with picturebooks both enhances children's reading and writing skills, as well as considering the role they play in developing empathy, knowledge and understanding. We consider the many different contexts for children engaging with picturebooks which include the classroom, after-school club programmes, libraries and the art museum, but also, as our studies show, homes, parks, hospitals, even refugee camps. The fact that 'reading can be marvellous anywhere' is beautifully illustrated in words by Salvadorean poet, Jorge Tetl Argueta, who kindly provided us with the 'Afterword'.

This third edition sums up what children have taught us after 20+ years of studying their responses and make the case that in a divided world, picturebooks bring us closer together because they afford 'more equal access to the world of story' and 'deeper levels of meaning through the interpretation of both word and image and the space between' (2003: 189), just as Kathy Couthard showed us in the first edition.

Notes

1. A detailed account of the way the original research design was conducted and justifications for it is included in the first and second editions of this book.
2. Letter from Sarah Gravestock, on behalf of David Shelley CEO Hachette, to authors, illustrators, translators and editors (6 December 2021).

Part I

The original study on children responding to picturebooks

1 The original research and guidelines for emerging researchers

Morag Styles, Evelyn Arizpe and Kate Noble

In the following quote, the art critic, Ernst Gombrich, draws our attention to the 'inquiring mind' that is required to understand and analyse the visual world:

> To read the artist's picture is to mobilise our memories and our experience of the visible world and to test [his/sic] image through tentative projections [...] It is not the 'innocent eye', however, that can achieve this match but only the inquiring mind that knows how to probe the ambiguities of vision.
>
> (Gombrich 1962: 264)

This book attempts to show that very young children have inquiring minds and that picturebooks are vehicles that can indeed 'probe the ambiguities of vision'. In this chapter, as well as re-presenting the most significant outcomes of our original research, we offer suggestions and guidance with new researchers, teachers and higher degree students in mind.

The aims of the original study

The principal aim of our original research was to investigate how multimodal texts were interpreted by children, to explore the potential of visual literacy and to find out more about the skills children needed to deal with visual texts. Some of the questions we set ourselves had not been asked before of readers aged 4–11. When confronted with complex picturebooks, how did children make sense of the narrative? What were the specific skills that young readers brought to interpreting visual texts? How did they perceive the relationship between words and images? How could they best articulate their responses? Did the reading background of the children affect their viewing? What part did visual texts such as films and other media play in their ability to analyse pictures? What did children's own drawings reveal about their perception of a picturebook? What did complex picturebooks teach them about looking? How did talking about a book in depth, with their peers and with adults, affect their responses? What was the relationship between thinking and seeing?

Research design

Our research design was based on the conclusions of a pilot study during which our research instruments were refined. The basic structure was as follows: we worked in seven primary schools serving varied catchment areas, interviewing two boys and two girls

DOI: 10.4324/9781003106326-3

per class from three different classes per school, one of which was early years (4–6), one lower primary (7–9) and one upper primary (9–11). This meant we worked closely with 12 children of varying ages in each school, usually requiring three whole-day visits as well as preliminary conferences with teachers. We also identified two further children from each age group in case of illness; these children were not interviewed but they were invited to take part in semi-structured group discussions. We used three picturebooks overall but only one with any given group of children.

The picturebooks

We spent some time trialling a range of picturebooks by contemporary illustrators to find examples of multi-layered texts which should appeal equally to children aged 4–11; this proved no easy task. However multi-layered and inviting the picturebook, so many were discarded as they simply would not straddle the wide age group. In the end, we settled on *Zoo* and *The Tunnel* by Anthony Browne and *Lily Takes a Walk* by Satoshi Kitamura,[1] all highly rated examples of picturebook art with an appeal to both younger and older children according to our pilot study and ideal for in-depth discussion. Each picturebook was to be used in at least two schools to allow for comparison: *The Tunnel* was read in three of the seven schools; *Lily* and *Zoo* were each read in two schools. Both artists were interviewed at length and were supportive of the project.[2]

The schools

Seven primary schools participated in the research, ranging from multi-ethnic and economically disadvantaged settings in north London to a suburban school in Essex. The schools were chosen to include those with differing intakes in terms of social class, though we did not systematically control for these variables, confining ourselves to collecting data on the proportion of pupils having free school meals.

All of the schools were to some extent multi-ethnic and multilingual, with the exception of School D in the south-east of England, where the pupils were predominantly white, monolingual speakers of English. This was in contrast to the London schools, where a whole spread of ethnic groups could be found, including a large percentage of refugees from the African and Asian subcontinents. Of the three schools in Cambridge, around 20% of the pupils spoke more than one language.

The children

The interview sample was constructed in order to produce an equal representation of boys and girls and to include children from diverse class and ethnic backgrounds. In addition, the class teacher's estimate of the reading ability of each child was obtained, providing a useful point of comparison when assessing children's ability to read pictures. Researchers had no knowledge of these reading abilities until *after* the interviews took place, though we had asked teachers to select two experienced and two relatively inexperienced readers. In the event, teachers took a fair bit of licence with our requests, including children who were fairly average readers and often selecting 'interesting' children whom they thought the experience would be good for. Overall, we had a sample of children from 4 to 11 years old with a wide range of abilities, responding to the same questions based on the picturebook used in their school.

Approximately 35% of the interviewed children were bilingual with varying linguistic backgrounds, from two pupils who had recently arrived in the UK with little knowledge of English to third-generation bilinguals.[3] Where necessary, interviews were conducted with a translator. A few children had slight learning difficulties associated with moderate dyslexia, autism and hyperactivity, but these were not found to interfere with their responses. Despite some shyness at the beginning of the interviews, and once they were assured this was not a test, most children were eager to participate, to answer the interviewer's questions and to draw, and by the time of the group discussion were almost always completely involved in the picturebook. When roughly one-third of the sample were re-interviewed a few months later, they remembered the initial interviews and could recall many details of the books even though most had not seen them for some time. We have changed the names of all the children in the study, the pseudonyms taking account of ethnicity.

In order to provide a context against which to set our results, we used a short questionnaire to find out about the reading habits of the 486 pupils (aged 4–11) in the seven schools that participated in the study. All told, the list of picturebooks mentioned by children was quite limited and seven seemed to be the peak age for reading them, with more girls than boys mentioning this genre. The data from the questionnaire suggested that most of the children's contact with images had occurred through media texts rather than through books. It would be interesting to see what differences would emerge if we applied a similar questionnaire now.

The interviews

In-depth semi-structured interviews were conducted with 84 children, 21 of whom were followed up in a second interview several months later. An interview schedule was closely followed, normally 45 minutes long, with about ten questions common to all, and a further ten which were book specific.

Before the individual interviews, we asked the class teacher to read our chosen picturebook and show the illustrations to the class as a whole, while we observed. The teachers had pointed out the students we would be interviewing in advance, so it gave us a chance to watch them responding to a picturebook before we actually met them.

The interviews began by asking each child about the appeal of the cover and how it showed what the picturebook might be about (later in the interviews we asked if, in retrospect, the covers were right for the books). We then read the book through, stopping whenever a child wanted to explore a picture in detail. Next, we read through the picturebook again, allowing the children to look more closely at the pictures if they wished, and asked them to tell us about each page or double spread that we had selected to focus on in turn, using both specific and open-ended questions. We also invited them to show us their favourite pictures, to tell us how they 'read' the pictures and to talk about the relationship between words and pictures. We questioned them about the actions, expressions and feelings of the characters; the intratextual and intertextual elements (without using big words); what illustrators needed to know in order to draw, and the ways in which they used colour, body language and perspective, etc. In addition, we took research notes that included references to the children's body language (pointing, gazing, tone of voice, use of hand, facial expressions) while reading the books. All the sessions were taped and transcribed.

Group discussions

After the individual interviews, the children participated in a group discussion with the other members of their class who had been interviewed, plus the two extra children who had been identified by the teacher in case of the absence of interviewees. In total, 126 pupils were involved in these discussions, which lasted up to an hour and which were normally conducted later in the same day. During these discussions, the researchers were free to review interesting issues that had come up in the interviews, open up new areas for debate, including those chosen by children, and give those who had not been interviewed a chance to grapple with the book.

Revisiting

Preliminary findings indicated that repeated readings of a picturebook could be an important element in pupils constructing meaning, so we were interested to find out whether significant changes in interpretation had occurred sometime after the initial research. Accordingly, we decided to carry out follow-up interviews three to six months after the initial interviews with roughly one-fifth of our original sample, i.e., one child from each class. The children were chosen to represent a range of responses to the first interviews – from children who had been outstandingly articulate or passionate about the book the first time round, to those who had barely been willing to participate, from children with specific learning difficulties to those who were described by their teachers as more or less average readers. In the revisiting, the emphasis of the questions changed from a detailed examination of individual pages to a consideration of the book as a whole.

Having selected a mixture of children, we set about asking questions which were more demanding than the first time round and which focused on the book as a whole and the artist's likely intentions. For example:

- What goes on in your head as you look at pictures?
- How do you think the artist decides what to write as words and what to draw as pictures?
- Tell me about the way Satoshi Kitamura draws lines.
- How do the endpapers of *The Tunnel* take you into the story?
- What do you think Anthony Browne might be trying to tell us about the differences between humans and animals in *Zoo*?

We also repeated a few of the original questions which the children had found challenging initially and asked for new drawings in response to the text. Our first impression was that although the children returned to the books eagerly enough and remembered a great deal about their earlier encounters with them, there was little evidence of any major new thinking. However, after we scrutinised the transcripts we became aware of small, subtle developments. Amy (now 5), for example, pounced on *Zoo*, declaring: 'I just noticed a funny difference I never noticed before… the colour helps you to find the differences between the animals and the humans'. Her statement about the mother was more clear-cut than before: 'Mum is sad and she thinks the animals should be going free'. She also told us that, 'I imagine the pictures. I see them with my brain', while Yu (4) concluded that, 'I think of pictures when I go somewhere else'.

Erin's (7) thoughtful interpretation on the first visit was again evident in the re-interview. Her summing-up of *Zoo* as a whole showed her usual insight: 'Humans change into animals to learn how it feels; animals look a bit like humans so they know what it's like to be free'. She liked Browne's work because 'it makes you keep thinking about things'. Perhaps most noteworthy was Erin's different style of drawing. Her first picture is spontaneous, attractive and expressive, full of the experimentation she enjoyed in Browne's work; five months later, she seems to have entered the phase which Davis (1993) calls 'literal translation' and she is now more concerned with naturalism and a sense of morality, so evident in the drawings of the older pupils. In all cases, the children went a little further in their understanding of the picturebooks.

The evidence for the points we have been making in this chapter about the often remarkable ability of children to interpret challenging picturebooks with great insight can be found in Chapters 2–8 to follow.

Children drawing in response to picturebooks

It was purely by chance that children drawing in response to picturebooks became such a major part of our study. We had noticed in our previous forays with children younger than seven that their powerful physical, emotional and social responses to picturebooks were not always borne out in what the children had to say about the books when asked direct questions. In other words, and as plenty of research has shown, young children cannot always articulate their ideas and feelings – but they *can* often show their meaning-making through their own artistic creations. We wanted to get as close as we could to understanding what the younger children in our study were thinking, so we decided to ask all the participants to draw in response to the book we had examined. The purpose of the drawing was to access some of the knowledge that might not have been verbally articulated during the interviews.[4] The researchers provided materials when necessary and the pupils were allowed time to draw, either while others were being interviewed or later in the day. Some of these drawings are analysed in Chapter 5.

Data analysis

The amount of data generated from the interviews and discussions was considerable and required many careful readings.[5] The transcripts from the initial and the follow-up interviews were analysed qualitatively, partially employing a Grounded Theory approach (Glaser and Strauss 1967; Strauss 1987), but also using codes derived from previous studies on response to text (for example, Thomson 1987). We also took into account the data analysis carried out by two of the most systematic studies on response to picturebooks to date – Kiefer (1993) and Madura (1998). Kiefer developed categories and subcategories of response according to four of Halliday's functions of language: informative, heuristic, imaginative and personal. Madura took Kiefer's framework into account but grouped responses to the particular books she used into three main categories: descriptive, interpretive and the identification of thematic trends.[6]

Although we found these categories useful, both as analytical tools and as a means of corroborating our findings, *the most useful codes were developed from our own data, which were successively modified through further analysis*. In order to facilitate this analysis, the oral response was divided into two groups – although it was clear that these groups were closely linked. We identified one group as 'categories of perception' because the responses were based on codes derived from what the children took from the picturebook, such as the noticing of significant details, intra- and intertextual references or the relationship between the text and the image. Responses in the second group, 'levels of interpretation', corresponded to the way in which the children made sense of these picturebook codes, for example, giving the interviewer literal, implausible or plausible explanations, interrogating or evaluating the texts and/or images. This initial categorisation served as a framework for organising the data. Once this was achieved, researchers took the analysis in different directions, for example, looking more closely at the response to visual features, ethical and moral issues, the interaction between written text and image (depending on the picturebook in question) or concentrating on the linguistic and cultural context of readers.

Implications for research and pedagogy

In what follows, we summarise some of the main findings from our original research as well as adding those from the last 20 or so years that have confirmed and supplemented these initial findings. We also provide some guidelines for those who want to carry out research on response to picturebooks, based on extensive experience with our own further studies and those of other researchers. Finally, we review the methodologies that guided our original research and are still widely used, referring briefly to implications for pedagogy and further research.

Summary of findings

In this section, we attempt to provide a concise picture of the evidence that supports the importance of children reading and responding to picturebooks. We start with a list of the most salient findings from our original study:

- Children as young as four were very good at analysing the visual features of texts.
- Most children were deeply engaged by the texts and keen to discuss the moral, social, spiritual and environmental issues they raised.
- Analysing visual text, and the relationship between words and images, made demands on higher-order reading skills (inference, viewpoint, etc.).
- There was no clear correlation between reading ability (as identified by the class teacher) and the ability to analyse visual texts.
- As well as learning through looking, we had clear evidence of children learning through talking, and the importance of enabling questions was underlined.
- There were many similarities between the responses of children in schools with completely different catchment areas.
- The younger children's drawings often showed understandings they were unable to articulate.
- While we were aware of the development in children's ability to interpret visual texts, the trajectory by age was not always clear-cut.

Our findings confirmed our original belief that careful looking and constructive dialogue enables children (including those who are very young or do not speak English fluently or do not read print confidently) to make worthwhile judgements about pictures which were often profound, complex and richly interconnected with other ideas or symbolic systems.

The children in our study learned effectively because they found the activity they engaged in to be worthwhile. Children can become more visually literate and operate at a much higher level if they are taught how to look, confirming Avgerinou and Ericson's argument that 'higher order visual literacy skills do not develop unless they are identified and "taught"' (1997: 280).

While recording the research sessions on video makes it easier to view the children's body language and physical gestures, there are ethical implications which need to be addressed in any data-gathering activity and relevant permissions must be sought.

We realised that we had been asking a lot of children under six and would recommend working for shorter periods with this age group and, if possible, working with younger children in pairs.

Five years after the publication of the first edition of *Children Reading Pictures*, we carried out a review of research on response to multimodal texts, discovering that most of our findings were now supported by the work of others (Arizpe and Styles 2008). We think it is worth reminding our readers about these similarities despite the differences in terms of texts, population and methodologies. Once again, the first thing to come through for many researchers was the excitement and pleasure shown by children engaging with picturebooks and the emotional bonds forged with the texts. Some of the other findings we highlight again here as they stress the importance of:

- using well-crafted picturebooks that have the potential to "teach" readers both literary and literacy skills;
- using picturebooks which engage readers deeply, leading to critical thinking and meaningful learning;
- taking time to look closely at images and do re-readings;
- valuing the intertextual knowledge and visual literacy practices that children bring to their meaning-making from outside the school context;
- providing meta-language to discuss the visual features of picturebooks as well as some reference to how pictures and words interact;
- asking about and discussing cultural references in picturebooks;
- considering the role of the mediator in the interaction between children and picturebooks;
- encouraging in-depth interpretation and understanding through talk and collaborative discussion.

Carrying out a well-crafted study

Since our original research, we worked at our respective universities with numerous students and classroom teachers who were eager to learn more about how children interpret picturebooks by setting up their own research studies, often based on our model but with much smaller numbers. We are now, therefore, very aware not only of the benefits of such research but also some of the pitfalls to which we alert readers in this chapter, especially those new to this type of research. We can also assert with confidence that a well-crafted research design linked to a well-chosen picturebook, an open mind, careful observation and the ability to listen to what the children have to say is likely to lead to worthwhile results. This applies not only to research in schools but also to research in other nonformal educational contexts.

Before we consider some pointers for a successful study, it is important to emphasise that research should take proper account of the aesthetic qualities of a picturebook. As Nodelman argues, it is fundamental to think about what the work is for and what it might accomplish (2010: 18), and we would add that simply recording the 'interesting' things that children say, without having a strong theoretical framework to carry out in-depth analysis, does little to contribute to understanding.

In all cases, issues of ethics regarding the reader must be considered as well as the crucial role of the researcher in this process and the specifics of the context and the participants. Efforts should be made to avoid the pitfall of overgeneralisation from limited data noted by Nodelman. This can lead to the neglect of the picturebook itself, or to a contrived context or to research that fails to fully incorporate the children's voices. Finally, as Nodelman adds, it is important that the researcher be aware of the 'unspoken and taken-for-granted assumptions about both children and literature' and engage in 'self-critical thinking' which has 'the best chance of producing knowledge that is, if not generalisable, nevertheless usefully shareable' (2010: 17–18). What follows should be most useful for new researchers, such as students engaged in empirical research as part of teacher education or higher degrees, or classroom teachers wanting to explore visual literacy within their own classrooms.

The picturebooks

1 *Choosing a picturebook that has the potential for rich exploration is essential.* Given the increasing number of picturebooks on offer, we recommend careful consideration and documenting of the decision-making processes behind the selection of the picturebooks used in research. This may include self-reflection on the researcher's positionality and stance regarding beliefs and values about certain topics. McAdam et al. (2020) note that three key elements tend to influence picturebook selection: "personal affective responses, an appreciation of the book as an aesthetic object (content and form), and expectations of the ways in which children would respond as readers/viewers of the book" (4). The selection process can be strengthened by discussing potential choices with others who have knowledge of the context in which they will be used (e.g., the classroom teacher). The selection will depend on the research aims but those that are multi-layered or display interesting tensions between words and images or have thought-provoking postmodern features or are aesthetically challenging often work best. Those fairly new to the appreciation of visual literacy often take some time to see the potential of picturebooks and they may need solid support and several good examples in order to choose well for themselves and the participants.

2 Having selected *a suitable picturebook*, the next requirement is *to analyse it insightfully* and to do so they would be wise to engage in critical reading by more experienced researchers. McAdam et al. (2020) recommend using a 'Critical content analysis' framework (Johnson et al. 2019) paying attention to the role of both the verbal and the visual text to ensure the texts are inclusive and any minority group representations are positive. Sharing plans with others, if possible, including a researcher with experience of working in this area. Analysing the key elements of the picturebook

intended for use with children is recommended before the full research design is attempted. Potential researchers need to be clear about their focus and what they want to find out from the children.

3. The next issue to be grappled with is *deciding on a focus likely to be of interest to the age group concerned*, as no researcher would ever be able to probe all the possibilities in a picturebook. Once this has been determined, then decisions need to be made about which pages or spreads offer the most potential. In our experience, new researchers begin by being too ambitious and have to learn to be more realistic about what can be managed in a limited timescale.

Eliciting response

Our experience shows that where interviews take place, and how they are set up, can make a huge difference. Researchers need to consider important details such as where the interviewer and interviewee sit, whether to share a book with a child or have one each, as well as avoiding noisy and distracting classrooms or problems that can be associated with the informality of working in children's homes. It is important to bear in mind how the researcher's positionality and interviewing style can influence the responses.

If the decision was made to talk to children about their responses using semi-structured interviews, either individually or in pairs, or to conduct group discussions, the most frequent problems relate to devising too many questions, often lacking focus and clarity, or questions which are too demanding (or too bland) for the age group concerned. A quick rule of thumb suggests that children younger than seven will find about ten well-constructed questions an ideal number, whereas 10+ can manage up to 20, the upper limit.

Apart from stamina and maintaining interest, another reason for not starting out with too many questions is that, depending on how the child responds, supplementary questions are likely to be asked. These can't always be prepared in advance so listening carefully to what the child has to say is essential. In terms of timing, half an hour is more than enough for under seven-year-olds, and an hour is the maximum time you might spend with 10+.

The crucial role of good questions in eliciting quality responses from the children was highlighted again and again in our discussions. In interview situations, children often think there are the right answers they need to supply and strive to give the researcher/teacher the answers they think s/he wants. Children need to be reassured that there are no right or wrong answers and that the researcher is simply interested in their views of the picturebook. The questions need to be carefully constructed and this is where a pilot study is beneficial so that they can be tried out on small numbers first and improved when necessary. Even so, children often needed a few easy questions, to which they gave straightforward answers, before getting into their stride. The simplest is often best: 'Tell me about this page'. 'Do you think Rosie might know she is being followed by a fox?' 'What makes you think that?' 'What' seems to be more comfortable than 'why?'

Most of our questions for the first edition of this book required children to probe the visual text analytically. Many school systems use a high percentage of information retrieval questions, which are not challenging to young readers. We concentrated on questions that required children to use inference and deduction. Some of our personal response questions were demanding: 'Did the cover make you want to read *Zoo*?' 'What do you find interesting about the gorilla picture?' 'Would you describe *Zoo* as funny or serious?' A typical example of a question requiring inference would be 'Why do you think Anthony Browne showed a hamster on the title page before the story begins, when it's a book about going to the zoo?' Other questions focused on explaining textual evidence. For example: 'Did you notice anything special about the way Anthony Browne used colour/body language/perspective in *Zoo*?'

Although the younger readers found some of our questions taxing, the overall response to all three texts in our original study was very positive and the children appeared to find the experience interesting and the questions inviting. They also seemed to respond well to the fact that, when they volunteered information, we would often encourage them to probe more deeply. The rigour of the analysis and the amount of time devoted to considering a single picturebook appeared to surprise the children, but they also seemed to enjoy rising to the challenge. By the time they had the group discussion at the end of the day, instead of understandable reactions such as boredom or 'we've done this already', on most occasions children were eager to contribute, especially when we made it clear we wanted to move on from the earlier interviews. Like Kiefer's respondents in *The Potential of Picturebooks* (1995: 24), we found that 'children in all settings displayed an enthusiastic willingness to immerse themselves in the contents of their picture books'; however, we would not agree so wholeheartedly that 'verbal language seemed to give them the tools to understand these complex art objects', as some young children were only able to show their response visually.

In the interviews, all the researchers asked the same prescribed questions, though we took a fair amount of licence in asking supplementary questions when replies opened up interesting channels of discussion. In what follows, the first interview question was scripted; after that further questions were devised by interviewers on the spot, if it seemed worthwhile to pursue a line of enquiry. The following examples are typical of how we responded to the children to help them keep probing the meaning. Sometimes all that was required was a simple 'Why?' or 'Is there anything else you would like to say?'

INTERVIEWER: Do you think Anthony Browne is a good artist?
CHLOE (8): Yes, yes.
INTERVIEWER: Why?
CHLOE: Because he like thinks about the animals, then he like puts all the detail in them. And like because he's all serious, he puts horns up there [picture of Dad where the clouds behind him look like horns, a visual metaphor for the devilish way he is behaving]. It's clouds, and like he gets all the detail in the floors [a reference to Browne's hyper-real style and famous attention to detail in wooden floors, brick walls, etc.].
INTERVIEWER: What do you think Anthony Browne wants us to imagine in that picture?
SIMONE (10): Erm... to imagine that you're there so you can see everything.
INTERVIEWER: Now is it just about seeing everything or...?
SIMONE: He makes us feel like you're in her shoes to make you feel how she's scared or you're in his shoes [the brother's] making her scared.

Other times the researchers asked thoughtful questions which meshed with what children appeared to be trying to express. Sometimes the questions had no effect and, despite our hunches that children were on the point of breakthrough, they remained clammed up. In this extract, the interviewer wants to know whether Erin understands that Browne is suggesting that pets are often kept in captivity as well as more exotic animals in a zoo. She suspects that Erin understands this connection, as she has noticed many other subtle things about the book. But on this occasion, her questions do not elicit any further understanding from Erin.

INTERVIEWER: Why does Anthony Browne show us a picture of a hamster in a cage?
ERIN (7): Well a hamster is an animal and at the zoo you see animals.
INTERVIEWER: Is there any other reason for choosing the hamster?
ERIN: They're also in zoos and got funny cages.
INTERVIEWER: So why might he have chosen to put a hamster in a cage?
ERIN: I don't know.

At other times, the questions seemed to release previously unarticulated ideas. Without the supplementary questions, much of the children's knowledge and understanding would have remained unknown to us. In the extract that follows, the interviewer finds out by further questioning, not only that Paul feels empathy for the orang-utan's unhappiness, but that he also associates it with being caged and reads the animal's body language correctly.

INTERVIEWER: Why do you think we are not shown the orang-utan's face?
PAUL (5): Because he's sad?
INTERVIEWER: Why do you think he's sad?
PAUL: Because he's trapped in a cage.
INTERVIEWER: How does Anthony Browne show us that he's sad?
PAUL: Because he's trapped.
INTERVIEWER: How do you know that?
PAUL: Because there's a cage there [pointing].
INTERVIEWER: Is there any other way that Anthony Browne shows us that he's sad?
PAUL: Because he's sitting against the wall and won't show his face.

We have already mentioned the importance of having a clear focus for any line of questioning. However, some of the worst examples of picturebook research is when the interviewer concentrates so much on their particular emphasis that they fail to notice the children's replies show a different line of interest. You always need to be alert to how the children are responding and expect the unexpected.

Methodologies

It is worth noting that almost all empirical research with picturebooks is based on the Reader-Response theories of Iser (1978) and Rosenblatt (1978, 1982). While other theories are brought to bear on the response, especially given the visual aspect of the texts, the view of reading as a transaction between the text and the reader (Rosenblatt) where response-inviting structures in the text encourage readers to 'fill the gaps' (Iser) is still at the core of most studies. However, the more recent visual literacy and picturebook theories that we go on to discuss in Chapter 10 are beginning to influence empirical research and what has been changing is the methodology for obtaining a response to picturebooks. The range of methods is perhaps one of the most exciting aspects of picturebook research because it has demonstrated a variety of possible pathways to explore response as well as the creativity that can be encouraged in responding to picturebooks.

Earlier methods were based on talk (from semi-structured interviews to literature circles) and this continues to be part of most studies. However, since the original publication of this book, visual and other types of response are now almost an expected part of the research. These methods remind us that we are dealing with picturebooks which are multimodal artefacts and are also a way of encouraging the development of 'new literacies' (Anstey and Bull 2009). The methods used in most studies to obtain readers' responses are sometimes difficult to distinguish from teaching strategies and many acknowledge the important role of mediation.

The research based on oral responses usually references the 'book talk' recommended by Chambers (1993) and his seminal request, 'Tell me'. These studies typically employ different types of questions, prompts or instructions, including retellings, and they range from discussions which were almost completely unguided (McClay 2000) to discussions in the classroom that follow a particular teacher's lesson plan. In some studies, the oral response is based on a page-by-page 'storybook picture walk' (Paris and Paris 2001) or 'Walk-throughs' (Arizpe 2010, 2014; McAdam et al. 2014; Møller Daugaard and Blok Johansen 2014), where the researcher and the reader(s) take time to look carefully at each spread. When wordless picturebooks are involved, readers are often asked to retell the story in their own words or create captions or speech bubbles (Mourão 2015).

Like Rabey/Noble (in Arizpe and Styles 2003), many researchers have elicited responses via drawing or artwork. This works particularly well with young children who find it hard to express themselves or for children who are not yet able to write. Another important reason for having a visual response is that words cannot necessarily sum up the aesthetic experience of looking at a picturebook. Written responses often are a part of the work done in the classroom (Pantaleo and Bomphray 2011). Drama and performance have been employed by Mackey (2003) and Adomat (2010). Carger (2004) used painting and clay sculpture. Carger observes the benefits for language learners of responding via art:

> When given the opportunity to use art, I consistently found the students to be focused and on task, often chatting informally about the book or technique at hand. They glided from topic to topic, made intertextual comments, and engaged in authentic conversations. For these young English Language Learners, the benefit of engaging art activities connected with literature was multifaceted.
>
> (288)

The next step in the research process is the analysis and in this field a variety of interesting ways of examining the qualitative data have been used. The analysis will depend on the researcher's aim. Many tend to start from an interpretative paradigm and use some version of Grounded Theory (Strauss and Corbin 1998), coding through close examination of the response, usually dividing it into 'conversational turns', to create categories and a typology. Others look for emergent or generative themes and discourse patterns (Freire 2008; Erickson 1986; Gee 2005). Some have used analytical elements from linguistics and semiotics (Kiefer 1995; Walsh 2003) or socio-cultural literacy theories (Arizpe et al. 2014; Martínez-Roldán and Newcomer 2011).

As Sipe (2008) points out, one of the drawbacks of Grounded Theory is the difficulty of applying typologies across other studies, so Sipe attempted to replicate his own 'system' across his own different studies. While this has made his typology one of the strongest yet, it should be noted it was only used for a particular age range and it is less certain that the conditions would be the same even when working with the same age range in other cultural contexts. Nevertheless, his typology continues to be referred to, proving that at least some of the categories work across studies (e.g., Braid and Finch 2015).

The emergence of new theoretical frameworks like cognitive criticism, as well as the use of new analysis software and the interdisciplinary nature of research collaborations, has begun to have an impact on research on response. One potential option would be to see how the more culturally oriented theories fit in with the recent research on cognitive criticism. The work on digital picturebooks (or picturebook apps) will also require new ways of looking at the transaction between text and reader and of obtaining a response. The considerable amount of research, as evidenced in this book, is now also something that must be taken into account and built on in any new study. There is also now a wider interest in international publications and issues around translation, which opens the possibilities of looking at the response to both words and images in other languages (e.g., McGilp 2014). Finally, the influence of marketing, consumerism and ideology could be more fully considered by scholars in the field.

For every aesthetically engaging picturebook, there are potential studies on readers' responses that could be carried out considering a number of theoretical frameworks and methodological approaches. This means that care must be taken in the selection of the text and in the decisions made regarding the research process. The work of Kiefer, Sipe, Pantaleo, as well as our own, has provided some of the initial paths that others have followed and taken forward in new directions based on new picturebook and visual literacy theories. After revisiting some of the original studies, in the chapters that follow we provide new perspectives and new evidence, as well as asking searching questions about this exciting field of study. What is not in question is the often remarkable ability of children to interpret challenging picturebooks with great insight. We will leave the last word to Dave, aged 8: 'The pictures look so good. You just *want* to read it…'

Notes

1 We are delighted that Scallywag Press has recently released a new edition of this picturebook.
2 The interviews can be consulted in the 2003 edition of this book.
3 Nationalities included Greek, Italian, Turkish Cypriot, Turkish mainland, Kurdish, Tanzanian, Nigerian, Afghan, Chinese, Colombian, Kosovo-Albanian and Sri Lankan among others.
4 Because of the difficulties involved in articulating a verbal response to a work of art, Gardner suggests that 'nonverbal means, preferably involving the medium itself, would seem preferable for determining the full range of the child's competence' (1973: 180).
5 All the interviews were transcribed. In the examples used throughout this book, the use of (…) indicates a gap in the transcription.
6 As far as we are aware, no previous study had analysed children drawing in response to picturebooks. The data analysis in this instance (Chapter 5) was based mainly on aesthetic interpretations of children's drawings.

2 On a walk with Lily and Kitamura

How children link words and pictures along the way

Evelyn Arizpe

> I think you need the words really, to take the story along.
>
> (Lauren 11)

Lily is a cheery little girl who likes going for walks with her dog, Nicky. She watches the sunset, buys groceries and flowers, looks at the stars, says goodnight to the ducks, arrives back in time for supper and finally goes happily to bed. This is Lily's story and it is the story told by the words. But to understand why the smiling Lily is accompanied by her anxious-looking dog, Nicky, we need to 'read' the story told by the pictures. As Lily and Nicky take a walk, the pictures show us that the dog encounters (or he imagines), among other things, a snake, a tree with a wicked grin, a fierce-looking post-box, lamp posts with eyes, a vampire-like man emerging from a poster on the wall and various monsters. When they get home, Nicky seems to be trying to tell Lily and her parents what he saw, but they are not paying attention. Exhausted, he finally lies down, only to be plagued by a group of mice trying to get into his basket with a ladder!

Seeing things from a different perspective

Like the hen in *Rosie's Walk* (Hutchins 1970) who apparently never notices the fox that is following her, Lily goes out and returns home seemingly unaware of the creatures that frighten her dog. The text tells us that 'even if it is dark, Lily is not afraid because Nicky is with her'. Is she so confident with Nicky that she is oblivious to danger? Or is Nicky so neurotic that he will see monsters wherever he looks? Is it irony? Or perhaps, as one of the young readers we spoke to speculated (and not without reason), Lily is not afraid because she and her family are also ghostly monsters, a point which we will take up later.

Lily is a postmodern picturebook in the sense that it leaves the reader to deal with the questions mentioned above, fill in the gaps and resolve the ambiguities of the pictorial text (Styles 1996). These aspects belie the apparently simple narrative and lead the reader into a world of alternative meanings where fears can be dealt with through humour and irony. This picturebook is also illustrating one of the defining aspects of its genre: the relationship between image and written text. Lewis writes that

> the picture book always has a double aspect, an ability to look in two directions at once and to play off the two perspectives against each other... the picture book is thus not just a form of text, it is also a *process*, a way of making things happen to words and to pictures.
>
> (1996: 109–110)

In *Lily* we have two characters, each literally looking in a different direction, and as their perspectives play off against each other, readers find themselves participating in the process of making a story happen. They perceive at least two contrasting versions of the same events at the same time and perhaps understand that reality is never quite simple. If this seems too complicated a concept for young readers, it is worth quoting Kathy (7) even if she is struggling to express her reply to why Lily and Nicky might always be looking in different directions: 'Because they might have different like… say if Lily heard a joke and Lily laughed but Nicky couldn't laugh because he didn't get it… so they might have different possibilities'.

Nikolajeva and Scott (2000) call this particular dynamic 'perspectival counterpoint'; it stimulates the reader's imagination because of the different possibilities of interpretation.[1] In the case of *Lily*, Nikolajeva and Scott argue that this dynamic is 'highly developed' and that '[t]he counterpoint between the two perspectives and the ambiguity of the actual events shape the book's impact and the reader's involvement in decoding it' (2000: 234–235). Certainly, we found that, when the readers became aware of the counterpoint pattern, they began to anticipate it and to show they appreciated the humour of 'the jokes in-between the pages' (Lauren 11).

As in many of his other books, Kitamura's 'jokes' are part of a serious game he plays with the relationship between the illustrations and the written texts. In this particular picture, he invites his audience to join Lily and Nicky as they walk along, encouraging readers to become aware of the complexities of a postmodern narrative. As Meek (1988) tells us, it is the text that teaches what readers need to learn. It may be that some inexperienced readers will require more help in this understanding, and this is where the teacher should come in, as the more experienced reader who listens to the children's responses and asks the questions that will lead them to develop a critical awareness of the text and of their role as readers.

But how do young readers learn how picturebooks work? How do they join the artist's game, if in fact they do? How do they make sense of the discourse of the pictures? How do they relate it to the words? And how do they deal with the incoherent and the incomplete? We now explore some of these queries as interviewers as the children we worked with followed Lily and Nicky's footsteps through the picturebook.

Walking with Lily and Nicky

At all ages, the children became interested the moment they saw the cover and became keener as they turned the pages. The cover sets the tone for the rest of the book: the seemingly innocuous title which is Lily's story, together with the threatening background of blank, dark windows, empty streets and frightening monsters. It shows a smiling Lily carrying her groceries towards the left side of the page while Nicky stands facing the opposite way with a frightened look on his face, his eyes are wide open, his nose, ears and tail are pointing upwards and his mouth crumpled into a worried grimace. From Nicky's expression, the children – from the youngest to the oldest – gathered that there would be something menacing to come. This lured them to find out what he was scared of and to read the rest of the book. As Keith (10) said, '[You think] what's the dog scared of? So you like turn the page and then look and then just carry on reading and there's some more monsters and you just want to see the rest of it'.[2]

Despite the sinister atmosphere, the children expected a 'scary' but, at the same time, 'funny' book, because they were reassured by the cartoonish style of the drawing. Colin

(8), for example, predicted it might be 'a bit like a comedy'. Readers become involved when they can form analogies between the text and their own experience. For example, Judy (6) was immediately interested because of a building which looks like a church she goes to; others spoke of their own or other people's dogs. Interestingly, for many readers (myself included), it was not until the first reading was over and the cover was scrutinised again, that they discovered what it was that Nicky was looking at: a frightening face made by trees with fierce-looking nostrils, bent lamp posts as eyes and a mouth full of tree trunks with iron railings for teeth. At this point, there was unanimous agreement that the cover was a good one for the book because, as Janet (4) put it: 'it looked like what was going to happen in the story'.

The title page belies the cover in that the dog is actually looking quite happy to be going for a walk. Perhaps this is because they are just starting out or because Lily is actually looking at him for once. Several children noticed the house in the background and wondered whether it was Lily's home. On the next page, back on the pavement, both characters are looking at the reader; Lily is smiling but Nicky is already looking anxious and seems to be inviting us to share in his apprehension.

Empathy also encourages involvement, and it was not surprising that most readers were more concerned about the feelings of the over-imaginative dog than with the child, while at the same time laughing – not unkindly – at him. This also allows quite young readers to enjoy the experience of feeling a little more mature than the characters in the book. Some of the children reasoned that the dog was worried because he was hungry or tired, but most of them realised it was because of what he might see on the walk. Several children commented on this direct gaze. Flavia (10) said it was as if someone was taking a picture of him from outside the book, while Selma (11) noted that they were looking at 'us, the reader'. Nikolajeva and Scott (2000) equate Lily's lack of observation or imagination to that of an insensitive parent (although they also question the dog's reliability), though this does not correspond to the representation of Lily as a child who enjoys the sunset and the stars and who likes animals (even bats!).

Next, we have a double-page spread (like all the remaining pictures in the book), which shows them once again in the country or a park. Lily has her back to us as she admires the sunset, but Nicky is startled to see a snake as he lifts his leg against a bush. Several children said this was their favourite spread because of the rich colours, especially the blues and greens, and they also commented on the way the grass and the trees were drawn. Carol (10) liked the 'texture' and the way the trees looked 'scribbled' but were actually 'very carefully done'. As Lily walks along towards the right-hand corner of the page, Nicky's imagination really starts working. He looks behind him to see a tree giving him a wicked grin. Then, when Lily stops at the grocer's stall, his eyes widen in terror when he sees a post-box leaning over, with its open top full of pointed teeth and letters dropping from its 'mouth'. Some of the children mentioned the empty can and other litter in these two spreads, and, as we will see, they followed this trail and later reached the conclusion that Kitamura was saying something about pollution.[3]

As it gets darker, we find ourselves in one of the more frightening places on the walk: while Lily looks up at the stars, Nicky sees a face in the tunnel, a wide gaping mouth with lamp posts for eyes and traffic cones for teeth (see Figure 2.1). The alley is dark and deserted like the rest of the streets, except for a skip full of rubbish. Most of the readers commented on the menacing atmosphere, the older ones being more specific about which details made it frightening:

It's kind of scary, but it's funny because… street lights with just a tunnel wouldn't scare you at all, but it's just because it's together it makes it look real, like it's actually alive… All the detail, like even the skip with the rubbish falling out, and another reason why it's frightening is because not only that the dog's not looking at her, but because the dog's on the other side of the wall looking at something and she's just kind of talking to herself.

(Keith 10)

A younger child, Judy (6), was probably making an association with her own fears: 'Scary, there might be baddies' houses and as it is dark I thought there might be a baddie in [the skip]'.

The evening has become purple and on the right side of the page, the moon appears and becomes one of the eyes, together with the clock on the tower, of an owlish-looking face with tree trunks for teeth and a lamp post nose. Nicky stares at it in horror while, on the other side of the page, Lily seems to be looking directly at us, although the written text says that she is waving to a Mrs Hall. Mrs Hall is not depicted; she would have to be facing Lily, where we, the readers are. This gap, the 'missing' Mrs Hall, was only a problem for the younger readers, some of whom said that she must be in one of the windows *behind* Lily. The older ones said rightly that she must be off the page: 'It's like you're Mrs Hall because she's looking at you, because you can't actually see the window… so she's waving to you' (Keith 10).

As she continues her walk, now almost in the dark, Lily points out to Nicky how clever the bats are, but he is shaking at the sight of a strange-looking man who is tipping his top hat with one hand and holding a glass of blood-coloured juice in the other. He seems to be coming out of a poster advertising tomato juice, bending a lamp post in the process and spilling tomatoes onto the pavement. Keith observed that the dog was not 'round' but 'fuzzy', which meant he's 'even more scared'. When asked what sort of man he was, the children used the picture's clues to define him as a witch, 'because it's got a witchy hat and coat' (Janet 4) or a vampire, 'because it's got very pale white skin and it's got a blood stain there [on the cuff]' (Hugh 9). Anne (9) even gave him a part in the narrative:

> He has that sort of spiky collar and maybe he's pretending that's blood, blood juice and also there is a bat swooping around and going "Oh do not get near this poster or the evil bloodsucking vampire will have you for dinner!"

(see Figure 2.2)

The next spread shows Lily saying goodnight to the ducks and gulls on one side of the bridge, while on the other a dinosaur or Loch Ness monster-like creature stares down at Nicky, who is rooted to the spot despite his fast-moving legs. All the children were able to explain why Nicky seems to have eight legs in this picture and some exemplified it by moving their own legs very quickly. In this spread, it is Janet (4) who gives a voice to the monster: '"Aaaggg!". He's getting burnt [as he leans over the lamp post]'. There are still a few more monsters to terrify Nicky, popping out at him from rubbish bins before he and Lily get home. According to Keith (10) they looked '3D' and Carol (10) described how Kitamura's lines make them look scary: 'he's made them all like all different angles and all different triangle shapes and all sticking out and stuff and this one's just all straight, then zig-zagged'.

26 *The original study on children responding to picturebooks*

Figure 2.1 From *Lily Takes a Walk* by Satoshi Kitamura. (Text and illustration copyright © Satoshi Kitamura, 1987, by permission of Scallywag Press Ltd., London).

Figure 2.2 From *Lily Takes a Walk* by Satoshi Kitamura. (Text and illustration copyright © Satoshi Kitamura, 1987, by permission of Scallywag Press Ltd., London).

Once at home, over dinner, Lily tells her parents about her walk. We can see the father smiling but we can't see the mother's face. On the opposite page, Nicky has his mouth open, surrounded by little bubbles with the pictures of the monsters he has seen. Many of the children again showed their familiarity with the cartoonish style by saying these were the dog's 'speech' bubbles (one compared them to those in *Asterix* and *Tintin*): 'Well you can see the mother asking Lily and she's just like saying some nice things and he's just thinking of the things he's seen' Martin (7) (see Figure 2.3).

As the text says, it's time for bed and Lily sleeps happily underneath the duvet with her name written all over it (only the older pupils noticed this). Nicky has also settled into his basket and is just about to relax when, as the flap over the last page opens, a group of mice give him a final shock by trying to climb into his basket with a ladder. When asked how they felt about this picture before and after opening the flap, some of the readers remarked on the cosiness and messiness of her bedroom (and immediately compared it with their own) and at the same time remarked upon details which reminded them of the uncanny atmosphere, such as the fact that three of the stuffed animals look rather worried and sad, that the tiger in what is presumably Lily's drawing looks scared and that dark, blank windows are looking into her room. As Anne (9) rightly pointed out, it doesn't seem that Nicky will be happy anywhere because he will always find something to be frightened of: 'It's a place that Lily can be really comfy in and very happy, but Nicky can be like "Ooh this room!" There's just something about everything that he can get very scared about'.

Doonan notes that 'The omnipresence of musical and artistic instruments reveals Kitamura's focus upon the inner life, as well as providing intertextual reference to the artist's own creativity, and indicates a source for the self-reliance and independence of his characters' (1991: 108). Although there are no musical instruments to be seen in this picturebook, Lily's room is decorated not only by a Kandinsky-like poster, a calendar and a seagull mobile but also by her own drawings (or maybe original Kitamuras?) and her table is covered in art materials and a sketch of Nicky. Perhaps Lily, unlike Nicky, channels her imagination into her drawing, making her unafraid of encountering monsters on her walks.

Figure 2.3 From *Lily Takes a Walk* by Satoshi Kitamura. (Text and illustration copyright © Satoshi Kitamura, 1987, by permission of Scallywag Press Ltd., London).

Reading further into the picture

As readers and researchers walked along with Lily and Nicky, the responses gave us an insight into the more complex discursive aspects of this book in particular and of picturebooks in general. As we have noted, the most distinctive feature of *Lily* is the counterpoint between perspectives and it was this aspect we were keen to explore with the readers. In other words, we wanted to find out how they made sense of the interaction between words and pictures. Other responses that provided insights in relation to this main aspect were the following: readers' appreciation and awareness of visual features of text and artistic intentions; the implied reader and the children's own reading-viewing process and appreciation of the significance of the book as a whole.

Interaction between words and pictures

Almost without exception, the children thought the pictures were more interesting than the words. They felt that the book would still be good if you only had the pictures, but if there were only words it would be boring, especially, they added, for 'children'. There was definitely a belief that books with pictures (lots of them) were for younger children and the amount of pictures in books decreased in inverse ratio to the words as books were intended for older readers. However, some children did realise that only having the words would change the meaning of this particular book. Hugh's (9) comment about having only words was typical: 'you wouldn't be able to see what was happening'.

About the relationship between words and pictures in *Rosie's Walk*, Nodelman says, 'In showing more than the words tell us, the pictures not only tell their own story; they also imply an ironic comment on the words. They make the words comic by making them outrageously incomplete' (1988: 224). A similar interaction is taking place in *Lily* and it means that the reader must link not only the two different narratives – that of the printed text and that of the pictures – but also what the pictures are telling us about the printed text. As Nodelman says, they are showing them to be incomplete and therefore enhance the comedy of the narrative. It is not surprising that most of the younger readers struggled to express their understanding of this interaction; what is surprising is that some of the older ones managed to explain it quite clearly.

I: Do you think the pictures are telling the same story as the words?
SELMA (11): Yes plus a bit more... [the pictures] seem to bring out the story.

When asked if the words and pictures told the same story, most readers found it hard to separate them and answered yes, but some of the more engaged ones recognised they were different:

I: Do the words and the pictures tell the same story?
KATHY (7): A bit of a yes and a bit of a no because it doesn't say that like Lily is pointing to the leeks or something, but it does say 'today she...'
I: So if the words are telling that story, who's telling the rest of the story?
KATHY: The dog.

The older pupils were more able to articulate the difference between the meanings derived from the written text and the pictures. For example, Flavia (10) pointed out that 'the pictures tell you about the monsters and the words just tell you what Lily thought'. Keith (10) described this in more detail, weighing up the contribution of both words and pictures:

> [If it were only the words] it wouldn't be good because it would just be a happy book because it doesn't say anything about anything being scary. It's just saying she's not scared and she'll do her shopping, she looks at the stars, she walks past someone's house and waves. You wouldn't see the bats or any of those things that make it scary... Some books are better without the pictures because then you can make up your own thing, but I think this is better with the pictures... the words need the pictures more than the pictures need the words.

Invoking his previous experience as a reader, Keith recognises the difference between the two signifying systems and how they work upon the reader (the pictures make it scary). His statement also shows us the analytical process by means of which he arrives at a conclusion and makes a judgement on the value of these systems. It is an indication of the processes that are going on in the reader/viewer's head as they attempt to construct a story structure using different kinds of 'building blocks'.

Appreciation of visual features and artistic intentions

Questions about visual features were asked throughout the interviews with prompts about colour, pattern, perspective and body language. We also asked if they had found similarities with other Kitamura's picturebooks. Most of the children mentioned colour, and referred especially to the different shades of the sky (later, many of them made an attempt to portray these skies in their drawings). They also noticed the cartoon-like patterns of the 'wobbly' lines, the uneven bricks, the flat wheels and the crooked windows. One ten-year-old boy described this style as 'realistic but not realistic'. This 'cartoon-like' style helps widen the distance between the straightforward textual narrative and the fantastic images. Other visual features that were mentioned included perspective (how the trees became smaller in the distance); where the characters were placed (for example, that Lily is always on the side furthest from the monsters and Nicky is nearest); and intertextual references (to other Kitamura's picturebooks, such as *A Boy Wants a Dinosaur*).

The less experienced readers tended to provide less plausible explanations (with no basis in the text) for the way in which Kitamura draws lines. For example, they said the steps were wobbly because: 'they belong to a witch', 'they've been there for thousands of years' or 'a heavy man stepped on them'. The more experienced readers tended to give reasons that had more to do with logic (rightly or wrongly) than with the author's intention. Kathy (7), for example, said: 'It is hard to draw steps so he might wiggle a little bit' cause he is worried about it, that he's going to do it wrong, so he's a bit shaky'. And Martin (7) considered how they added to the atmosphere, 'it's to make it scarier and to stand out more'.

Other children commented on the atmosphere created by the continual appearance of dark colours, the blank windows and empty cars. They described it as 'spooky' and 'upsetting'. Carol (10) spoke of the difference between these dark backgrounds and the way in which Lily and Nicky 'brightened it all up'. Martin (7) also remarked on this contrasting effect:

It's very good, his use of colour, because he's like used all bright colours on her… I reckon he could have picked different [flowers] like roses or daffodils… but he probably just chose a really bright colour: yellow. And he's chosen a really dark colour for the houses.

Both Kitamura's characteristic colour and line were reflected in most of the children's drawings as they attempted to recreate the atmosphere in his pictures. Further examples can be seen in Chapter 8.

The implied reader and children's own reading-viewing processes

Perhaps because the 10- and 11-year-olds had little opportunity to look at picturebooks both at home and at school, *Lily* was initially considered a book for younger children. This was also true of some of the eight- and nine-year-olds, because, they argued, if it were for older children it would have more writing and 'a bit more detail'. However, by the end of the interview, this opinion was revised by many of the older readers, such as Peter (9):

> I think this book's interesting because… children enjoy picture-books but I think it's also better for older people because if they read it carefully they can like spot things, like what we're doing now, they can sort of have fun with it and spot things.

This and other answers show how their previous experience of books and their knowledge of the type of fiction we were reading comes to bear on their responses. Kitamura's cartoon-like style was an indication that it would be both a fictional and humorous book. Anne (9), for example, when asked if the monsters were real or imaginary, said: 'Well in books really anything can actually happen, it's just your own imaginary world so that could actually be happening'.

Asking a reader to describe what happens when he or she reads is always fascinating, especially when they are young children who are searching for a way to describe it (these processes are described further in Chapter 7). Many answers revealed the importance that detail has for them. The older children described how they spot 'the problem' or the unexpected and then return to the 'normal' and put the two together:

PETER (9): I look carefully and I see what may be the problem because you see the dog notices things that the girl isn't noticing so then I split the book into half and I see what Lily's seeing and really what she's saying… seeing and doing, and I will look at the dog and see what he's doing.
I: So you get sort of one side and then the other side?
PETER: And try and put them together.

Peter's description of what is going on in his head as he reads gives us an indication of what children are noticing as they look at pictures. As they read, they are looking at the whole picture and connecting it to the words, as well as seeing through the characters' eyes and trying to pull all this information together. Their processes of deduction involved both imagination and common sense. Judy (6), for example, spoke of looking for clues to 'get things right'.

Readers were aware that they were joining in a kind of game which allowed them to go back and forth through the book to look for details they had missed in order to solve the puzzles. In this case, they had to work with two different characters, comparing and contrasting their actions and words (at least Lily's words) with the written and pictorial narratives (which also meant imagining what Nicky would say if he could). They were willing to work hard at making connections and coming up with explanations; evidently they were deriving great satisfaction from participating in the meaning-making process by piecing the picture together.

Significance of the book as a whole

One of the most difficult tasks for any reader is to be able to stand back from a text and view it as a whole; it is perhaps even more difficult when we are dealing with a book where two different discourses must be dealt with at the same time. Yet, the children in the study showed that they were beginning to consider overall meaning at various levels. To begin with, we asked children whether they would describe *Lily* as 'funny' or 'serious'. Many of the younger readers said it was simply 'funny', while some of the older readers said it was both. They pointed out the humorous elements of the picture-book and the way in which Kitamura 'makes you laugh'. Hugh (9) summed it up by saying 'It's funny because the dog keeps getting scared and the little girl smiles'. In the children's drawings, Nicky is depicted as worried and Lily always smiles.

As the interviews and discussions progressed, the children raised moral and ethical issues which demonstrated that they were able to perceive more profound implications of this deceptively simple story. This occurred mainly in the group discussions. Often the researcher led up to some of these issues, but in other cases, the readers arrived at some surprising conclusions as they discussed possible and alternative meanings. For example, in the following extract from a group discussion, six- and seven-year-olds are debating whether the 'monsters' were really there or if they were a product of Nicky's imagination:

KATHY: I think he's just looking at it and then he thinks 'Oh no!'
JUDY: No, because it is in the dark, because he's staring in the dark and it makes them look different to what they really are.
JOHN: No, I think he's been watching TV about all this stuff... He's thinking of all this stuff and when he looks he sees them there, when they are not really there.
MARTIN: (Maybe it's a) person holding things up...
SEAMUS: I think that it's that he looks at them and then he imagines that they're scary.

The children put forth their hypotheses, trying to explain it to themselves and the others, based on their own experience of dealing with imaginary terrors. Together they are struggling to reach beyond the literal to a level of understanding that shows psychological insight into the dog's behaviour.

The environmental issue was raised by some children who noted that litter appears in many of the pictures. Carl (8) read this as a message Kitamura was trying to put across through his book: 'he might be trying to tell people in just a picture in a little way to clear up your rubbish... he might be saying to people who read the book to clear up your rubbish'. This idea was also brought up in the group discussion between seven- and eight-year-olds, and for one girl it involved an important consideration of viewpoint and perspective:

I: So the dog does notice all the rubbish doesn't he?
LAUREN: Because he's so small he might see it more, because it's a bit bigger than him.

By means of the two stories running alongside, Kitamura leads us to understand that the world can be seen from different perspectives. Selma (11) applied this idea to the fact that the 'vampire' and Lily's dad look quite similar. It is interesting to note that she also speaks of the importance of looking carefully at the text in order to notice this sort of detail and understand what she called 'the moral': 'People may look different in a different suit but they could be the same person. Some people may not realise that, they just look through it and they don't actually see the dad'.

The interviewer picked up on the idea of 'the moral' and as the children worked collaboratively, they reached a more satisfying explanation of what is going on in the book:

I: Would you say that there were any other morals in this book?
LAUREN (11): People believe in things but not everybody.
ANGUS (9): From the dog's point of view when you are little things scare you more than when you are bigger... when you are little sometimes your imagination just wanders and then when you are older you can tell things look like that or not.

The last statement shows a grasp of how characters' perceptions can be different and how these differences may be responsible for their emotions and actions. It also shows an analogical understanding of how the ability to discern between reality and fantasy develops with age. Like Angus, by the end of the group discussions, many other children were showing signs of a much broader comprehension of the picturebook.

Looking and walking with Kitamura

In English schools, picturebooks are not often re-read and re-discussed because of the constraints of the curriculum. This means that many children remain at a more literal level of comprehension, in which they understand the plot sequence, facts and details, but find it difficult to construct meaning at a more critical level. We found that at first the children were trying to make literal sense of the gaps and incoherences, instead of being able to take a step back and comprehend how they worked within the whole of the story structure. The reading of books like *Lily* confounds the reader's expectations in a playful and at the same time thought-provoking manner. It forces even older readers such as Keith to look more carefully, resulting in a greater understanding of how the visual and verbal narrative can work together as well as a greater enjoyment of the text.

We also found that some of the children who were considered by the teachers to be 'struggling readers' turned out to be some of the more experienced and articulate interpreters of the visual; even those students who had particular learning disabilities were able to make meaning and in some cases actually expanded the possibilities of Kitamura's pictorial text. Such was the case of Charlie, whose slight autism made him speak slowly and not very distinctly (his extraordinary drawings are analysed in the vignette). It was Charlie who reasoned that Lily's white face, the fact that the family were drinking the same tomato juice as the vampire and the father's resemblance to this vampire, meant that Nicky was, ironically, living with a family of ghostly monsters. No wonder Lily wasn't afraid of the dark!

An earlier version of this chapter appeared in M. Anstey and G. Bull (eds) (2002) *Crossing the Boundaries,* Sydney: Pearson.

Vignette – 'getting the pictures in my head' (Charlie 9)

Charlie was not one of the four children interviewed individually about Kitamura's *Lily*. I first met him for the group discussion, where his extremely slow and hardly intelligible manner of speaking, as well as his reluctance to meet my eye, made him stand out from the rest of the children. He spoke so slowly that he was constantly interrupted (something he seemed to be used to) and it was a struggle to make the others let him finish. I was intrigued, however, by his interventions – short as they were – and particularly impressed when I saw his drawing. So much so, that I decided to re-interview him five months later after a brief talk with his teacher. She described him as 'slightly autistic' and said that he was registered as having special needs. However, she added, 'although he's slow, it's all up there'.

Charlie's first drawing is based on the 'tunnel monster' picture, where Lily is looking up at the stars (see Figure 2.4). All of it is drawn with thick, determined lines. The left half of the picture is dominated by a brick-lined arch filled with vivid turquoise blue pencil crayon. On either side of the arch stand, two lamp posts bent inwards underneath the top of the arch giving the impression of two staring eyes. Inside stand two nearly identical houses with a perfectly balanced window and door in the centre of each. Nicky's state of mind is revealed by the squiggly, uncertain line that is his mouth. As with the rest of the drawing, Charlie has paid great attention to detail and the dog is carefully patterned with spots and black paws. Both Lily and Nicky are drawn in profile and this is particularly interesting because only a few of the other children attempted to draw the characters from this perspective. In his attempts to get it 'right', Charlie has rubbed out Lily's face once before carefully redrawing her hair and the shape of the side of her nose.

At the beginning of the re-interview, I asked Charlie why he had chosen to draw this particular picture. He said it was because that page 'looked really spooky, because it looks like a horrible monster, like the mouth'. It was also his favourite picture in the book because of 'the way the path goes like into the mouth' and the way Kitamura had drawn the lines. As these comments reveal, Charlie was very perceptive about Kitamura's actual drawing style. He mentions the 'lines' twice and also that 'the colours are good and like that's quite scary… because her [Lily's] skin is very white'.

The other aspect of Charlie's reaction to the pictures revealed by these comments was his sensitivity to the atmosphere in the book. He explained that the lines made things look scary, 'and the black walls too, the rubbish on the ground is also scary, and kind of crooked tyres and crooked sticks'. He mentioned that he often had trouble going to sleep after watching a scary video. Kitamura's images also haunted him: 'When I read this book it made me think of bats when I was in bed'.

Figure 2.4 By Charlie (9).

During the group discussion, he scrutinised a copy of the book, pointing out the monsters to the others. After several interrupted and unintelligible remarks, he pointed out that the father in the penultimate picture looks 'just like' the man in the poster and that Nicky was feeling 'a bit sick and thinking, "No, go away!" to those horrible things in his mind'. When at the end of the discussion I asked the children what they would like to ask the artist, Charlie said 'Well I'd like to ask him if that was Lily's dad and were these things actually really happening or Nicky was just thinking he'd seen them'. It seemed to worry him whether the monsters were 'real' or just a product of Nicky's imagination. When I spoke to him five months later I asked him what he remembered most about the book. He said: 'the looks of things… they look like spooky things'. I asked him what Kitamura wanted to make the readers think. He replied: 'that the town is haunted… he's trying to say that there are monsters and horrible scary things, or maybe he's [Nicky] just imagining them'. Charlie thought he could make out more monsters in Lily's room (made of windows) and claimed: 'If [Nicky] looked out the window he would see more scary things'.

During the re-interview, I read the book to him slowly, letting him comment during the reading if he wished. Then I asked him the same questions I was asking the other re-interviewed children but tried to give him as much time as possible to answer. Even so, he did not say very much because of the effort it took him to speak, and much of what he said was refining the ideas he had tried to put across during the group discussion. He had no problem understanding what the story was about: 'Lily is having a good time but Nicky is not having a very nice time on the walk… the pictures tell his story and if he tells it the people wouldn't believe him'. So he has noticed that the words and the pictures are telling different stories.

The picture he chose to represent in his second drawing is the one with the 'vampire' man and the bats, which had evidently made a strong impression on him and, like the first one, it shows an outstanding ability to draw as well as an understanding of Kitamura's style. In this drawing, there is also an example of his handwriting, which reveals his meticulous interest in shape. The letters have been laboriously delineated as if he had been thinking carefully about each of them. The drawing bears many of the characteristics of Kitamura's original drawings such as the accurately hatched blue sky which dominates the composition. Apart from the predominant blue colour, the picture is drawn almost entirely in black felt tip, with a red sea of tomatoes on the poster spilling down onto the pavement.

In this drawing, Lily has become more 'ghost-like' because only her yellow hair and red shoes are coloured. The man coming from the poster is very similar to that of the original, with his round cartoon eyes, U-shaped nose and arching semi-circle smile – again, carefully thought-out shapes. Lily and Nicky are drawn in a similar position and profile to the first picture but here is a more accurate depiction of the side on view with only one arm showing. Charlie's drawing also shows development in terms of movement (another aspect which few pupils tried to depict) with Lily's back leg bending at the knee as she walks forward.

Of all the drawings we showed him, it was Charlie's that most caught Kitamura's eye when he saw them; he even said he wished he had thought of the composition himself! Kate Noble, who analysed the other 'Lily' drawings in the study (see Chapter 8) also found that Charlie's artwork stood out, particularly in its attention to detail (e.g., the lamp on the post is shaped exactly with the pointed pattern on the top, split into two panes and anchored on three triangular-shaped supporting struts). She was also surprised by the boldness of his line and use of colour, suggesting it reveals a confident, definite use of drawing materials. She surmised this must be a child who draws a great deal (noticing, for example, the repeated schema of the house and the figures, almost identical but subtly improved in between the two sessions). It also seemed to me that he was carefully trying to reproduce the menacing atmosphere which so impressed him.

Not surprisingly, Charlie told me that he prefers pictures over words 'because they help you with the story, only words would be boring'. When faced with books without pictures, his approach is to 'get the pictures in my head, imagine them'. He certainly did not lack imagination, especially when he reasoned that Nicky was so afraid because he realised the whole family were ghosts! He came up with this idea after pointing out Lily's face is 'white' (colourless), that the father is like the 'vampire' and that the family were drinking tomato juice.

Fortunately, Charlie's teacher was aware 'it was all up there' and the fact that she selected him for the interviews meant she was confident that he would have something to say about the pictures. The obstacles in verbally expressing himself completely disappeared when he communicated through the visual. His engagement with the picturebook was intense and it is this intensity he manages to express to us only through his drawings.

Notes

1 Nikolajeva and Scott (2000 and 2001) include a section on *Lily* both in their book and in an earlier article.
   Their insights on the word/image dynamic are useful for understanding *Lily*, however, we differ in the interpretation of some of the images, as they see the 'monsters' as more menacing than humorous and seem to have misinterpreted some of them, such as the 'giant', which is not emerging from a shop window but from an advertising poster (and playing with advertising billboards is a common feature in Kitamura's work).

2 Keith was described by his teacher as of 'middle ability'. He was a bright, articulate boy who spoke of *Lily* as a book for younger children, yet he became more and more involved in it and particularly in the relationship between words and images. He is therefore frequently quoted throughout this chapter as an example of the way in which picturebooks can stimulate older children's understanding of visual literacy.
3 When asked about this particular point, Kitamura admitted that he might have made the reference unconsciously.

3 A gorilla with 'grandpa's eyes'

How children interpret ironic visual texts – a case study of Anthony Browne's *Zoo*

Morag Styles

I always remember pictures. I sometimes forget words.

(Amy 5)

He doesn't just want to say the animals want to be free – blah, blah, blah. He leaves you to find it out a bit better... makes you keep thinking about things.

(Erin 7)

A visual analysis of *Zoo*

The story is an account of a family visit to a zoo, which interrogates the ideological concept of zoos, and of man's relationship with animals, delivered in a multi-stranded narrative... The family and its backgrounds are depicted in comic book style, with clean outlines, minimal modeling and (with the exception of Mum) in plenty of bright, saturated hues, in lightly framed pictures generally, which occupy about a third of the page area. The animals and their enclosures are portrayed in black framed full plates, painted in Browne's meticulous non-photographic realist style, with intense care to selected details and textures. Each animal has a grave and beleaguered natural beauty set in contrast with unsympathetic materials – concrete, brick, cement shuttering – from which their environments have been structured... The composite text both questions the value of caging wild animals for the casual pleasure of the majority of visitors, and at the same time communicates the sad truth that humans also construct metaphorical cages through the ways in which they construct the world.

(Doonan 1999)

With her usual flair, Doonan gives a telling description of Browne's prize-winning book. The dramatic cover features black and white, vertical, wavy lines which most children interpret as reference to a zebra which is, in fact, missing from the list of animals encountered in the book. 'Well, it's just like a zebra, the stripes of a zebra I think and... that's kind of symbolising a zoo really' (Joe 10). It is also suggestive of the sort of puzzling optical illusions so favoured by artists like Escher. It could be a postmodernist joke, as *Zoo* is an unstable text with surrealistic fantasies side by side with hyper-real illustrations. Instead of zebra stripes, those lines could represent the bars of cages dissolving before our eyes. Nothing is what it seems. From the cover in, it is clear that this is not going to be a conventional family outing (although that is more or less what it is in the written text) and the reader will be taken on a confusing but rewarding journey.

There is also a book-shaped insert of the central family on the cover with an oversized father, a small, young-looking mother, plus two boys. The male family members are in the foreground looking happy and confident, wearing bright, colourful jerseys, whereas Mum (reminiscent of the mother living in a sexist household in Browne's *Piggybook*) almost disappears into the background, looking straight at the reader with a serious face. Unusually, the only lettering on the front or back cover is the title and the name of the author which are in large, white, bold print. The typography hints at eyes (gazing on the reader?) in the two 'O's of ZOO. In contrast, the word 'Zoo' is picked out in black lettering on the title page, which also depicts a hamster in a cage full of accoutrements, the same colours as the clothes of Dad and the boys.

The dominance of black and white is further emphasised in both endpapers, one side white, the other black, an unusual choice and clearly there for a purpose. It suggests that there is going to be a debate in this book; or perhaps it is raising the issue of right and wrong, good and bad, two sides of the same coin? It is for readers to decide by analysing the pictures; Browne raises questions rather than providing answers and the story told in words is often at odds with what is revealed in the pictures. Young readers soon learn (if they haven't already discovered from earlier encounters with Browne's books) that everything in the visual text is significant and they are going to have to work hard to carve out the meaning for themselves. Fortunately, this is an enjoyable process, as Browne is extremely funny and children laugh a lot as they read the book.

Ironic picturebooks

Most children read *Zoo* as a book which is severely critical about animals being held in captivity, but there is no reference to this in the written text except for Mum's final comment: 'I don't think the zoo really is for animals. I think it's for people'. Otherwise, all the evidence for an authorial stance critical of zoos comes from the pictures. For children to judge that this is a book about how humans treat animals and about captivity and freedom, they have to be able to interpret irony and read moral ideas into pictures.

Zoo could be described as a prime example of an ironic picturebook as Kümmerling-Meibauer explains: 'Ironic meaning comes into being as the consequence of a relationship, a dynamic, performative bringing together of the said and the unsaid, each of which takes on meaning only in relation to the other' (1999: 168). This irony makes demands on the reader to use inference to detect contradictions between what is said in the written text and illustrated in the picture. She goes on to underline the difficulties irony poses for younger readers, suggesting that:

> children do not acquire a full understanding of this concept in comparison to other linguistic phenomena until relatively late... The groundwork for understanding irony is often laid first not in verbal but in graphic images that act as visual equivalents to tone in oral storytelling and that can serve to play with or cast doubt on a straight-faced text.
>
> (1999: 167)

Nodelman (1988: 222) devotes a whole chapter of *Words About Pictures* to consider the irony in multi-modal texts: 'They come together best... when writers and illustrators use the different qualities of their different arts to communicate different information. When they do that, the texts and illustrations of a book have an ironic relationship to each other'. While Nodelman argues that picturebooks are 'inherently ironic', Kümmerling-Meibauer prefers to highlight the reader's role in recognising irony through paratextual clues and other visual hints which often contradict or subvert the written texts. These operate as triggers to suggest that the viewer should be open to other possible meanings, thus encouraging the development of metalinguistic skills. She also draws attention to the hard intellectual work involved in the interpretation of such indeterminacy which forces the reader 'to prise open the gap between the text and the pictures, working on the relationship between them' (1999: 167–176).

Nikolajeva and Scott (2001) also talk about the tension between the two different sign systems creating 'unlimited possibilities for interaction between word and image in a picturebook', also using the term 'counterpoint' to describe the dynamic between them. They go on to outline different kinds of 'counterpoint', many of which apply to *Zoo* – i.e., counterpoint by genre (e.g., realism and fantasy side by side), style (e.g., use of different artistic styles), in perspective (e.g., contradiction between ideologies), of paratexts (e.g., titles and covers). It was evident in our study that most of the children, even the very young, were aware of, and responded to, tensions within *Zoo* and that this was one of the features of the book they found so challenging and absorbing.

Seeing and thinking

Browne uses surrealist techniques to make connections between human beings and animals; people begin to metamorphose as the visit progresses. At first, there is just the hint of a tail, a banana or a fur coat, but soon we have people growing webbed feet, hooked noses and monkey faces. On most double spreads animals, sometimes alone, are presented within their cages with the colours, light, caging and body language accentuating their isolation. On the left-hand pages, in contrast, Dad, the boys and other visitors to the zoo appear in bold colours, often in bright sunlight under a blue sky with billowing Magritte-type clouds, something the children always notice. The visitors often behave thoughtlessly, intent on their fun and dismissive of the animals. Throughout the book the animals are portrayed sympathetically in contrast to the bizarre-looking humans, displaying (often most amusingly) shallow and boorish behaviour. Although the zoo is newish, architect-designed and relatively clean, the focus is on harsh, synthetic materials; the reader is positioned outside the cages until halfway through the book when the standpoint moves just inside for an even closer experience of the misery of captivity.

What came over most forcefully in the interviews and group discussions based round Browne's *Zoo* was the children's engagement with the text and their willingness to spend time analysing its meaning. What we saw, even with the young children, was what can only be described as intellectual excitement with the ideas raised by the book and aesthetic pleasure in the images. It was as if *Zoo* offered an invitation that children felt compelled to take up. Here are Lara (10), Joe (10) and five-year-old twins (part of the pilot study) explaining why the pictures were a priority for them.

LARA: The writing doesn't explain everything what you think about… the writing only explains what the book is about and what is happening, but it doesn't explain what you feel and what they feel. *So I like the pictures better because then you can think more stuff* [our emphasis].

JOE: I think I found the pictures more interesting really because the text does help me to know what is going on in the family, *but the pictures show what it's really like* and what's going on with the animals [our emphasis].
R AND F: Pictures are better.
F: Cause we can understand it more. We can't read very well, but *we can understand it by the pictures* [our emphasis].

The motivation was high from the moment children started looking at the front cover of *Zoo* and, almost without exception, they were eager to engage with the book after it had been read to them by their class teachers. Although this enthusiasm was evident in all the children (whether they had seen the book before or not did not seem to make a difference), those below the age of 7, unsurprisingly, found it much harder to answer the questions in interviews than those of 7 and above. Furthermore, children below the age of 7 were usually satisfied with seeing things in the text; older pupils wanted to pursue the how and why of Browne's artwork.

By the group discussions at the end of each interview day, it was always evident that the children's thinking had moved on. Aspects of the book that individuals had failed to comprehend in interviews were often sorted out when they began talking together. Group dynamics were interesting. For example, Joe was regarded by his teacher as a very good reader and was the most academic of the 10- and 11-year-old children. He made thoughtful responses in the interview, but held back during the discussion. This could be the reasons of personality; perhaps he was confident enough to form his own opinions without voicing them aloud, or perhaps the more forceful members of the group held him back? However, if there was any doubt about his emotional investment in *Zoo*, a glance at his powerful drawing of an elephant would cast it aside.

The children were assiduous at noticing details in *Zoo* and were keen to interpret every last image. They all enjoyed the humour but thought the book was more serious than funny. This is probably one of the reasons for Browne's popularity with young readers: the combination of intellectual challenge, aesthetic pleasure, amusement and intriguing 'puzzles' to unravel.

Perplexing features of visual texts

There were some instances of imagery which adults tend to find straightforward, once they have been pointed out, but which proved perplexing to most children. For example, on the first page, a snail is poking out of the top right-hand section of the picture, ahead of the traffic jam leading to the zoo, while cars and people acquire animal characteristics. This is presumably an ironic joke by Browne, saying that the traffic is moving so slowly that even a snail could go faster. We should not have been surprised that children found this difficult since Kümmerling-Meibauer reminds us that such irony requires sophisticated metacognitive awareness and, perhaps, familiarity with metaphorical linguistic terms and their application, such as 'going at a snail's pace' or 'the traffic was crawling along'. Children came up with every conceivable suggestion for the snail's role on the opening page. Here are some examples by groups of five-, eight- and ten-year-olds:

YU (4): To make it beautiful.
ASHOK (5): Because *Bear Hunt* had lots of different things and perhaps he thought he could put lots of different things into this book as well [a nice example of intertextual awareness].
PAUL (5): I think he's jumping off the roof.
ASHOK: Because he wanted to get to the lions first.
SOFIA (8): Well, the man in the van must have like pushed him off.
EYLEM (8): It shows you to like… change the page.
I: It tells you to… go to the next page. Is that what you mean?
EYLEM: Yeah [a good try, but incorrect].
MIKE (10): Well he might like snails.
GIOVANNI (10): 'Cause he can see the traffic jam, people shouting and arguing and it gives you an idea of the snail is fed up and he's trying to get away from it.

In the final discussion, most children of seven and above solved the snail conundrum together with some guided questioning by the interviewer. The children's problems with interpreting the snail serve to highlight the extraordinary analytical ability shown elsewhere by so many children about other pictures in the book.

Affective and moral dimensions of *Zoo*

One of the reasons the children were encouraged to work at an analytical level in examining *Zoo* is that they were emotionally involved with the book. Vygotsky taught us about the interrelationship between the intellect and emotion, arguing for 'a dynamic system of meaning in which the affective and the intellectual unite… every idea contains a transmuted affective attitude towards the bit of reality to which it refers'. Vygotsky believed that thought processes were inevitably linked to 'the fullness of life, from personal needs and interests, the inclinations and impulses of the thinker'. And he goes further:

> Imagination and thought appear in their development as the two sides of opposition… this zigzag character of the development of fantasy and thought… reveals itself in the "flight" of imagination on the one hand, and its deeper reflection upon real life on the other.
>
> (Vygotsky 1986: 10)

There were some features of the book that most children, regardless of age, were able to comprehend and articulate. Perhaps most noticeable was an empathy with the suffering of the animals, often linked to statements of personal analogy. This was generally accompanied by criticism of the way humans behaved towards animals. Joe (10) summed up the book's message neatly. 'I think he's trying to get across that we are more like animals than animals really… like it says on the last page… the zoo is more for humans than animals'. Most of the children interviewed were critical of the poor conditions in which the animals were held and very concerned about their apparent unhappiness. (Again, this is never mentioned in the written text and has to be inferred from the pictures.) The older the children, the more concerned they were with the ethics of keeping animals in captivity. This strong moral viewpoint was also evident in the drawings of this age group, which either showed humans and animals in role-reversal situations or pictures which contrasted the misery of the animals in captivity with the joyousness of freedom, expressed in the use of bright and dull colours. Sue (10) joined the discussion, but was not an interviewee. She had only had one brief reading of *Zoo*, but she quickly gets straight to the heart of it:

SUE: Well, it was about how lonely (the animals) were in the zoo… and the people were being nasty and just wanted to look at the animals… They didn't seem to realise how miserable the animals were… it is not just a trip to the zoo. It is thinking about how the animals feel and how the people… They should be given more freedom… The animals are acting better than the people. The people are acting like animals or what we think animals act like.

The children read emotion in Browne's pictures with great subtlety and their empathy was often extended towards the mother who shows concern for the animals' plight and appears ashamed of the bad behaviour exhibited by her husband and children. Here is Sue again, observant of Mum, and understanding what it means to show rather than tell: 'Perhaps she felt sorry for the animals, because all the way through it suggests it'. Les (10) also noticed that Mum might be disapproving as 'she's just standing there and everyone else is smiling'. Even five-year-old Amy was able to articulate in her second interview that 'Mum is sad – she thinks the animals should be going free'.

AIDAN (10): She doesn't like the animals being in the cage 'cos when they was looking… I think it was at the gorilla or something like that… she said 'poor thing'.
I: Right. So she doesn't… like the animals being caged in the zoo?
MIKE (10): Because she's a very serious-looking lady that she thinks the animals should be free, so she probably ain't in that picture because she's like wandering off all upset that the animals are trapped.

Many children found the image of the orang-utan very moving. Browne emphasises a sense of desolation as the animal crouches dejectedly in a corner of a domestic-looking cage with his back to the jeering visitors. The only objects in its space are bits of faeces and empty shells. In contrast, the increasingly animal-like visitors (who include Magritte, Catwoman and D. H. Lawrence!) bang on the glass in derision. Here is an extract from the discussion of ten-year-olds who humanise the orang-utan, perhaps for greater identification with him:

SUE: Because he is sort of similar to a human, he should be treated like a human.
LARA: Because he looks like he's got hair coming down… it has got really long hair.
SUE: And it has got hairy ears.
TONY: And it has got grey hairs like an old person.
SUE: He looks like he's got his hair in a bun at the top and like…
I: How do you know he's sad?
JOE: Because you don't just crawl up into a corner, just turn away, for no reason. You can't be happy when you're like that, you can tell that he is not happy.

A seven-year-old in an interview showed how she could read the environment:

I: How do you think the orang-utan is feeling?
ERIN: Very sad.
I: What makes you say that?
ERIN: Well if he's not showing his face then it might be because he's sad and he just doesn't feel like it.
I: Is there anything else that suggests he might be sad?
ERIN: Well if you look really, he hasn't got anything around him. Like the elephant, no natural habitat.

The four- and five-year-olds in the interview also realised the orang-utan was unhappy:

I: How do you think the orang-utan is feeling?
AMY: Sad.
I: You think he's feeling sad? And what makes you think he's feeling sad?
AMY: Because he's sitting in the corner.

Analysing visual imagery

Kümmerling-Meibauer discusses the textual markers and paratextual clues that encourage readers to recognise the irony in picturebooks operating 'as triggers to suggest that the viewer should be open to other possible meanings, thus encouraging the development of metalinguistic skills' (1999: 168–176). What follows in the next few sections are some examples of children recognising textual markers, noticing switches in artistic styles, analysing colour imagery, noting changes in points of view and filling in semantic gaps.

Younger children were fascinated by the changes that kept appearing in Browne's humorous, comic-style artwork. They also kept commenting that reading this text was like solving a puzzle.

ARJANIT (10): You know where the 'em the gorilla is… that looks like a puzzle and it's like… he's puzzled they're looking at him like that.
I: Why do you like his pictures?
AMY (4): Because he hides things.

There were many examples in the transcripts of the children's understanding of how Browne used frames to highlight the captivity theme. Doonan (1999):

> There are hand-drawn frames thin as threads (depicting humans), their outlines wavering and bulging at times almost like breathing… There are rigid frames (for the animals), black save for one yellow, and one grey. The apparently small detail like type of frame becomes a vital sign in the discourse.

I: Why do you think he puts that big black line round the animals?
AMY (4): Because the edge of the cage is black.
ERIN (7): They're all barred up like they can't get out, and it's not very nice.

TINA (10): Yes, on the little picture there is hardly any, but then on the big pictures (of the animals) there is a big, black outline round the pictures... on this page it hasn't got a border at all, so it is like he's an animal and he is also free.

The children were also able to talk about how the viewer was positioned, confirming their hunches about the text with reference to Browne's use of colour imagery, perspective and body language.

TINA (10): I've got two things to say. That the big animals have got little bits of wood and the things like the gorillas and the monkeys and the lions have all got bars, so really they haven't got much freedom. And it doesn't look very healthy around there, because it is all really grey on the page.
SUE (10): He's chosen quite pale colours and nothing too bright...
TINA: It is like the giraffe; it's got all dull skies around it, so it seems like there's a factory somewhere near the zoo and letting lots of fumes just near it.

They were also quick to notice Dad's behaviour linked to body posture.

SUE: Because he's a more dominant person and he's shouting and bossing people about all the time.
TINA: He's always big in pictures and there's one picture where he is standing up and he's got two clouds like that and he looks like the devil.

The children had no difficulty in analysing most of the visual metaphors. For example, Browne is clearly making a pointed analogy when he paints a butterfly, perching freely on fresh green grass in identical colours to the tiger who paces across the parched grass of his high metal cage. This was not lost on some ten-year-olds.

LARA: He is kind of like saying the butterfly is free but the tiger isn't.
TINA: It makes you think the tiger has been walking around that bit for ages and made a shape of himself.

The seven-year-olds:

ERIN: Well outside they're free and happy, but inside he's really sad.

And the four- and five-year-olds:

AMY: The butterfly's the same colour as the tiger.
I: Why do you think he put a butterfly out there on the grass?
AMY: Because butterflies live outside.
I: And do you see the colour of the grass there [lush green outside]? But what about the colour of the grass in his cage [dull green inside]?
PAUL: Because it's like a desert inside his cage.

This example shows the development of visual understanding linked quite clearly with age. The youngest children have noticed connections between the butterfly and the tiger and the first glimmerings of understanding that they represent the concepts of captivity and freedom. Although this is a sophisticated idea for four- and five-year-olds to grasp, we believe their responses show that they do. This is backed up in the children's drawings. Five-year-old Amy observes the size differentials between the family members looking at the tiger with fierce claws dwarfed by his large cage. She also notices the grass outside the cage. Ten-year-old Bella is trying something quite sophisticated and 'Brownesque' as the tiger's stripes appear to be melting into the background. Both depict the butterfly outside the cage (the children's drawings appear in Chapter 5).

Paul's analogy, likening the grass to a desert, shows his imaginative interpretation of the picture. By the age of 7, children were able to provide a simple explanation, linking freedom with happiness and captivity with sadness. (The word 'sad' was probably the adjective used most frequently in relation to *Zoo* by children from every age group.) By the time they reach ten years old, children are capable of articulating the visual dichotomy. 'He is kind of like saying the butterfly is free but the tiger isn't'.

A gorilla with 'grandpa's eyes'

The image of the gorilla is one of the most powerful in *Zoo*. The dignified, thoughtful, wise-looking gorilla seems young at the top of the picture and older at the bottom, depicted against a structure which could be a cage or a window, but also forms the shape of a cross. (Browne himself once described this picture as 'my first crucifixion'.) Adults may be familiar with such symbolism from religious paintings and visits to churches, though most do not see the connection until it is pointed out to them. None of the children were aware of the religious iconography suggested by the gorilla framed within a cross during individual interviews. Joe (10) came closest and did notice it in his interview, but he wasn't quite ready to go one step further to make the connection with the crucifixion.

JOE: I think it's interesting the way they've made a white cross right through the middle of the picture and I think it's to show that he's trapped inside this cage. That he drew this thick line to show the cage lines... and he can't get out and he looks... he's got a really sad expression on his face.
I: What might the cross symbolise?
JOE: I think it symbolises that he's just... he can't get out because there's all these wires stopping him... and he just doesn't have the freedom and he can't run around in the wild. He can just sit there while there's all these people staring at him.

One researcher did not pursue this line of questioning in the group discussion since none of the children had made reference to it. The other researcher, however, was very interested in the symbolisation of the gorilla as a Christ figure. Consequently, she was tenacious in her questioning on this issue, not least because she believed the children themselves were aware of some symbolic meaning, judging by their voices and their body language.[1] After discussing Browne's use of frames, cages and bars in the group discussion with the ten-year-olds, she draws their attention back to the cross:[2]

I: Look at this shape. Does it remind you of anything else? We've said windows; we've said bars of cages. Is there anything else this shape reminds you of?
TINA: It reminds me of a sad thing that happened, when Jesus got crucified on the cross and like the monkey is thinking that he might... [voice tails off]

Children as young as 7 eventually noticed the connection in the group discussion.

I: Yes, but there's something else. There's something else. Look at that cage. There's something else in that cage.
ERIN: There's been no white bits in between… because like it looks sad and kind of like he don't want to see in his…
CHLOE: It's like Jesus's cross.

Finally, here's Amy (now 5) and Yu on a second interview, answering the question, 'Why do you think Browne makes us look at things this way in the gorilla picture?'

AMY: It's like a cross… makes me feel sad…
YU: He's got like… a grandpa's eyes.

Empathy and personal analogy

In the final spread, the boy who is the narrator of *Zoo* sits with his head in hands while the bars of a cage are shadowed against his body. All the mischief seems to have ebbed out of him and we are left with a small boy in a subdued and reflective body posture. On the opposite page, we see the zoo buildings in silhouette, dwarfed against a beautiful moonlit sky with two wild geese flying off into the distance. The buildings are angular with straight lines; there are, perhaps, echoes of concentration camps – even a tree appears to be imprisoned – which contrast with the soft roundness of the moon and the curved lines of the geese in flight. The images made a big impact on young readers. Here is Chloe (7), an inexperienced reader who is struggling to articulate her thoughts.

I: What do you think the last two pictures are about?
CHLOE: Like he's a little bit sad because we're leaving the zoo now…
I: How do you know he's sad?
CHLOE: Yeah, because you know he's going like that (points to his crouched position and bent head) he don't feel very well.
I: So you're reading his body posture, aren't you?
CHLOE: Yeah… and he feels like sad because he's like left the zoo and he's like thinking like a dream. He's thinking like a dream. He's like thinking about the gorilla and he's dreaming about it at the same time.

Similarly, Dan (7), also an inexperienced reader, felt a sense of moral injustice on reading *Zoo*, again linking it sensitively with his own experience.

DAN: He's in a cage and been all sad and all that lot.
I: Do you think the boy was feeling bad about the visit to the zoo?
DAN: Yeah, and sometimes when your worst dreams, you like cry in the middle of the night and all that lot… I like this page because it's all black, dark and all that lot. And then birds come along and fly away. And it's nice and peaceful in the dark, I find it is, and I just like these mountains and all that…
I: What do you think Anthony Browne wants us as readers of the book to feel about it?
DAN: Well I think they should read it…

By the age of 10 some children, like Joe, were able to express their ideas more forcefully.

I: What do you think Anthony Browne wants us as readers of the book to feel about it?
JOE: He wants us to stop and think about that zoos may be fun to go to and look at all the animals but it's really horrible for the actual animals... they need to be happy. But they're just stuck in cages for our own entertainment.
I: Do you agree with him?
JOE: In the end I agree with him and when I go to zoos I just don't stop and think about how they might feel.

As we have tried to demonstrate, a significant finding from the research was that, while some children who were fluent readers of print were also good at reading image (such as Joe), it was also noticeable that many children in this study labelled as below average readers (such as Lara) were capable of subtle and engaged analysis of visual texts within an enabling environment: with an interested, experienced reader who listens carefully to their responses and gives them time to think; in a situation where the focus is on talk and image rather than written text and writing; where carefully constructed questions supportively challenge their thinking; through the facilitating process of talking in a focused yet open-ended way with peers and a teacher/researcher with high expectations of what the children could achieve; using a text that is intellectually, affectively and visually interesting and that motivates engagement and scaffolds learning – in other words, a text that teaches (Meek 1988). Indeed, as we read the transcripts, it is almost possible to watch the children working through their particular zone of proximal development into deeper understanding.

LARA: It's a good book because it gives you the feel of what it's like, because I never thought what it would be like in a cage.
I: You've never thought of that before.
LARA: No, but then when I read this book it made me feel different. *It's a serious book* [our emphasis].

An earlier version of this chapter appeared in *Children's Literature in Education*, 32 (4) 2001: 261–281.

Vignette – 'I think she feels the pain of the animals' (Lara 10)

Lara was impressive from the outset. She listened and watched eagerly as her teacher read *Zoo* to the class and clearly couldn't wait to contribute to the discussion. Her answers showed her to be alert, sensitive and fairly articulate. As I knew that one of the two girls I was interviewing must be an experienced reader, I assumed (wrongly as it turned out) it was Lara, and was very surprised to discover later that she had literacy problems. Lara was eager to be interviewed and took an active part in the group discussion later in the day. Her drawing in response to *Zoo* was ironic, featuring a defiant, fashionably dressed woman with a bare midriff behind bars, shouting 'What's everyone looking at?' as families of pigs, foxes and bears jeer at her with cheeky, speech bubble remarks – 'Look at that thing!' 'Hey kids, look at that'.

The most noticeable aspect of Lara's response to *Zoo* was her empathy for the animals' plight which she often highlighted through powerful personal analogy. Looking at the picture of the penguins, she remarked, 'If I had to live in a cage, I would live in the penguins' cage because it has got nice turquoisy colour water and it looks like it's been looked after'. Speaking about the elephant which she has described as 'lonely... because it is in the dark in the corner doing nothing', Lara goes on to say: 'I think he [Browne] is trying to make us feel what you would feel if it was you being trapped in a cage'. She imagines the orang-utan

> is missing his family and wants to be at home where he used to live instead of being trapped in the zoo, because most probably he doesn't want everyone looking at him all the time... and staring and shouting and waving and looking at him all the time. He just wants to be left alone.

Unsurprisingly, Lara was sensitive to Mum's feelings: 'I think she feels the pain of the animals. They want to be left alone and not pushed about and shouted at'. And later: 'The Mum is looking very miserable still because she has got dark patches around her eyes'.

This attention to pictorial detail also helped Lara analyse visual metaphors. She realised that Browne created a dramatic cover for visual impact: 'it makes it different from other books'. She correctly identified the imagery of wild geese on the final page: 'making it look like they're free, but the animals in the cages aren't'. She was also able to read the silhouette of bars against one of the boys: 'they've swopped around, so the boys are in the cage instead of the animals'. Lara was strongly aware of colour symbolism and the emotional intentions of the artist.

I: How do you think Browne shows us the elephant's loneliness?
LARA: Because it is in the dark, in the corner doing nothing. It is all bright then they just go to into this other page and it's all dark...
I: And do you think Browne did that deliberately?
LARA: Yeah, to make you feel what it is like to have everyone looking at you... it doesn't look a very nice place to be in, so that makes you think what would you feel if you were trapped up all the time in a horrible little cage.

Lara's teacher was surprised that she had made such a positive impact on our research, yet the extracts above show that she was deeply involved by the ideas in the book and articulate in exploring them. Did this largely pictorial text enable Lara to show what she was capable of when not held back by problems with decoding print? Did the images provide an enabling structure in which she could develop her ideas? By analysing a sophisticated picturebook (unlike the relatively simple fiction she could manage on her own), was it the case that, for once the complex ideas, images and issues thrown up by this text matched Lara's need for challenging literature? She was so absorbed by this book that it led us to question the diet of texts struggling older readers like Lara exist on, how many chances they normally get to engage with satisfying texts, and whether visual texts should not have a greater part to play in reading development? It also raised questions about whether the short, highly focused approaches to extracts from books in Literacy lessons had replaced more ruminative exposure to literature, where there was more time for young readers to explore texts in their own ways.

We had intended to re-interview Lara, but on the day in question she had the chance of taking part in a special maths game and chose that activity above ours. (Another child was re-interviewed in her place.) It was a useful corrective for a researcher all too ready to make assumptions about Lara's passionate commitment to picturebooks!

LARA: How would you feel… trapped up in a cage and everyone looking at you, staring at you, shouting at you. Treating you really bad… If you think about it, if you had to be put in a cage, that is where you would stay. You would stay there and I can't imagine living in that sort of conditions.
I: Did you think of that before you read the book?
LARA: No, I just thought about it a moment ago.

Notes

1 This shows the difference the knowledge and preferences of teachers can have on learning outcomes even in a situation where teachers were trying to follow a common script.
2 This was certainly a leading question, but one that the interviewer had used regularly with adults on other occasions, many of whom had failed to see the connection.

4 Picturebooks and metaliteracy

Children talking about how they read pictures

Evelyn Arizpe

> I think that stained-glass windows in church help you understand pictures too. Sometimes I go to church to look up at the stained glass windows, just look and try and tell the story, that's all I do. Because before you read a book you can understand a stained-glass window, because you just look. You can learn on a stained-glass window and then when it comes to a book you're ready and you can look at the pictures and know what's happening.
>
> (Tamsin 8)

In *A History of Reading,* Manguel (1997: 104) mentions the similarities between the reading of pictures in the Biblia Pauperum (the first books with biblical images) and those in stained-glass windows: both allowed the non-literate to participate more fully and at their own pace in the interpretation of biblical stories – stories they had previously only had access to through someone else's reading. Even today, with so many images around us that the pleasure derived from this freedom is now so commonplace we take it almost for granted, we find that a child refers to these same stained-glass stories in order to describe how she looks at pictures.

Tamsin's explanation of how she 'read' pictures and the comments made by other children about the way in which they interpret the image, and also what they say about how the author intends us to look, are clues to understanding how they make sense of pictorial narratives. These clues are usually based on children's previous book knowledge and on their experience with other types of media, from comics to computer games. This type of knowledge comes together with metacognitive skills when children answer questions about their expectations of a picturebook, its implied readership and their understanding of artistic techniques. It also reveals their perceptions of the complex relationship between word and image, one of the defining aspects of picturebooks, but also present in other types of media texts.

In this chapter, we will analyse some of the comments children made about reading visual texts in an attempt to understand the thought processes behind these skills. We shall discuss how the children described the artistic processes involved in making a picturebook and how they relate this process to their own creative experiences. Finally, we shall try to pull all these observations together in order to understand how children make sense of their own meaning-making processes and suggest ways that these metacognitive skills can be built on, in order to help young learners become more critical and discerning readers.

'You can also read by pictures': How to read a picturebook

Not all the children were able to answer the question we asked about how they read pictures, perhaps because this was a new idea to them, or because they found it hard to articulate an answer. Generally, it was the more experienced readers or children of 9 and upwards who were able to describe the steps by which they approached a picture. This is a metacognitive ability which involves stepping back, an objectivisation of themselves as readers, something which is not easy to do even for adults.

The first distinction to be made is between the words and the illustrations. Greg (6), already a keen reader, was one of the few young children who was able to take this step back when asked what he looked at first in a picture. 'I look at the picture to give me a clue of what's happening. And then I read the story, the words'. Jim (7) looks first at the writing within the illustration: 'I look if they have speech bubbles and then I read the bit that it says, then read the writing and then look at the picture'. Joe's (10) description is perhaps the most accurate in terms of the eye going between the image and the text, not once, but several times: 'First I look at the picture just for a short while, then I read the text, then I take a longer look at the picture and see what's happening in it and see if there's anything going on'.

This distinction reveals the powerful attraction of the image and the fact that it is often easier to understand than the written text. But what happens when children look at a picture? Where do their eyes go first? Karen (7) demonstrated for the interviewer how her eyes rolled around the picture; other children described their eye movements in various ways. When asked how they read a picture, Corinna (10), Jason (9) and Erin (7) explained that they look first at the 'main parts', such as the characters and the 'things that stand out' or the actual objects and then they look at the background. Kevin (10) looks 'at the overall thing and then the detail'. Dave (8) revealed his scientific knowledge about how the eyes work: 'in your head you translate it from upside-down to the right way, 'cause when you see it, it's the other way'. Alice (9) said she first notices the usual things and then the unusual, like the 'normal' picture of Lily feeding the ducks and then the dinosaur on the other side of the canal. This way of looking, at the norm and then the exceptions, was also applied to *The Tunnel* and *Zoo* by other children. Another way of looking was to first follow the movement of the characters as described by Eva (7): 'I think you look at the people that are walking, see where they're going. It tells you where they're leading you to in the book'.

As with the reading of the text, the reading of images is not a simple left-to-right movement. The eyes tend to focus either on the largest identifiable object or on an object that has a particular interest for the viewer. When Jess (6) was asked what she looked at first in the spread in *Lily* with the vegetable stall, she said 'the bike, because I can ride a bike'. Looking is also affected by the narrative in terms of expectations: a few pages into *Lily*, the children were ready to find both the central characters, but also to search for the monster. So even if Lily was on the left-hand side of the spread, they would look for the monster first. In *Zoo*, they learnt to expect the family on the left-hand side of the gutter and the animals on the right, and they were usually drawn first to the more colourful family side. In *The Tunnel* their eyes followed the sister and brother; as Sean (9) said, 'I look at what is actually happening, like the main characters, and then I look like round the edge to see if there's anything I missed, and then I look at the background'.

Older children are not used to having time to look at a book slowly. Because they read so fast, they sometimes missed details which they only saw when they were pointed out. As Joe (10) admitted:

> Well at first I didn't notice that all the humans didn't look like animals, I just thought they looked like normal people at first. The thing I first noticed was the family because they're the main characters, but then when I looked back I could see all the other people in the background and them looking like animals.

Kiefer (1993: 277) refers to studies of visual perception which found that 'children's eye movements within a pictorial plane are quite different from adults'. The reason for having 'many more and longer eye fixations' may be a learning function, not a sign of immaturity, and the result of this is that children notice more details than adults do.

'Working out things on the page': Deductions

Metacognitive skills were also needed to explain the process by which one tried to make sense of the pictures. Only a few of the older children were able to give detailed descriptions of how they thought they did this. Talking about *Lily*, Carol (10), a struggling reader according to her performance at school, pointed out: 'It seems like you take ages on the book but you're actually looking at the picture and you're trying to know why, working out things on the page'. She goes on to say that what you start looking for in the book is the 'problem. Kind of like you want to know what's wrong with the dog'. Carol has already worked out that a reader forms expectations – about narrative patterns in this case – and looks out for them throughout the book.

Usually, the readers' deductive processes were implied through other comments about the book. For example, when Ruth (8) noticed the fairy-tale book on the cover and endpaper of *The Tunnel*, she thought they 'must tell us that whoever likes the book [is] the main person in the story'. A few pages later, she said she was looking for clues about how this person was feeling. So she is aware that the artist is using symbolic clues, which the viewer must interpret to understand a character and also to signal their importance in the narrative. Later, as she described the pictures of the forest, we can follow her thoughts quite accurately:

> Well one picture is nice and jolly and happy and just trees, and this picture is in darkness, forest, the trees there are very ugly, all swirls and squiggles. And you've got some weird trees at the back and they make you think why is that there, those vines? And someone must have been there, chopping wood. There's a rope. Someone must be climbing.

As she talks about the pictures, Ruth first contrasts their atmosphere, based on colour, light and pattern. She notices the background (weird trees) and then zooms back into the beanstalk and some of the most noticeable details such as the axe and the rope.

Many children told us that the process of reading a picture seems to involve first noticing the ordinary and expected; next, there's the unexpected and extraordinary (there's always plenty of that with Browne and Kitamura); then asking questions, making deductions, proposing tentative hypotheses and then confirming or denying them as the reader moves on to something else, reads the verbal text or turns the page.

Tamsin's (8) account, for example, follows this process closely, though she also considers the main characters' actions, as well as detail and colour, as she tries to find the meaning in the pictures. She emphasises the effort this requires:

> I just look at it and I think, OK now, this is a picture of a stone boy and a little girl with her arms around him. What can that mean? Then you just think the boy's been turned to stone and the little girl's come to save him. That's what I think it is and then you see the stones turning to little flowers, so I think, OK now, this girl has saved her brother and the stones have turned into daisies and the background's changed colour too. So you just need to look really hard.

'Getting the words off of the pictures': The relationship between image and text

Valuing the contribution of the two signifying systems in a picturebook, the words and the pictures, also leads to insights into how children look at them, both at each system on its own and in conjunction. When we asked about the relative merits of word and image, pictures were usually declared more interesting because they were, of course, colourful and eye-catching. We followed up by asking the children whether the book would work if it just had pictures or if it just had words. Most children gave greater significance to the pictures and said that the book would not be as good without them, because the pictures help to show 'what's going on' and also 'what the characters look like, because some people can't read'. Several children thought that a good artist would need fewer words because it is all there in the pictures. As Denise (9) put it: 'The words are interesting because you can read instead of just trying to get the words off of the pictures'.

Most of the children expected picturebooks to have both words and pictures and found it no problem to 'make up' one or the other if missing (many had participated in these sorts of exercises before: drawing pictures for words or making up words for pictures). However, they thought that getting the pictures 'right' was more important than getting the words right. To find out what's happened with just the pictures 'you have to use your head more' (Jason 9), whereas with just words 'you'd have to picture it all in your head, and you could see it would be a lot fatter book because there has to be more writing, describing and everything' (Dave 8). So images are translated into description and detail in a verbal text and are a more economic way of getting a message through, as Tamsin (8) pointed out: 'It would be really hard if he said [wrote] everything that was in *The Tunnel* so he just put in the pictures everything that was in there'.

Another revealing question was whether the words or the pictures told the same story. This proved difficult for many children who simply said 'yes'. However, many of them revised their answer either in the group discussions or in the re-interviews. Because the word/picture dynamics is different in each of the three picturebooks in this study, the pupils' responses were also different. In *Lily*, there is what Nikolajeva and Scott (2000) call a 'perspectival counterpoint' where words and pictures employ different perspectives to tell the story and involve both contradiction and ambiguity. Lily's story is told by the written text and Nicky's by the pictures. In *Zoo*, the written text gives the narrator's point of view (one of the boys visiting the zoo) and the pictures tell the story of the animals; this could be described as a counterpoint in characterisation (humans/animals). Finally, in *The Tunnel*, the text and images tell a similar story except that the text is fairly bland and the pictures reveal much more.

With some prompting, the children who read *Lily* noticed that the words did not explain what was happening to Nicky and why he was frightened or mention the monsters which were only evident in the pictures. The pictures also provide 'the atmosphere' (Angus 9). Without the pictures, said Kevin (10), 'it would just be a happy book'. One of the children with learning difficulties pointed out that 'the pictures tell his [Nicky's] story and if he tells it the people wouldn't believe him'. On the other hand, Lauren (11) thought the words were needed 'to take the story along', to provide the narrative thread.

The responses to *Zoo* were similar because (again, with some prompting) most children realised the words and pictures were not telling the same story. Frank (5) noticed this at an elementary level: the words don't tell the same story as the pictures 'because when he said he had lots of food in the writing it didn't show in the picture. They look at the giraffes and the rhinos but they didn't say in the words'. Cristina (9) knew there was a distinction between the pictorial and verbal discourses even though she found it hard to express it: 'I think the pictures give more description about all the animals and the writing tells you a bit about the zoo, more of the zoo'. Older, more articulate children Lara (10) and Joe (10) really got to the heart of the matter. When asked which she preferred, Lara replied:

> the pictures, because the writing doesn't explain everything what you think. The writing only explains what the book is about and what is happening, but it doesn't explain what you feel and what they feel. So I like the pictures better because then you can think more stuff.

Joe also found the images more interesting because 'the pictures show what it's really like and what's going on with the animals'. He then refers to the perspectival counterpoint described by Nikolajeva and Scott (2001):

> I think they do tell the story in different ways, because the text is more like their [people visiting the zoo] point of view, but the pictures are more of the animals' point of view.

These responses contrast with *The Tunnel*, where both words and illustrations were felt necessary to understand the story. However, readers noticed that, although the words helped to 'guide' the reader through the book, the pictures created the sense of unease. This was particularly apparent in the spread in *The Tunnel* without any words, where Rose is running through the menacing forest. It was also one of the favourite images in the book for many children. Shanice (10) had to 'make up the story… it's making me think why the author put them [the various strange objects and figures] there'. Shanice also pointed out that, by looking at the pictures and making up your own story, 'you can understand more things than the writing'. Tamsin (8) summed up many of her peers' observations about the relationship between the visual and the verbal texts:

> Every book needs a bit of picture to make you understand. I mean if this book didn't really have much pictures except for the one in the front, you'd get lost a bit… if it was just writing you wouldn't really feel like you were in there because there was nothing to show you what it was really like. OK you could use your imagination, but if you want to know what the girl's point of view or the boy's point of view is you'd have to have pictures to see.

It is worth noting that at school Tamsin was considered a 'weak' reader, someone who had difficulties reading 'long' books, according to her teacher. However, as we can see here, her awareness of the reading process was far greater than any of her classmates and, indeed, of most children in the study. She had not seen *The Tunnel* before, but was familiar with other picturebooks and especially with fairy tales.

'He moved his imagination': The artistic process

The relationship between the words and the pictures leads to another element involved in the act of reading and viewing: the implied author/artist and his creative process.

The children's observations on the artistic processes involved in composing a picturebook not only indicate how they understand the pictorial text but also how they use metacognitive skills in doing so. In the following quote from four-year-old Janet, she speculates about the steps Kitamura took to write and illustrate *Lily*:

> Well he first wrote the words and then he drew. He read them and then he drew what he thought might be what he wanted to draw and he looked at the pages. He had a first sketch there and then he looked at them and then he drew them with colours and put them in the book. I always draw people like that [and] if I can write them, I put words. I can write quite a lot of them.

The sequence, as Janet describes it, involves a lot of looking and thinking at various stages, as well as writing and drawing. The words come first and then an attempt at the drawing and finally colouring. She is also aware of the 'sketch' stage which implies the artist might make changes (there was only one other child who mentioned making a sketch first, 'in case he got it wrong'). In her last sentence, Janet reflects on her own attempts at drawing, implying she is somewhat aware of the thinking, looking and revising involved in the process. The only difference is that she adds the words later because, at four years old, she is more confident about her drawing skills than her writing. This was reflected in her second drawing when, after finishing the pictures, she laboriously began to write a text above the drawing.

Throughout her two interviews, Janet attempted to explain her movements, talking about sequence and comparing the way she drew houses (square with triangle on top) with the way Kitamura draws them. She was also very articulate when describing her drawing of the tree monster with strikingly coloured squares above it, representing the warm colours of the curtains in Lily's room (Janet had told me she had similar curtains in her room and her favourite colour was purple), then a yellow square and a black square representing the lit and dark windows in the houses on Lily's walk. Although Janet struggled to talk about the pictures in the book, her sensitivity to Kitamura's use of colour (which unfortunately we cannot represent here) and pattern, is evident in the drawing. Her awareness of the steps involved in the process is also a recognition of the sophisticated cognitive skills which bridge writing and drawing when it is a creative act.

However, behind the children's comments, one can also sometimes hear the cautionary voices of teachers or parents. Browne and Kitamura will be relieved to hear that 'he's very neat', 'he colours in nicely', 'he stays in the lines' and 'there are no mistakes'! This is Carol (10) (mentioned above as a struggling reader), talking about the way Kitamura has drawn the grass at different angles and the way she has been told to do it at school.

Note the choice of vocabulary such as 'texture', which she may have picked up from the interviewer:

> I like the texture of the grass. When I was little I got told to never do it all different ways, so like I've already done that because I've been learned to do that... if I was an artist I wouldn't have done that because I've been learned from school when I was really little.

In general, comments on the artistic process can be divided into three groups: those that have to do with the actual techniques that the artist used; those that refer to the way in which he expressed his ideas; and those that show how the children understood his intentions. In the first group, we find mention of specific paints and techniques, such as the possibility that Browne used a 'blow-pen' to spray the paint in one of the pictures, or that Browne used watercolours and Kitamura used crayons. It does not matter if these speculations are right or wrong, what really matters is that children are not looking at the illustration merely as a finished object but as the result of a process that begins with using a particular medium. Eisner is making a similar point in relation to drawing in his Foreword to Arnheim's *Thoughts on Art Education*:

> In the course of drawing, for example, the child must not only perceive the structural essence of what he wished to draw, which, Arnheim points out, is at the heart of skilled reasoning: the child must also find a way to represent that essence within the limits and possibilities of a medium.
>
> (1989: 4)

Children also regularly commented on the use of shadows, line and, perhaps most frequently, colour, in the pictures. For example, Corinna (10) pointed out the importance of Browne using red for Rose's coat because of its reference to Little Red Riding Hood. Martin (7) said the same thing about Kitamura choosing yellow for Lily's tulips to stand out among the darker colours of the evening. Lara (10), an inexperienced reader commenting on *Zoo*, made many insightful references to Browne's use of colour.

> You can tell they [the animals] are upset because there is this dark one, not many colours, not bright beautiful colours, and it makes you think well... when it's people, it is happy, and it makes you feel oh we're happy, so we should be on the happy page. And the animals are really upset and are on the black page.

Other comments revealed what the children thought was going on in the artist's head as he drew. According to some children, first the artist has to 'imagine' the pictures in his head before he can draw them. Luke (5) thought that Browne writes the words for the story first and then thinks of a good picture to 'match' because 'words and pictures match exactly'. Sofia (8) believed that Browne drafts the written text first, makes a few changes and then draws pictures that match the text. Like others, she believed in the 'matching' of words and pictures because 'you wouldn't have a picture that says this, that doesn't match it, that doesn't quite make sense'. This thinking encapsulates the more literal engagement that some children had with Browne's work, in which words and pictures were perceived as telling the same story. Some of the older, more experienced readers like Lauren (11) had a more balanced view of how the artist went about his work: 'As I am reading it, the pictures link very well with the text, so he needed to know what was happening in both, both in the pictures and in the text'.

Pupils reading *Zoo* and *The Tunnel* were very aware that the author had to 'really think about it'. For example, as Erin (7) said, 'in a way the boys behave like monkeys and Browne chooses to draw monkeys rather than another animal'. In the group discussion, she also spoke of how Browne would have planned ahead carefully before doing it. Dan (8), who participated with Erin in the group discussion, agreed that Browne must have taken his camera to the zoo and then 'wanted to do something very very careful with this book' and that even if he did make a mistake he would not 'give up'.

One question that children found hard to answer was what the artist had to know in order to do the illustrations. Many chose not to speculate but Carol's (10) reply condenses those who did. She spoke of the research Kitamura would have had to do before being able to create his story:

> Well he needed to know a dog that looks like that and he needed to know a family that has a dog and how they kind of look after their dog and somebody that likes walking. You needed to interview somebody, to kind of know more about people and… how they kind of look after their dogs, or do they get scared and what do they do when they are scared and do you have any kids, do they walk the dog…

In other words, like Erin and Dan, there is a sense of the planning and time the work involves, the need to know your subject and then how you are going to set it down on paper.

This links to the third set of comments that imply an awareness of the artist's intentions behind the writing and drawing. Generally, it was considered that the artist had drawn in a particular style to make a picture 'more lively' or 'interesting' or 'funny' so 'people get excited and want to read on'. In some cases, this was linked to enjoyment, but in others it was linked to a commercial interest – creating a desire for reading would also make people 'buy it'. Sometimes their interpretation of the author's motives were linked to the story itself: one child thought Kitamura wrote *Lily* because he had a dog like Nicky (in fact, Kitamura got the idea for this story when he was living with a family who had a small girl he often took for walks in a pushchair). Others thought Browne wrote *The Tunnel* because he had a sister who was very different from him, or *Zoo* because he wanted people to go and see one.

Perhaps the questions that most revealed this awareness about intentions were those about the inclusion of the 'unusual' and this applied to all three books. Most readers suggested that the artists did it for the atmosphere, to make it look 'scary'. Several agreed that Browne and Kitamura draw in a way that makes you want to look carefully and not just turn over pages quickly. However, there were a few children who could only make literal sense of these features. One pupil kept insisting that Browne's 'brain must be off'! Finally, there were also those who said the artist put the things there 'because he wanted to' and as far as they were concerned, that was that.

Thinking, reading, looking and learning: Conclusions

It is important to remember that these comments were made by children from different ages, as well as different socio-economic, cultural and linguistic backgrounds. It was impossible to do any further research into how each of these variables might affect viewing, but it is evident that they were all trying to make sense of the texts in front of them and most were able, to a degree, to express how they were actually doing this.[2]

The children's answers reveal how the eye scans a picture, roaming over it, focusing on what they perceive are the salient features, then looking at the background and other details. They also reveal how the eye moves between one part of the picture and another, piecing together the image like a puzzle. The eyes also move back and forth between the words and the images, leaning on each other for understanding, confirming or denying hypotheses about what is happening in the story. These movements correspond to some of the compositional elements described by Kress and van Leeuwen (1996) in their 'grammar of visual design' where, for example, the informational value of the left-hand area of an image is linked to what is already known or expected and the right-hand side is linked to the new or unexpected.

The children were aware of the thinking, looking and planning required to achieve all this successfully and of the possibility of making and rectifying mistakes. They also revealed an ability to put themselves in the artist's head to imagine how he wanted the reader to react by creating images that inspired humour, fear and other emotions. The children were also able to go inside their own heads to describe what they were thinking and feeling as they read a picture (and also as they drew their own).

Their critical comments and observations suggest how these metacognitive skills can be developed and built on in order to help them become more critical and discerning readers. In the first place, their knowledge needs to be taken into account in the classroom. Once there is a space for them to articulate what they know and to discuss it with the teacher or their peers, they will feel more confident about their own skills and more interested in how the teacher can complement it. This can be done by looking at more picturebooks, comparing and contrasting them, as well as through children's own artwork. Finally, children can be encouraged to bring their experience with other visual media to the classroom and use it to understand the processes of reception and creation and, in turn, reflect upon it, whether it be the latest computer games or ancient stained-glass windows.

A version of this chapter appears in M. Styles and E. Bearne (eds) (2002) *Art, Narrative and Childhood*, London: Trentham.

5 Thinking aloud

Looking at children drawing in response to picturebooks

Kate Noble

> Sometimes I practise when I draw. I draw a lot and it gets much better, I hardly scribble now, you see. I love drawing and colouring in 'cause it's really fun.
>
> (Polly 5)

Polly's comments show one young artist drawing, talking and 'thinking aloud' in response to a picturebook. Sedgwick and Sedgwick (1993: 29) assert that 'however it works, drawing is thinking aloud, a powerful route into knowledge'. Both quotes demonstrate the role of thinking in the creative process, but Polly also captures that unique pleasure that young children can derive from drawing. In this chapter, I will look at how the children in this study drew in response to *Zoo*, *The Tunnel* and *Lily*. Through their drawings, we can see them 'thinking aloud' and begin to understand more about the metacognitive processes involved in creating visual texts.

Children can communicate what they see through their drawings and their drawings, in turn, reflect their responses to the visual stimuli they encounter. In *Art as Experience*, Dewey states that:

> Thinking directly in terms of colours, tones, images, is a different operation technically from thinking in words… because the meaning of paintings and symphonies cannot be translated into words… There are values and meanings that can be expressed only by immediate visible and audible qualities, and to ask what they mean in the sense of something that can be put into words is to deny their distinctive existence.
>
> (1978: 73–74)

A visual experience demands a visual response true to its original form. From Rousseau onwards, we have seen an unprecedented interest in children's art, which has been both celebrated for its aesthetic qualities and explored as a tool for understanding cognitive development. Psychologists such as Arnheim (1966), Kellog (1979) and Gardner (1980) have demonstrated how children draw to make sense of the world around them. In simple terms, the toddler starts by drawing the world she knows and a waxy, circular scribble with two dots eventually becomes her mother's face. Early drawings form a bridge between the concrete world of experience (mummy) and the abstract world of symbols and signs (waxy scribble) and open the way into the other forms of symbolic representation such as reading and writing.

DOI: 10.4324/9781003106326-7

My involvement with the project began as a class teacher and art specialist. This chapter is both a description of my experiences working on *Zoo* with my own class of four- and five-year-olds and an analysis of the drawings of the other children in the study. As the only class teacher/researcher, my pupils had the advantage of being able to spend more time thinking about one picturebook. Our work formed a mini-project where the children were given the opportunity to look at and discuss the illustrations and text in great detail and make their own 'zoo' stories through play and art and craft. I was also able to watch them drawing. As well as working on *Zoo* at the time the researcher visited my classroom, we returned to it a few months later and spent further time discussing the text and drawing our responses.

Analysing the drawings

I have divided my analysis of the drawings into several sections, based on categories adapted from Davis (1993), Parsons (1987) and Lewis and Greene (1983). I start by looking at *literal* understanding, which constitutes a basic level of response, whereby the child draws people or events from the text to communicate the story and content. Next, I looked at the *overall effect* of the drawings, considering qualities such as the aesthetics of the image and a discussion of colour, tone, form and line. Finally, I looked at the *internal structure* of the drawing, examining the composition for balance and the relationship between objects or characters and their relative scale. I found that some of the most interesting *developmental differences* appear somewhere between the overall effect and internal structure. (I will explore these differences later in the chapter, focusing in particular on one exceptional class of ten-year-olds.) Through their individual details many of the young artists move closer to what Parsons describes as the final autonomous stage of appreciation and judgement (see Chapter 1). A case study of an exceptionally gifted child, Yu, exemplifies some of these categories in more detail.

Literal responses

Children drawing in response to all three books showed literal understandings of their narrative content. The vast majority of children studying *Zoo* picked up on the central issue and drew animals trapped in cages. At all ages, children highlighted the contrast between the worlds inside and outside the cages. In many of the drawings of the younger children, an animal subject formed the focal point, often occupying a large part of the centre of the picture plane. Amy's drawing (see Figure 5.1) was made in response to her first reading of *Zoo*. On a literal level, her simple pen-and-ink sketch indicates that she knows that the story is about a family visit to the zoo. Both animals and humans are given equal status in the composition and occupy the same space.

The majority of drawings in response to *Lily* and *The Tunnel* also depicted people and events from the texts, communicating the children's understanding of the narrative. Many of the *Lily* drawings showed a child walking a dog, often placed within an urban scene and feature many of the strange monsters such as the snapping pillar box, the river monster and the grinning tree (see Figure 5.2). Drawings inspired by *The Tunnel* picked up on the sibling relationship and focused on references to fairy tales and physical environmental features, such as the tunnel, the bedroom and the woods.

Looking at children drawing in response to picturebooks 61

Figure 5.1 By Amy (4).

Figure 5.2 By Seamus (7).

Overall effect

The overall effect of each of the three books is very different. In Browne's books, the illustrations are painstakingly drafted and contain meticulous detail of everything from the stripes on Dad's polo shirt to the stony pattern on the surface of the tunnel. Browne's almost photographic realism and skilful control of the composition give a solid overall effect which is heightened by the sensitive use of colour. In *Lily* Kitamura uses colour and line in a very different way. His pictorial style is more direct and cartoon-like with black pen lines encasing a wash of bright primary watercolours. In all three books colour, pattern and line communicate a strong sense of mood and atmosphere and open up many avenues for discussion. Looking at the drawings it does seem that the children have picked up on some of the different stylistic qualities of these two artists.

Will's (9) drawing evokes a disturbing overall effect and vividly characterises Dad from *Zoo* as the devil using light, unstable pencil strokes; the big empty eyes and dark grimacing mouth form an eerie focal point (see Figure 5.3). Will also captures Dad's brightly coloured shirt which contrasts with the nightmarish features on his face. As a finishing touch Will captions the drawing, 'dad the devil are you scared?'

Tony (10) drew one of the most articulate emotional responses to *Zoo*.[1] It is also worth noting that he was one of the children judged to be an inexperienced reader by his teacher and his interview was hesitant and uncertain. A black line down the centre of the page

Figure 5.3 By Will (9).

Looking at children drawing in response to picturebooks 63

clearly divides the picture into two halves which stimulate very different responses. On the left-hand side, he uses a faint pencil line to draw a small human figure and a pig. The figure appears behind long vertical bars whereas the pig is positioned outside the bars and is carefully coloured in a soft pink crayon. On the other side of the picture, a large tree marks the division, negating the existence of any bars in this new world. A large hairy gorilla stands smiling underneath the tree in the centre of gentle, curving arcs of warm light coloured in yellow, blue and red. This side of the picture is coloured in bold, bright felt tip and the overall effect is a potent image of containment versus freedom. Both Will and Tony have moved away from a literal representation of the story and added their own evocative details.

The younger children's drawings in the study were generally freer and less inhibited than the older pupils' in overall effect, and they often used the space more boldly. In response to *Zoo*, for example, Sara (4) (see Figure 5.4) recreates the family, each member occupying equal space across the horizontal picture plane. Her lines are curvaceous and free, enclosed and protected by a large beaming sun in the left-hand corner, complete with a stretch of sky punctuated by one cloud and a flock of round-shaped birds. Her simple pen drawing is happy and spontaneous and the four smiling faces beam out at the viewer.

After reading *Lily* Janet (4) explored the expressive qualities of colour. The top left-hand half of her first picture is covered in a coloured stripe. The first section is made up of thinner strokes of purple, blue, red and brown before a square of intense black and then yellow. Cutting into the yellow square is a large green vertical form which echoes the long neck of the sea creature in the river in Kitamura's story. The green form stands in a large purple square. Janet has worked with a great degree of care and control and the resulting image is both imaginative, original and highly symbolic. Her detailed explanation of the

Figure 5.4 By Sara (4).

composition backs this up; she described the horizontal stripe of colour as representing her curtains, the black square acting as a dark window and the final yellow square showing light pouring through a window. Her second drawing three months later is made with the same concentration, but now shows more interest in planning. Her drawing has become an exploration of forms laid out horizontally across the page, highlighted by a thick purple stripe of the night sky along the top. Drawing this time in felt tip, Janet again uses colour to articulate feelings but her drawing has become more realistic as she experiments with and re-creates the twisted shapes of Kitamura's lamp posts, clock towers, buildings and trees.

Internal structure

Many of the drawings collected in the study show children beginning to experiment with the structure to introduce new viewpoints. Christina (8) (see Figure 5.5) starts by drawing a large orange tiger in the centre of the page and, having rubbed out her first attempt, tries hard to make her picture as realistic as possible. Although she has clearly had difficulties with the head, which is large and awkward, the hind legs and tail are drawn with greater accuracy, with the far leg placed behind the front leg in a convincing way. This thoughtful drafting corresponds with her interview when she talked about the way in which Browne positions a baboon to show it is sitting:

> I think the way he draws the baboon that's sitting down like a lion with his mouth open. He draws all the fur first then he draws two legs and draws two more legs on the front to make it seem that it's sitting up.

Figure 5.5 By Christina (8).

The tiger's tail and paws are carefully shaped, as is the butterfly fluttering outside the cage. The threatening grey felt-tip bars of the cage stretch vertically across the whole piece of paper and are reminiscent of the thick black lines around the animal pictures in *Zoo*. Although Christina has drawn green grass in the cage she makes a clear distinction between inside and outside by the position of the butterfly, shaping the grey felt tip so as not to cover its pink wings. It is also interesting to note that she has continued these games in the top right-hand corner of her picture where she has written 'ZOO', doodling eyelashes and eyeballs on the two 'O's. On a third line, she has written, 'enjoy' a neat little joke of her own which demonstrates not only a real understanding of her drawings as means of communication but also an understanding of the role and position of the viewer.

Several children drawing in response to *The Tunnel* depicted the boy turned into stone, one of the most haunting and compositionally sophisticated images in the book. As in the original drawing, Bobby (8) (see Figure 5.6) has framed the image in a rectangular box, and the reader, peering in on the scene, empathises with the girl's sense of loss and isolation as she finds her brother 'still as stone' and sobs, 'Oh no... I'm too late'. Bobby has drawn in a grey pencil except for a thin stripe of blue on the horizon blended into the grey clouds. The internal elements in the drawing have been placed with care: the jagged grass in the distance, the tree stumps and the circle of stones around the boy's feet. The figure has been re-drawn several times, but Bobby has successfully depicted the boy frozen in motion, arm and leg outstretched to run away and, most chillingly of all, mouth and eyes wide open in fear.

Figure 5.6 By Bobby (8).

66 *The original study on children responding to picturebooks*

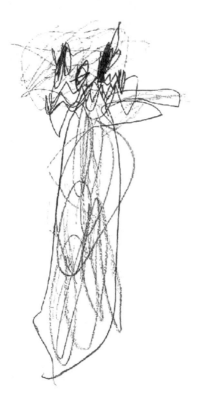

Figure 5.7 By Ashok (4).

Figure 5.8 By Anne (9).

Ashok (4) and Anne (9) chose the grinning tree from *Lily* as the central point in their composition, but a comparison of their drawings demonstrates the differences between the two ages. Ashok draws with great energy and his large green scribble tree is placed in the middle of the picture, complete with its menacing black mouth and dark eyes (see Figure 5.7). The picture is as graphic and direct as might be expected in the drawing of a young child. In contrast, Anne has drawn the tree as only part of the whole composition (see Figure 5.8). Repeated rubbings out around the figure of Lily and the dog show that this young artist has placed considerable emphasis on 'getting it right'. Her colouring in is more accurate and controlled, and, unlike Ashok, she uses careful, solid blocks of colour. The arrangement of the internal elements is more worked out and more skilfully arranged and executed. However, her drawing lacks the direct aesthetic response of Ashok's tree. This deliberate planning brings us to an interesting point about developmental changes.

Developmental differences – Polly 'switches her brain on'

In *Artful Scribbles,* Gardner's young son explains the difference between the drawings of older and younger children: 'As you get older, I think you look differently. You look more carefully at things. Also you think a lot, you plan before you actually make the drawing' (1980: 17). This notion of the role of thinking and planning in drawing comes through in several of the interviews and is evident in the pictures made by some of the older children, such as Christina, Bobby and Anne. However, we found that even younger children such as Polly and Janet were capable of engaging in the metacognitive processes involved in the creation of images. Here are more of Polly's (5) comments whilst drawing[2]:

> I'll just switch my brain on... that's the house in the distance that's why it's really small... Now here I am going to use another green. Isn't grass two different shades of green? This is a lime shade of green...

Unfortunately, Polly's was the only transcript which captured a child talking aloud while actually drawing[3] but Erin's (7) comments to the interviewer also capture an awareness of the role of thinking and planning in the production of images, as well as showing her enjoyment of picturebooks:

ERIN: I really love his books.
I: I want to know why you say that, Erin.
ERIN: Well he doesn't just say, 'I'll just write a story, I think I'll do it about this' and then he writes it. He actually thinks about it. Or he plans it ahead and then he really does good pictures and the pictures tell a different story, the same story only in a different way.

Erin's first drawing (see Figure 5.9) uses bold colours and composition and is emotionally direct. However, by the time of the re-visit, her drawing had lost some of this earlier confidence becoming more concerned with a moral message (like most of the older children) than from an emotional and aesthetic response towards a greater interest in the internal structure of the composition.

Davis (1993) explains this change in terms of 'U-shaped' development. In middle childhood (8–11) children reach the trough of 'literal' translation and are held back by the desire to capture the 'realness' of an object; they are no longer satisfied with a

Figure 5.9 By Erin (7).

drawing which provides the essence or an impression of what they see. Benson (1986) also describes this period as an important time of conventionalism, a preoccupation with the rules of language and of graphic representation. The expressive qualities of the younger children's drawings are, perhaps, a direct result of a lack of restraints and rules. Gardner suggests another possible factor:

> Once writing mechanics and literary accomplishment have advanced sufficiently (as they ought to have by the age of 9 or 10), the possibility of achieving in words what was once attempted in drawings comes alive: the stage is set for the demise of graphic expression.
>
> (1980: 155)

Gardner suggests that the child's drawing is affected not only by the development of concrete operational thinking and increasing awareness of the self and its surroundings but also by teaching methods which emphasise the primacy of the written word as a means of communication. Echoing Gardner, Davis fears that, 'Although artists thrive and survive the literal stage, most individuals are lost in the trough of the U' (1993: 90). The desire for realism is impossible to achieve and only a few very gifted artists ever attain the degree of pictorial accuracy so craved in middle childhood. Most children are defeated by pictorial forms of representation, thus considering themselves unable to draw. This can be seen in the majority of the older children's drawings in the study which seem more constrained than those of the younger children.

The humanities project

As the U-shape model suggests, middle childhood does not necessarily have to herald 'the end' of aesthetic artistic response as long as children are given opportunities to continue to explore, accept and understand the uniquely expressive qualities of art and other aesthetic forms of communication. One class of ten-year-olds in the study proved it was possible to emerge from the 'U'. Working with an experienced and charismatic teacher, these pupils had taken part in an extended humanities project: over the course of the year they had examined the portrayal of refugees from World War II – and more recent conflicts – in a variety of media texts including photographs. The drawings they produced in response to *Zoo* were powerful and visually fluent, as their characters scream and glare out of the picture plane, demanding attention. Their interviews also showed that the children understood and used a wide variety of visual terms:

MAL: ... she probably feels sorry for the animals...
I: So how do the colours signal that?
MAL: 'Cos she's wearing that black and dark... dull and dark colours.
I: So what does that mean? Black, dull, dark colours?
MAL: They're like... you usually wear black for funerals.
I: Right. So you wear black for funerals. And what do black and purple represent?
MAL: Sad and sorryness.

They also discussed compositional devices such as the use of different borders around pictures:

BELINDA: It's like saying that like he probably says that the humans aren't really important, so he put like wavy lines round the picture. That the animals are more important than the humans so he's put like a straight border around the picture...
AIDEN: The animal pictures are all edgy and it's like you know, it gives the... really there's a tension...

This knowledge of picturing devices and techniques is also evident in their drawings. Sally (10) has attempted a complicated composition inspired by the close-up image of the caged gorilla in Browne's original text (see Figure 5.10). She has drawn the cruciform bars of the cage so that they show up white against the grey fur of the gorilla and form a cross two-thirds up the vertical picture plane, deliberately positioning the gorilla's eyes on each side of the top section of the cross. This careful composition is strengthened by her clever use of colour. The drawing is executed entirely in graphite pencil apart from the deep brown eyes and gaping red mouth which form the focal point of the picture and draw the viewer in.

In Belinda's (10) drawing (see Figure 5.11), she experiments with the striped pattern of a tiger. Browne's style is characterised by his attention to the minuscule details of the daily world and many of the children's drawings echo this sensitivity to pattern and design; like Belinda, they experiment with stripes and marks on the animals' coats, playing with ideas about camouflage. A large number of children depict striped animals, tigers or zebras, which echo the bars of the cages, the black-and-white cover of the book and even the stripes on Dad's shirt. In Belinda's drawing, the stripes have slipped off the tiger and metamorphosed into the cage itself, providing an interesting metaphor for the

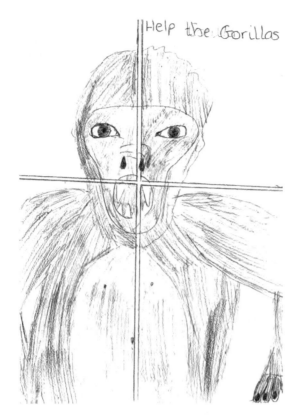

Figure 5.10 By Sally (10).

relationship between environment and animal. As it loses its stripes the tiger becomes unclassifiable to the human eye and the cage takes on a strange, organic and fluid quality of its own. This is cleverly juxtaposed by a lonely butterfly which has been positioned on the bare white paper underneath the cage. The issue of camouflage and the naturalness of the surroundings are the key to many of the drawings from this class and show an understanding of composition, content and message as well as the deeper philosophical and moral implications of the story.

Many of the drawings by these pupils explored the moral dimension of *Zoo*. Some show a clear visual portrayal of human versus animal viewpoints and incorporate words into drawings to increase impact. One unsigned drawing (see Figure 5.12) is divided into two parts named FREEDOM and ISOLATION. On the 'freedom' side of the page, a monkey swings upside-down on a banana tree prophesying, 'no cage will spoil the world!' A smiling, colourful earth is drawn next to a person wearing clothes bearing slogans 'I hate zoos' and 'I hate animals in zoos'. This person says, 'it's great not to be in a cage'. The 'isolation' side shows a caged black-and-white earth with a mouth drooping downwards. Although the images in this drawing are strong and eloquent in their own right, it is interesting that the child felt the need to back up his or her moral view with the written word. This ties in with Gardner's point about the move from visual to verbal forms of communication.

Looking at children drawing in response to picturebooks 71

Figure 5.11 By Belinda (10).

Figure 5.12 Unsigned drawing.

All of the drawings by these older children contain striking individual details representative of the particular interests and motivations of the artist. They show the effects a gifted teacher and an in-depth analysis of visual image can have on the way children think, write and draw. As Gardner says, 'The capacity to consider various intellectual and social possibilities confers fresh powers on an individual's artistry' (1980: 213).

The *Zoo* project

As my class's understanding of *Zoo* developed, so too did the sophistication of their drawings and I can see many parallels between their work and the work of the ten-year-olds described above. This change took place in the context of a series of visual exercises and experiments which were designed to encourage the children to deepen their existing understanding by talking, looking and making. Their work also demonstrates the cognitive link between seeing, doing and knowing.

During our re-readings, I talked to the children about Browne's pictures using direct questioning, and I also allowed the children to ask questions in return. One of the strongest compositional devices and the easiest for the children to see is the juxtaposition of the two worlds inside and outside the cages. We also talked about the way in which the artist uses the left (verso) and right-page (recto) spreads to illustrate the two different sides of the zoo debate. As our discussions about the book continued, many children began to place different emphases on the relative size of animals to humans.

In addition to our focused work on *Zoo,* the class had wide experience of creating their own images, both from their imagination and in response to familiar objects, pictures and stories. Over the course of the year, we carried out a series of experiments with colour, pattern, tone and form which encouraged the children to develop their own visual vocabulary. They were also encouraged to draw their own stories, make books and use their own images as a starting point for writing. This particular class was also characterised by a wonderful capacity for focused looking and great concentration. Just as they were happy to sit for half an hour on the carpet analysing a picture or a book, a simple pencil exercise could occupy them for a whole afternoon. During class drawing sessions, they were often so absorbed that they worked in total silence. Our return to *Zoo* enabled my class to use their newly acquired visual skills, having developed the confidence and control to produce drawings that were closer to their actual understanding.

Revisiting *Zoo*

After the initial in-depth study, I wasn't sure how the children would respond to *Zoo* several months later. When they came in from lunch many of them spotted the book resting on my board and a few started a discussion about which Browne's book was their favourite. When I reread *Zoo* with them I was conscious of a strange shift of power and felt that they were reading the story *to* me, often eager to interrupt my reading of the text with knowledgeable and confident observations and suggestions. During the initial sessions, we had talked about the gorilla picture in some detail, although none of the children had drawn it afterwards. This time they were obsessed with it and one of the most striking observations was made by a normally silent child

Looking at children drawing in response to picturebooks 73

with additional needs, Louis (4), who talked to the class about the compositional similarities between the gorilla picture and the family portraits at the start of the book (see Figure 5.2).

Lyle (4) was an exceptionally articulate child; in the class discussion, he talked in depth about the visual symbolism in Browne's book, particularly the penultimate page which focuses on the gorilla's face. The children noticed how the page is split 'like the bars of a cage' and described the gorilla as 'looking like a king' and 'his eyes look like a person'. When I asked the class whether it reminded them of anything, Lyle responded, 'Jesus. Jesus died on a cross'. When asked why the artist had chosen to draw the gorilla like that he replied, 'Because God made Jesus and God made all the animals'. The children also compared the animals and people: 'The gorilla looks wiser, more like a person'. Lyle concluded, 'I think the animals are becoming wiser and the people are like animals'. His comments tie in with his own deeply religious home background. In *Art and Illusion*, Gombrich writes: 'Whenever we receive a visual impression, we act by docketing it, filing it, grouping it in one way or another, even if the impression is only that of an inkblot or a fingerprint' (1962: 251).

Lyle has drawn on his own bank of visual experience, something all readers do in their own idiosyncratic ways when interpreting or responding to images. Although this particular child was frustrated by his attempts to communicate what he saw and understood visually, his verbal responses showed a proficiency in interpreting and understanding visual references and metaphors. This is a good example of what Kress is saying in *Before Writing* where he describes reading as a transformative action in which the reader 'makes sense of the signs provided to her or to him within a frame of reference in their own experience' (1997: 58). The reading process is multi-modal and, as we have seen, visual meaning can be communicated and interpreted in many different ways.

In *Zoo*, the facial expressions and body language of the family and the animals are powerful communicators of the isolation and pointlessness felt by Mum and the apparent lack of concern of Dad and the boys. As we have noted elsewhere, many of the youngest children were able to talk about facial expressions and body language. My class and I discussed in detail how the individual protagonists within the story were feeling. Initially, only a few of the children were able to articulate these feelings in their drawings, a finding backed up by research cited in Gardner (1980). However, on revisiting *Zoo,* I was intrigued to see that the children now had the confidence and skills to depict some of the more challenging and complicated images from the book. Many chose this time to draw the image of the gorilla within a cruciform frame. Louis (4) made a quite outstanding drawing of the family and the caged gorilla (see Figure 5.13). Although his figures are still very immature and tadpole-like, he has deliberately drawn bemused frown lines on Dad's forehead. A strong white crucifix separates the gorilla from the family and his eyes have been skilfully placed on either side of the top section. Louis has also attempted to write the title of the book. Many others made similar developmental leaps to achieve levels of expression and fluency unusual in such young children. The confidence evident in the discussion is also reflected in the children's drawings as they explore the theme of suffering on the cross – one of the most distinctive and poignant images of the western world – and relate it to the gorilla in the cage. The children were symbolically representing captivity and suffering in their drawings and communicating empathy for animals (and elsewhere

Figure 5.13 By Louis (4).

for people, especially Mum). This finding runs contrary to beliefs about the egocentric perspective of the pre-operational young child.

The final drawings are by Jane (5), who made a quite remarkable leap between the two sessions. Her first drawing shows a literal understanding of the story and depicts a grinning elephant centred on the page inside a square box surrounded by a happy but androgynous 'tadpole' family (see Figure 5.14). Her later drawing is an attempt at the gorilla's face seen through the crossing bars of the cage (see Figure 5.15). Jane has made a deliberate decision about the composition and internal structure of her drawing and has halved the page horizontally and vertically with two thick bars in the shape of a cross. Her drawing focuses on the gorilla's eyes, placing each in the top quarter of the page. She works in graphite pencil to capture the texture of the gorilla's fur, hatching tiny lines in different sizes and directions, using darker, stronger lines on the bottom half of the face to emphasise the gentle sadness of the eyes. Her drawing explores not only Browne's dramatic composition and viewpoint but also his realistic rendering of every tiny hair on the gorilla's face. In both drawings, Jane uses the compositional devices of the cage to communicate entrapment. However, in the later drawing, she is intrigued not only by the positioning of the humans to the animals but also by the psychological dimension. The detail in the fur and the eyes reveals how important she understands the individual animals to be. Her sophisticated composition creates drama and pathos articulated by skilful attention to texture and detail. By experimenting with and talking about artistic devices and conventions, Jane has developed her visual knowledge and is now trying out these devices in her own work.

Looking at children drawing in response to picturebooks 75

Figure 5.14 Drawing 1 By Jane (5).

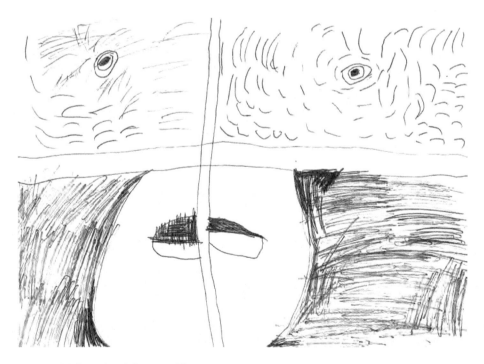

Figure 5.15 Drawing 2 By Jane (5).

Final thoughts

Kellog (1979: 13) points out that 'children's hands and eyes must be active for intelligence to develop'. Looking at the drawings in this study has demonstrated to me that even the youngest children can interpret, comprehend and communicate the visual – far beyond what they might be assumed to know. The young artists in my class came to a deeper understanding through their visual explorations. What seems to happen when we draw is similar to the process that we experience through writing: by doing we come to understand.

Although many children draw spontaneously from a young age, adults have a role to play by allowing space for experimentation and practice. By focusing explicitly on external visual elements such as composition, line, form and colour, the teacher can develop children's capacities to internalise this visual language and, in so doing, come to understand and communicate through their pictures. These explorations should take place by looking at art, as well as developing children's graphic skills. Our study provided opportunities for children to explore what they saw through playing, talking, making and drawing, thus enabling them to demonstrate the sophisticated thinking of which they were capable. Drawing is a serious enterprise for young children; combining drawing with careful looking offers the intrinsic pleasures derived from all creative activities and the special way in which art nourishes 'the invisible realms of our mind' (Gombrich 1962: 239).

Vignette – 'it makes you feel you are trapped in a cage' (Yu 4)

Of all the drawings in the study, some of the most interesting in terms of overall effect, content and understanding are by Yu (4). She is a quiet and thoughtful child and, although both her reading and writing are advanced for her age, she said very little in the interviews or the class discussions. However, her drawings communicated a deep response to *Zoo* and an indication of some of her own preferences, feelings and experiences. In many of her early drawings, the figure of Mum is drawn particularly carefully. As a middle child of a young family of five children, her drawings perhaps indicate the importance and power of her own mother as primary carer.

Yu's early drawings reveal that she has understood the main themes in *Zoo* by depicting the family side by side with animals caged inside their enclosures. Yet, she also shows a striking level of sensitivity to visual elements such as composition, design and characterisation. Yu's first drawing shows a giraffe and a large tree fenced in by a bold, three-barred gate (see Figure 5.16). On the other side of the fence, to the right of the tree, stand Mum, Dad and the two boys who take up the last vertical quarter of the picture. Yu's composition shows an understanding of the contrast between the freedom of those outside the zoo and the unnaturalness of the animals' enclosures. The tree and the fence form a clear barrier between the animals and humans while a small, smiling bird sits on the fence next to the giraffe.

This distinction is reinforced by environmental details. A large sun, a few clouds and birds in the sky of the animal section form a marked contrast to the bars which separate them from the human protagonists. There even appears to be fruit on the

Looking at children drawing in response to picturebooks 77

Figure 5.16 Drawing 1 By Yu (4).

giraffe's side of the tree and on the floor of its enclosure is a nondescript shape, reminiscent of the dirty cages in *Zoo*. Yu has taken the greatest care over the figure of Mum, who is drawn bigger than the rest of the family with details such as her eyes which are drawn with lashes and tiny pupils. Yu skilfully controls the relationship between the different actors in her story by placing one in front of the other. Cox (1992) and others have discussed how very few young children achieve this partial hiding or occlusion in their pictures and will draw, for example, the whole object rather than partially obscuring a hidden object. Luquet used this example to demonstrate that 'children draw what they know rather than what they see' (quoted in Cox 1992: 88).

Later on the same day as the interview, Yu began her second picture, which is an example, not only of her widening understanding but also of the way in which children continue to explore what they see through drawing. Sitting at a table with a group of other children, she began with an exploration of bubble writing which she placed in the top horizontal section of the picture. (I had noticed before how children enjoyed experimenting with typographic conventions and bubble writing is a good way of exploring both the shapes and conventions of text.) Next, Yu started drawing an animal, a cheetah, which was then carefully contained in a cage, along with the bubble writing. As she drew in the bars of the cage she tried not to go over the lines on the cheetah before adding a few thin, dusty strokes of black dirt to the base of the cage. By now she had filled nearly the whole piece of paper, so she reached for another piece on which she redrew the family. Again the tree forms a powerful divide, this time between the parents and the boys who are now squeezed into the left-hand vertical plane of the picture.

As with the first drawing, Yu reapplies carefully practised schema for her figure drawings. While the boys are treated in exactly the same way in both drawings and are nearly identical, once again it is the figure of Mum who receives the greatest attention; she is the largest character, occupying nearly half the picture plane. However, the figures of both Mum and Dad demonstrate changes in her schema. Mum is drawn in profile with her back to the children and her arms outstretched towards Dad to whom she is saying, 'Come back!'. Drawing figures in the profile is very unusual in young children's drawings as once again the child is required to draw what they see rather than what they know. A long, diagonal sweep of hair draws the character in towards the rest of the family. Mum's hands, arms and hair are emphasised, whereas on one of the boys the arms have been forgotten altogether. Dad's face is drawn in greater detail, his eyes are big and open and he has an angry, fuzzy mouth and expressive, upturned eyebrows, more reminiscent now of the father in *Zoo*. While Mum looks at Dad, Dad looks out of the picture towards the viewer. As in the book, he is fooling around and making silly noises, as do the children. Finally, Yu went back to the drawing of the cheetah and added a speech bubble for the animal, 'ha, ha ha'.

Three months later, Yu drew again in response to *Zoo* after re-reading the book in the classroom (see Figure 5.17). In this drawing, a large rhinoceros stands alone in the centre of the page in a dirty, barren enclosure. The cage has no bars and is bare except for the grey bricks of the top right-hand corner and a few mouldy, insipid green patches on the floor. The cage is dirty and scratched with graffiti. Yu has placed the viewer in the cage with the animal, a compositional device employed by Browne in *Zoo*. The most significant change in this later drawing is the facial expression of the animal. This time the eyes are slanted and angry, its mouth is open and teeth bared. The total effect is both unsettling and disturbing – similar to feelings evoked by the neglected, lonely orangutan in *Zoo*.

In the final drawing after the second interview, Yu depicts a tiger and four birds (see Figure 5.18). Three brown baby birds sit inside a nest perched on top of a palm tree while a much larger, rainbow-coloured bird flies towards the right-hand side of the page, pointing in the same direction as a dramatic, elongated tiger. Yu's positioning of the bars of the cage gives an ambiguity to her picture, as the reader is not entirely sure whether all the creatures are inside or outside the cage. Such indeterminacy is, of course, a feature of Browne's work.

Since Yu's first reading of *Zoo*, she has spent time studying not only this book but other natural history books. In her later drawings, the animals are more anatomically correct and individual for each animal type. The tiger is depicted in profile and is angry with a long, wavy mouth and upturned eyebrows. Yu is now working in felt tip and the bright blues of the sky and careful, multi-coloured pattern on the bird produces a powerful aesthetic response in the viewer.

Yu is clearly a gifted artist and her mature understanding of the story is communicated through sophisticated, detailed drawings. She has begun to grasp some of the complex relationships between the actors in the story and her drawings show a striking degree of sensitivity to the emotional state of the main protagonists and the beginnings of characterisation. It is very unusual for such a young child to draw a figure in profile, to represent movement and to layer the composition by deliberately placing one object behind or in front of another. By continuing to provide her with

Looking at children drawing in response to picturebooks 79

Figure 5.17 Drawing 2 By Yu (4).

Figure 5.18 Drawing 3 By Yu (4).

> opportunities to express herself visually, to draw what she sees, Yu will be able to communicate her considerable knowledge as well as adding to it. She is also able to express her powerful reactions to *Zoo*, strong feelings which she was unable to communicate in any other way.

Soon after writing this chapter for the first edition of this book, I left full-time teaching to embark on a PhD, examining the development of visual literacy in young children. My research built on the findings of the original study to explore how 24 children aged 5, 7 and 9 responded to three picturebook versions of the traditional tale *The Frog Prince*. I videoed the children as I interviewed them reading the books, talking about the words and pictures and drawing in response. I then analysed their talk, drawing and actions to explore the dual processes of reception and production in response to picturebooks.

There are many parallels between the findings of my doctoral study and those of the original research below. The most visually literate children I interviewed exerted the greatest control over their drawings and interpretations. The seven- and nine-year-old children demonstrated greater self-awareness of their own drawing repertoires and were able to offer each other advice and support as they drew. They were not always the most confident readers in the group but there was some correlation with reading ability. They set themselves achievable personal goals, monitored and planned their own performances, and demonstrated a complex knowledge of their own capabilities and skills. This 'thinking aloud' through drawing is evidence of complex and sophisticated thinking in action, as has been explored in detail throughout this chapter. The most visually literate children were able to look closely, carefully and deliberately at the picturebooks we read and isolate salient features within the visual images to support their interpretation of the central narratives. They did this with speed and confidence, drawing on a wide textual knowledge to make sophisticated predictions, hypotheses and deductions.

While the older children made more use of real-world knowledge to inform their reading, younger children were more likely to empathise with the characters as we read. This enabled them to make personal and immediate connections with the protagonists as the story unfolded. I found that individual children's level of knowledge was more dependent on personal experiences and interests than upon chronological age indicating the importance of providing opportunities for young readers to experience a wide range of different texts. What was more significant developmentally were the metacognitive differences in the ways in which the children used their intertextual, textual and intratextual knowledge to make connections, comparisons and deductions. Older children were more likely to make more sophisticated connections, distancing themselves from the immediate to locate the narrative within a broader context, while the younger children's responses were rooted in the concrete world of personal experience.

Alongside these cognitive skills, I also found that children of all ages had strong personal and affective responses to the picturebooks we looked at together. These individual preferences, interests and motivations impacted on their meaning-making. The children I worked with took great pleasure in the drawing process, deriving satisfaction from the colours, patterns and shapes they created and as they drew they often sang, joked and shared related memories and events. Individual case studies of three children of different ages within the study further revealed the importance of the role of personal choices, aptitudes and preferences within their meaning-making process. I found that when young children were presented with age-appropriate visual texts they were capable of reaching some of the higher stages of response outlined in the developmental models of aesthetic response described by Parsons and others which will be explored in detail in the following chapter.

In line with socio-constructivist accounts, I found that visual literacy developed through both individual experience and collaborative activity. The social world of the children set the context for their looking, thinking and drawing, both alone at home or with friends and family and at school. Many of the children I interviewed told me that they spent more time drawing and talking about drawing in their leisure time than they did in the classroom. Several children commented on my interest in their drawings, and compared this to their experience of drawing at school where they said they were often only given opportunities to draw when rain prevented outdoor play or in response to a directed, structured task. They were not used to being invited to draw freely at school, or to having an adult talking to them about what they were doing. As in the original study, it was clear that my questioning deepened their engagement with both the process of drawing and with the picturebooks themselves. The process of looking and talking to young children about what they could see allowed them valuable time to think, reflect and create their own interpretations.

Since completing my PhD in 2007, I have worked as an art museum educator. I am committed to ensuring children are given opportunities to develop their visual literacy through art. In the next chapter, we will explore this work in greater depth to unpick some developmental models of aesthetic development and to examine how children can be given valuable time and space to look, think and make in response to pictures.

Notes

1. Unfortunately, this drawing is not included.
2. Polly uses bold colour and line to represent Rose and Jack in the forest, the figure of the wolf in the tree, the tunnel and the siblings' mother shouting, 'Children', (written by the interviewer at Polly's request) from her house at the top of the hill.
3. When I planned my doctoral work soon after, I ensured that observing and taping the children while they drew in response to picturebooks was the main focus of my study.

Part II

New developments in research on children responding to visual texts

6 Young learners looking and making in the art museum and classroom

Kate Noble, Evelyn Arizpe and Morag Styles

There is a buzz of activity as a group of children come into the gallery and sit on the floor in front of the painting, A Village Festival, by Brueghel (See Figure 6.1). A museum educator stands at the front and asks the class to make themselves comfortable. Once they have settled and are still, the educator invites them to focus their attention on the painting in front of them and sets them a challenge to look closely and deeply. She asks them to focus their concentration by scanning the painting from top to bottom, from left to right. As she describes the task, she traces her finger above the surface of the picture to demonstrate the direction in which their eyes will travel. She encourages them to work at their own speed, to move quickly over some parts and to stop, to dwell, to spend time where they find something of interest or intrigue. They look together, in silence, for several minutes, each member of the group deeply absorbed as they discover the details of the picture in front of them. The calm and quiet in the room contrasts with the earlier noise and movement as the group now work together in silent contemplation. The minutes pass slowly until some of the students break away from their looking and turn their attention back to the room and their surroundings, signalling that it is time to move to the next part of the session.

This vignette invites us through the doors of the art museum and describes the experience of reading a painting with a group of school children. Nodelman describes a museum as being a 'sort of picturebook, and the images in it like illustrations within it' (2018: 19). There are similarities between this example and how a classroom teacher might introduce a new picturebook to a class for the first time before moving on to a class discussion. The educator sets the challenge of careful looking and scaffolds the children's exploration by modelling a structure for their enquiry. Due to the public nature of the art museum and size of the painting, this act of reading is a shared experience, similar to reading a picturebook with a child or group of children. Once the group have formed a personal understanding and connection with the themes and content of the painting, they will share and reflect on their ideas with the rest of the group.

Since the first publication of *Children Reading Pictures*, other researchers have demonstrated how developing children's awareness of the principles and elements of visual design enhanced their understanding of picturebooks (Pantaleo 2020; Sipe 2008) and helped students to become proficient in visual analysis of a range of different media. For example, Serafini (2015: 453) describes the complementary relationship between fine art and picturebook art and how they can serve as both an accessible introduction to fine

Figure 6.1 A village festival in Honour of St Hubert and St Anthony by Pieter Brueghel the Younger © The Fitzwilliam Museum.

art and the world of the art museum in the classroom and as an extension of the reading curriculum. He points out how visual references in picturebooks both increase children's exposure to fine art and help young readers to understand the visual codes necessary for interpreting contemporary picturebooks (2015: 452). This chapter explores this relationship further, drawing on art museum research and practice and exploring different methodologies for supporting children to look at, understand and respond to works of art. We start by introducing the concept of slow looking within the art museum to demonstrate the link between looking and thinking before considering the findings of our original research in relation to developmental models of response to pictures. We will then conclude by considering the power of making and the importance of providing opportunities for children to produce their own art in response to pictures.

Slow looking together in the art museum

The careful work of the museum educator in the example above reminds us of the difference between looking and seeing. When we first walk into an art museum, we might notice a picture on a wall in front of us. We can glimpse a few shapes or colours or pause to read the label as we walk past, but we won't actually get to know the painting from such a fleeting, casual encounter. Research shows that the average museum visitor spends between 15 and 30 seconds in front of a work of art and much of that time is spent reading the label (Smith, Smith and Tinio 2017). In contrast, the group looking at *The Village Festival* is supported by the museum educator to take time to get to know a picture through prolonged, careful observation. As described in the previous chapters, the act of looking is a serious cognitive task. In *Slow Looking: The Art and Practice of Learning Through Observation* Shari Tishman explains,

> Whatever sensory form that it takes, slow looking is a way of gaining knowledge about the world. It helps us discern complexities that can't be grasped quickly, and it involves a distinctive set of skills and dispositions that have a different centre of gravity then those involved in other modes of learning.
>
> (2018: 2)

The discipline of slow looking crosses traditional subject boundaries. Careful observation informs the work of scientists, writers and artists alike. Take the example of a pebble, washed up on a beach. The scientist, artist, writer might all pick up the pebble and take the time to examine it closely. The scientist might look at the texture and structure of the rock, notice small imperfections in the surface and make a field drawing to record their observations, accompanied by notes about its geological origins and properties. The artist might also spend time appreciating the shape, lines and textures, noticing the colours and how light falls and reflects on its surfaces. They could make a drawing of what they have seen – thinking carefully about which colours to mix, what materials to use and how to replicate the smooth surfaces of the stone on the pages of their sketchbook. A writer might also pick up the pebble and turn it around in their hand, contemplating the weight, texture and colours they can see. They might then think about which words they would use to describe and capture this visual and sensory experience. All three are engaged in the process of slow looking but in each example, this process is mediated through their distinct knowledge, understanding and expertise. In all three examples, the initial act of slow looking is vital to their understanding of the pebble. By looking closely and thinking carefully about what they see they begin to create their different and individual meanings.

'The intelligent eye': The link between looking and thinking

Tishman worked with Gardner as part of the Project Zero Team at Harvard University who have produced much evidence and ground-breaking theories on arts education, including work on multiple intelligences and visual analysis. In his attempt to link human development and the artistic process, Gardner studied the moment in which children begin to understand and use symbolic systems. He thought it probable that, by the ages of three or four, children could experience 'discrete emotions', including those in response to a work of art, though they would not be able to articulate those emotions. Perkins, who was also part of Gardner's Project Zero research team, provided us with illuminating observations about how looking at art engenders thinking and set us off on a fruitful line of inquiry as part of the original reading pictures research. In *The Intelligent Eye: Learning to Think by Looking at Art*, Perkins shows how this works:

> looking at art has an instrumental value. It provides an excellent setting for the development of better thinking, for the cultivation of what might be called the art of intelligence… [and] a context especially well suited for cultivating thinking

dispositions... as [works of art] demand thoughtful attention to discover what they have to show and say. Also, works of art connect to social, personal and other dimensions of life with strong affective overtures.

(1994: 3–4)

Perkins is interested in how exposure to works of art encourages children to think analytically. Rather than produce a model of aesthetic appreciation, he cites the characteristics offered to viewers by works of art and relates them to young learners. First, he talks about the *instant access* offered by a work of art which 'can be physically present as you think and talk, providing an anchor for attention over a prolonged period of exploration... The image is here and now' (1994: 85). Instant access is followed by *personal engagement*: 'Works of art invite and welcome sustained involvement... by their very nature [they are] likely to stimulate one kind of spasm (sympathy, revulsion...) or another... thinking is a passionate enterprise [calling for] concern and commitment, spirit and persistence' (1994: 13). Although many of the theorists recognise the importance of personal engagement in looking at visual texts, Perkins alludes specifically to the powerful reactions this can provoke, such as genuine passion in the eye of the beholder, something we observed in many of the children in our study.

Perkins goes on to talk about works of art addressing a range of symbolic systems through *wide-spectrum cognition*, which generates the involvement of multiple sensory modalities (e.g. spatial, pictorial, verbal). Finally, Perkins argues that art is *multiconnected*, linking social issues, aesthetic concerns, trends of the times, personal convictions, different cultures, 'creating opportunities to bridge thinking dispositions across to diverse other contexts explored in tandem with the work of art' (1994: 85). He is particularly excited by 'the challenge of transfer' where learning in one context impacts on another. We noted this multiconnectedness in the responses of children from different cultural backgrounds. (Chapter 9 makes reference to more recent findings in relation to cultural transfer.)

This 'model' is prefaced on Perkins' concept of *experiential intelligence*, 'the contribution of applied prior experience to intellectual functioning', and *reflective intelligence*, which refers to the knowledge, skills and attitudes that contribute to mental self-management.

> We can prompt our experiential intelligence, cajole it, aim it, redirect it, to arrive at more varied and deeper readings of the work before our eyes... By cultivating awareness of our own thinking, asking ourselves good questions, guiding ourselves with strategies, we steer our experiential intelligence in fruitful directions.
>
> (1994: 82–85)

Perkins' two kinds of intelligence saw many echoes in our study, with the second, richer vein of thoughtful interpretation emerging after some time had elapsed from first looking at the visual text.

Developmental theories on looking at art and links to the original research

When developing our original research, the most substantial developmental theory we found about the way people come to understand art is by Parsons (1987). He contends that children respond naturally from a young age to the aesthetic qualities of art. On the evidence of about ten years of somewhat eclectic research with a wide variety of adults and children, Parsons sets out stages of aesthetic response to art. The first stage he calls *favouritism* as 'an intuitive delight in most paintings, a strong attraction to colour, and a freewheeling associative response to subject matter... Most young children understand paintings at this level' (1987: 22). This stage is characterised by simple responses such as liking the subject matter or the colour of the picture. The second stage is characterised by *beauty and realism*, where the viewer recognises other people's viewpoints as well as her own. At this stage, realism tends to be favoured above other styles of painting. The third stage Parsons describes as *expressive*, when the feelings provoked by the work of art begin to become more significant and the viewer becomes more interested in the artist's intentions. The fourth stage focuses on *medium, style and form*:

> The new insight here is that the significance of a painting is a social rather than an individual achievement. It exists within a tradition, which is composed by a number of people looking over time at a number of works and talking about them.
>
> (1987: 24)

In Parsons' final stage, *autonomy, judgement* and *dialogue* are the keystones: 'The result is an alert awareness of the character of one's own experience, a questioning of the influences upon it, a wondering whether one really sees what one thinks one sees' (1987: 25). This Parsons links with dialogue and reflection.

While we would agree with Parsons that most children's initial responses to art fall within categories 1 and 2, using his own criteria, we can provide several examples of children fulfilling stages 3–5 in many regards. Accepting that all children reach level 1 as of right, let us take one of the key criteria in each stage and examine it in the light of our evidence.

Stage 2: Realism

It is true that most children like realism in pictures. We had many examples of children making comments to that effect. One of the three picturebooks in our study was mainly realist in style (*The Tunnel*), while in *Zoo* Browne depicts the animals with almost photographic realism, contrasted with a mixture of realism and surrealism, as people turn into animals. However, the non-realistic aspects of *Zoo* were as appealing to the children as the realistic: while they loved the pictures of the animals, they were often fascinated by the strangely metamorphosing humans growing webbed feet, stripey bodies and tails. Kitamura's *Lily* does not use realism at all, drawing instead on a highly stylised method of painting, with many characteristics in common with the cartoon world into which most children have been saturated by exposure to television. None of the children seemed to find *Lily* less interesting or enjoyable because it deviated from realism. Our findings suggested that, although children do favour realism as a style of painting, they can find other styles of art equally absorbing and understandable. Many other best-selling picturebook authors, such as Eric Carle, Maurice Sendak, Emily Gravett, Shaun Tan and Mini Grey do not use realism in their work. It seems more likely that children favour styles of art that amuse, delight and challenge them and that the range of styles, which they take pleasure in and understand, is much wider than Parsons suggests. Of course, the fact that his study only included paintings by famous artists, rather than narrative texts geared to children, may make a significant difference.

It is also interesting to reflect on different attitudes to visual aesthetics internationally. In *Children's Picturebooks: The Art of Visual Storytelling* (2012), Martin Salisbury describes the success of the Italian artist Beatrice Alemagna in several European countries as well as East Asia but notes that her work is only just beginning to break into the English language market. He suggests that this might be due to the long tradition of British illustration for children which is firmly rooted in representational painting which 'has led to narrower perceptions of graphic "suitability" in picturebooks' (2012: 69). This point further demonstrates the need to be critical and reflective about the range of picturebooks we share with children in order to give them experience of a broad range of visual styles through picturebooks which represent different visual cultural heritages.

Stage 3: Expressiveness

Children from 4 to 11 showed strong emotional reactions to the picturebooks. *The Tunnel*, a tale of conflict and reconciliation between siblings in a part modern/part fairy tale setting, provoked fear, sympathy and joy in equal measure; empathy and revulsion were the strongest feelings expressed about *Zoo*, which unleashed a debate about captivity and freedom; whereas the children who read *Lily* were aware of the menace in the text, but could distance themselves from it through the humour and the contrasting viewpoints of the two central characters. In response to all three books, the children not only talked about their feelings or related the subject matter intelligently to their own experience, but often considered the artist's intentions most thoughtfully when invited to do so by the interviewer (see Chapters 2–5). Our evidence suggests, therefore, that many of the children in our study reached level 3 of Parsons' hierarchy in the interview and discussion situation. How much this was brought about because of the nature of our questions and how much the children would have spontaneously achieved this by themselves remains a question.

Stage 4: Medium, style and form

In this category, Parsons is concerned with understanding the social and artistic context of a work of art and the sense of the artist working within a tradition. This is a sophisticated position which Parsons assumes only a minority of viewers will achieve. However, we should like to emphasise the number of times pupils made references to other books by the same artist, comparing and contrasting what they were doing in the book in question with his other work. For example, four-year-old Amy is devoted to examining *Zoo* for the 'changes' she knows Browne makes in other books, including *Changes*. Before she was three years old, Evelyn's daughter, Isabel, on entering an exhibition of picturebook artists, shouted 'Lily' on seeing examples of Kitamura's work on the walls. These particular pictures were not taken from *Lily*, which she was familiar with: Isabel had simply recognised Kitamura's style of painting. Many of the children in our study were very interested in how the artists had painted the pictures, what medium they were working in and why they used a particular style, voicing their opinions with confidence ('He's a good artist because…'). We would suggest that many of the children in our study fulfilled significant elements of stage 4.

Stage 5: Autonomy, judgement and dialogue

We want to emphasise the serious, careful way most children examined the texts in our study. The interviews gave children the opportunity to take their time to think about the books in the supportive context of a one-to-one conversation with an interviewer. The discussions gave them the chance to listen to what others had to say, to exchange views with their peers and generally to collaborate in their learning. In so doing, their judgement was being extended by the research situation.

Using image-based thinking routines in the classroom and the museum

Since the publication of the first edition of this book, the 'Visual Thinking Strategies' (VTS) approach has been developed and adopted by art educators as a way to support discussions around works of art. Developed in the early 90s by museum educator Philip Yenawine and psychologist Abigail Housen (Housen 1999) VTS draws on Parsons' model, and describes each stage of interpretation as sequential. In the words of Housen, the approach,

> is not about dispensing facts and modelling expert performance. It is about facilitating the aesthetic response as it naturally occurs at each level of development and creating an environment to experience art viewing in a new and richer way.
> (1999: 28)

Within this developmental account, the viewer is only capable of seeing and understanding in line with their existing cognitive and aesthetic capacity. Within stage I of VTS, *Accountative* viewers are storytellers, using their senses to make personal associations and concrete observations. At Stage II *Constructive* viewers set about building a framework for looking at art, using their own perceptions, knowledge and values. At Stage III, *Classifying* viewers adopt the more analytical and critical stance of the art historian – identifying each works' singular place, school, style and time. At Stage IV, *Interpretative* viewers seek a personal encounter with a work of art, allowing critical skills to interact with an understanding of feelings and intuitions. At the final Stage V *Re-Creative* viewers build on substantial experience viewing and reflecting on works of art to 'willingly suspend disbelief' (Housen 1999: 11). The VTS approach encourages the use of 'developmentally appropriate questions' in order to help viewers to move through each of these five stages to develop a more sophisticated understanding of how to look at art. VTS offers useful strategies and guidance to support looking closely at art with young children. However, our original research on children reading picturebooks contradicts theories about a rigid developmental model of visual literacy by demonstrating that even the youngest children are capable of reaching sophisticated understandings of visual imagery which have much in common with Stage IV and V of the VTS model. This was supported by the findings of Kate Noble's doctoral research as described in chapter 5.

Educators and researchers have drawn on the VTS framework to support close looking at picturebooks. In her work at The Eric Carle Museum of Picturebook Art, was inspired by VTS to develop The Whole Book Approach, designed to help concentrate readers' attention to the picturebook as art form and engage with the visual elements of the design. She stresses the importance of reading picturebooks 'with' children by asking carefully considered open-ended questions and giving them the time to follow, develop and explore their own ideas and observations. Pantaleo (2020) cites VTS alongside other interpretative frameworks in her case study of eighteen nine-year-old students exploring the development of their meaning-making skills and competences by studying the visual elements of design in picturebooks. She found that students were appreciative of being given the opportunity to slow down and look carefully at the visual features and details of the illustrations. She concluded that slow-looking pedagogies had the potential to both support students' visual literacy to develop deep thinking and deep looking. However, she warned of the need for educators to both recognise the importance of this work and to teach slow looking as a learnable practice within their setting. Pantaleo's work demonstrates how students can be taught slow-looking strategies to interpret picturebooks by using different frameworks for guiding visual enquiry.

Another popular strategy to scaffold close looking and careful consideration is the toolbox of visible thinking routines created by researchers at Project Zero. Routines such as, 'See, Think, Wonder' or 'Connect, Extend, Challenge' encourage students to develop their thinking skills. These offer different frameworks to help students to go beyond their initial observations, to interpret and question what they see before moving into more creative, imaginary realms of investigation (Perkins 1989, 1994; Ritchhart 2011). Kate Noble worked with colleagues Holly Morrison and Rosanna Evans at The Fitzwilliam Museum to adapt the 'See, Think, Wonder' routine to create digital learning resources to support children, teachers and families to engage thoughtfully with works of art when the museum was closed during the pandemic (Noble, 2021). Using open-ended prompts and questions with the three-step prompt 'Look, Think. Do', the resources encouraged children to consider what they saw and apply these observations, to make connections and links with other knowledge and ideas. Many of the simple routines in Project Zero's Toolbox can be adapted and refined for use with picturebooks to help focus a discussion or investigation and to provide an anchor for creativity and deep thinking.

Supporting the development of visual literacy by looking at and talking about pictures together

As seen earlier, the art museum and classroom are social spaces that offer many opportunities for individual and collaborative explorations of this complex multimodal world. Many art educators draw on Vygotsky's socio-cultural theory to acknowledge that knowledge is socially constructed, and that the use of language and art are connected to the development of cognition (we unpick this further in chapter 10). Within this framework, participatory art practice has the potential to enact change, to empower, to strengthen and to bring people together, as described by Francois Matarasso,

> Art is the creation of meaning through stories, images, sounds, performances and other methods that enable people to communicate to others their experience of and feelings about being alive.
>
> (2019: 46)

Through the process of creating meaning, many voices are better than one and all have the opportunity to contribute. In *Teaching in the Art Museum*, Burnham and Kai-Kee

(2011) describe how a group works together to reach a shared understanding of an artwork. Through this collaborative enquiry, some will see things, others do not and by working together they will reach a deeper understanding of the ideas and stories represented and of visual elements of design such as composition, colour, technique, symbolism and style. An educator can guide and support this process by creating opportunities for engaged and extended dialogue through careful and thoughtful questioning. This approach has parallels with dialogic teaching principles such as those described by Robin Alexander (2020), which can be used to plan and guide classroom talk. When conversation is participant-led, the experience of close looking and meaning-making will be different each time. A skilled art educator makes this process seem easy, as conversation ebbs and flows and appears to be naturally propelled by the insights and observations of the group focused on a work of art or picture. McLeod et al. (2017), found that the artist-led programmes at Tate Liverpool gallery gave children valuable opportunities to express their ideas and develop their creativity, and noted that, 'knowing how and when to respond, model, extend, stand-back or interrupt is significant for motivating and encouraging children's involvement in creative thinking and learning' (2017: 942). This finding is echoed within the UK-wide Creative Partnership Project, which found that arts practitioners were often highly skilled in supporting pupil talk, allowing crucial wait and thinking time (McLellan et al. 2012). In this way, approaches used by art museum educators to support art-making and close looking at images and objects can provide insight into how to encourage collaborative creative enquiry around picturebooks.

There are very few studies exploring the direct link between looking at paintings in an art museum and the development of wider literacy skills and dispositions. Lefroy (2018) found that her 11 and 12-year-old students' understanding and appreciation of symbolism and style in art increased after studying paintings as part of a visit to an art museum and that this had some impact on their ability to analyse these features in written language. She also reported the positive effect the museum visit had on students' confidence and motivation. She reflected on how students found that seeing one image at a time rather than flicking through them made them more accessible and so empowered them to draw out their own interpretations. An art museum-based visual literacy programme developed by Barbot et al. (2013) aimed to improve writing skills in a group of six to eight-year-olds through museum workshops and teacher training. They found the programme led to an improvement in the use of vocabulary, narrative structure and originality and a better sense of observation and increased inferential thinking. They employed a specially designed Perception, Interpretation and Expression (PIE) teaching framework which emphasised skills which were transferable to writing. The framework supported children to move from observation and representation through perception of visual images, to develop their spoken expression through interpretation and to express themselves through writing based on the visual stimulus. They found that this approach encouraged children to use evidence to support their ideas and develop their confidence and self-expression. It is interesting to note that they also found the positive benefits of using sketching as pre-writing to support the generation of ideas, planning of characters and plot, as well as other creative processes. This finding is supported by the CLPE Power of Pictures research (2021) which found that when children were given opportunities to draw as part of the writing process it helped them to formulate, develop and extend their ideas and made their independent and self-initiated writing richer.

Thinking through making and materials: Responding creatively to picturebooks

As the MAMBO case study demonstrates in the next chapter, museum educators often use picturebooks and art-making as a bridge between the world of home and the school and the world of the art museum. The familiar act of sharing a picturebook together can be reassuring for new visitors within the unfamiliar context of the museum. Once the story has been shared, the group can explore the gallery together, looking for links between themes and subjects within the narrative and the museum collection and make their own art in response. In their Early Years residency research at The Fitzwilliam Museum (Wallis and Noble 2022), *The Gruffalo* by Julia Donaldson and Axel Scheffler was read to the group as an introduction to some of the animals represented in the ceramics gallery and to set the scene for story making. After reading the book together in the gallery with puppets and other props, the children were invited to go 'on safari' around the room to find the different characters in the cases as shown in Figure 6.2.

This exploration was then extended through a drawing activity on a long roll of paper laid out on the gallery floor. Using a range of drawing materials to re-imagine the story, children were invited to use lines and movement to represent the footsteps of the different characters and collaborate to invent new stories.

In the example depicted in Figures 6.3–6.5, the act of drawing became a story in its own right as the children experimented with line, colour, shape and movement. Through the enactment of non-representational meaning-making children created their own sensory and embodied narratives tied to their experiences of the picturebook

Figure 6.2 Sharing The Gruffalo in the gallery.

Figure 6.3 Drawing together in the gallery, *Figure 6.4* Drawing with a friend, *Figure 6.5* Drawing with pencils and string.

and the museum objects and generated their own lines of enquiry. Drawing on Haynes and Murris' (2019) post-humanist re-configuring of the picturebook, this example demonstrates a move beyond the human and discursive to explore the 'more-than human and the material': the space, the floor, the atmosphere, the sounds, the cabinets, the museum objects, the art materials and the movement and entanglement of the children's bodies. These elements intra-act and fuse together and have a power of their own, 'overflowing with possibilities' (2019: 305). Matter is not just being, it is ongoing and un/doing capable of endless (re) generative possibilities (Barad 2015: 411) and meaning emerges from the 'intra-action' between the child and the materials with which they are working. This example can be held in contrast to the idea of the museum viewing experience as distant and untouchable (Nodelman 2018). Children's encounters with picturebooks within the art museum are transformed by harnessing the power of making and materials. Art-making experiences of this kind can also enrich understanding and experience of picturebooks within the classroom or library. Through making, we explore our experiences, feelings and sensations, and conjure up emotion and sensation through our use of colour, line and shape. Making art enables children to develop their creativity, imagination and curiosity and to explore and tell their own stories.

Pictures all around us: Why we need art and visual literacy education

The human desire to make pictures in response to what we see, feel and experience in the material world can be traced back over 40,000 years to the cave art of our ancient Palaeolithic ancestors. As Hockney and Gayford (2020) tell us, our picture-making history includes paintings, photographs, illustrations, advertisements, computer-generated images, virtual and augmented reality and traverses the boundaries between home and school, high and popular culture, moving and still images. Since the first edition of this book more than 20 years ago, there has been an unprecedented growth in visual forms of communication. Children's textual worlds have become increasingly multi-layered and complex, mediated through many different modes of sound, image, word, gesture and movement within a rich pictorial landscape.

Although children and young people are often characterised as digital natives, we cannot assume that their visual competence will develop spontaneously. Pavlou's (2020) study on digital storytelling in primary education reveals the potential of empowering students to use visual media critically and creatively in the classroom but she stresses that, these competences do not evolve automatically – the educator must provide opportunities and support children's efforts. This is supported by Pantaleo's work (2020) which demonstrated how young children were taught to read images by focusing on the visual elements of picturebooks. The ability to engage critically with complex and multi-layered texts within our visual culture is all the more important for these 'digital natives' (Prensky 2001) as the internet and social networks are carried around in their pockets. Piotr Czerki describes this in his Web Kids Manifesto,

> […] we do not 'surf' the Internet to us it is not a 'place' or 'virtual space'. The internet to us is not something external to reality but a part of it: an invisible yet constantly present layer intertwined with the physical environment.
>
> (cited in Meyer 2017: 378)

For today's young people, there is no separation of the digital and physical. In the UK, 69% of 12–15-year-olds have a social media profile (Orben 2020). Social media platforms such as TikTok, Instagram and Snap Chat send a steady flood of images, text and sounds into their phones connecting them with friends and providing games and entertainment. Visual literacy skills, the ability to understand, to interpret, to engage critically and to create multimodal visual narratives are vital and urgently needed for the young citizens of the 21st Century.

Ironically within that same 20 years, time spent teaching visual art in primary schools has been on the decline. The 2016 National Society for Education in Art and Design survey of UK state schools reported that 43% of KS1 and 38% KS2 teachers indicated that in the last five years the time allocated for art and design had decreased (NSEAD 2016: 12). 17% of KS2 respondents reported that the access to art and design for pupils in their schools was only one hour a month or less. There has also been a reduction in the time spent training teachers to teach the subject (Gregory 2019) and a decrease in opportunities to take part in subject specialist professional development opportunities and this trend is also the case in other European countries (International Society for Education Through Art 2015). This decline in art teaching and training is concerning, but is even more worrying when set within the context of both a rapid evolution and growth of digital, image-based media. The failure of school-based literacy programmes to address multimodal definitions of literacy means that a generation of children are missing out on vital opportunities to learn about and make pictures. It is clear that visual modes can provide a particularly powerful tool for even the youngest children to access their thinking and communicate their perspectives. Looking at, responding to and making pictures supports children to develop their visual literacy, and builds knowledge, skills and confidence in interpreting pictures. It might also help to prepare for their immersion into the visual elements of the digital world.

From picturebook to museum and back again

This chapter has demonstrated some of the different strategies and approaches educators use to support children to look carefully and think about pictures. However, it is important to start by creating the right environment for looking. Perkins describes four dispositions to looking at art which can be applied within both the art museum and classroom:

1   Give looking time
2   Make looking broad and adventurous

3 Make looking broad and deep
4 Make looking organised (1994: 34)

The first point about making time for visual enquiry is key and was found to be so important within our original research. The second and third points emphasise the importance of using carefully considered questions to encourage children to think deeply, speculate and take an open playful and adventurous approach to meaning-making. The final point about making looking organised is central to providing training in visual enquiry. As we have seen, slow looking is a learnable practice and there are many different approaches for educators to draw on to support teaching and learning in this area.

It is a wonderful experience for children to be taken to a museum or gallery to look at original artworks and every child should have the opportunity to do this at least once in their school career. However, it is now possible for educators to bring the art museum into the classroom in a way which we could only imagine when we first published this book in 2003. Schools have a range of technology available such as whiteboards, visualisers and projectors which enable them to enlarge images and artworks from picturebooks, museums and galleries to share with a class of children. The closure of many public museums and galleries during the coronavirus pandemic enabled many museums and galleries to prioritise making high quality, downloadable images of artworks and objects from their collection easily accessible (Feinstein 2020). These resources can introduce children to their rich visual heritage, support the teaching of close looking and thinking about pictures and provide inspiration for them to explore their ideas and to create their own interpretations and artworks.

Award winning Czech illustrator, Květa Pacovska is said to have described picturebooks as 'timeless mini art galleries for the home', and although we could not find a direct reference for it, this description captures the significant role picturebooks play in linking viewers at home with readers in an art gallery or museum. Sharing a picturebook with a child introduces them to pictorial representation, to ideas, feelings and stories which can transport them to new imaginative and creative realms. Art museum pedagogy can inform the way we talk about and respond to picturebooks with young children. By following simple thinking routines, children can be supported to look closely and deeply at pictures together. Encouraging children to make their own discoveries, to look, to think, to feel and to make their own art in response to pictures, will help them to develop their visual literacy by gaining a better sense of *how* works of art might be understood (Burnham and Kai-Kee 2011: 10). These early adventures with art can support children on their journey beyond the world of the picturebook and into the complex and multi-layered visual environment of the 21st Century.

7 Psyche, picnics and penguin

Case studies of children responding to visual texts

Kate Noble, Marcela Escovar, Luisa Naranjo and Kim Deakin with Morag Styles

Our initial research on children's responses to picturebooks revealed that we often learned more from group discussions and inviting drawings from children than from conventional semi-structured interviews. Since then researchers, teachers and museum educators have convinced us that there are many other means of providing evidence of children's responses to picturebooks, paintings and other visual texts by using a variety of data collection methods and engaging in art or visual projects which draw on them. These include annotating copies of spreads from a picturebook, adding text to blank speech bubbles, games with simple puppets of key characters, dramatic play based on picturebooks and many more.

It is encouraging to find that our results of more than twenty years ago are largely borne out by more recent researchers. As in the original *Children Reading Pictures*, we were impressed by the commitment of the children to the tasks and the insightfulness of their responses. The case studies which follow offer further illuminating examples.

Case Study 1: 'Inspire' at The Fitzwilliam Museum: Narrative Art and Storytelling – Kate Noble

The Inspire project at The Fitzwilliam Museum explored how one painting could be used as the starting point for creative enquiry across the primary curriculum and took inspiration from the National Gallery's flagship project, *Take One Picture*. Over 3800 children from 40 primary schools across Cambridgeshire studied the painting at school

Figure 7.1 Cupid and Psyche by Jacopo del Sellaio © The Fitzwilliam Museum, Cambridge.

DOI: 10.4324/9781003106326-10

and the end of project exhibition was visited by over 30,000 people during its 16-week run. This case study describes how the project was developed in two different settings and shares some of the extraordinary artwork which was created by the children who took part.

About the focus painting

Inspire was based on a wooden panel painting of the story of Cupid and Psyche that was painted in Florence in 1473 (Figure 7.1). Beautifully decorated panels like this often depicted stories from classical mythology or of famous contemporary events. For the young children growing up in these richly furnished houses, these images would have fulfilled a similar role to the modern-day picturebook, telling classical and contemporary stories of drama, romance and bravery. The painting would have originally been a fashionable piece of furniture from a Renaissance bed chamber (Cooper and Noble 2020). Like a picturebook, the image is a sequential narrative, read from left to right and the key characters appear multiple times as the story develops (Campbell 2009).

While the action in a picturebook might be divided into different frames or pages, the Cupid and Psyche story is taken from classical mythology and draws on the visual conventions of the classical vase or sarcophagus to tell the story through sequential narrative in one long picture, with several overlapping scenes. On the left side of the painting the hero, Psyche, depicted in her white dress, is visited by suitors who have heard tales of her legendary beauty. A jealous Venus sends her son Cupid to curse Psyche, but instead, he falls in love with her. In the middle of the composition, Psyche is blown off a hill and lands in a soft bed of grass where she falls into a deep sleep. When she awakens, she finds herself outside Cupid's palace where she is met by servants who show her kindness and offer fine food and riches. Cupid invites Psyche to live with him in his palace on the condition that she never looks upon him so she remains unaware of his identity. They live together in this way for some time before Psyche's sisters visit and persuade her to uncover the identity of her secret companion. That evening, as Cupid sleeps, Psyche takes a lamp to look at him and instantly falls in love with him. However, a drop of oil from the lamp burns Cupid's skin and he awakens, furious at Psyche's betrayal. In the last scene of the panel, he leaves the palace, determined never to see Psyche again.

The story continues on a second panel which is now in a private collection. Venus enslaves Psyche but Cupid asks Zeus to intervene. He then rescues and marries Psyche and they live happily ever after as befitting a story for a family bed chamber. The painting would have been a powerful visual reminder to the new wife of her duty to her family and husband. Psyche must swear allegiance to her 'husband' and in return for the safety of his palace and protection is rewarded with gifts and riches. If she questions his authority and breaks her promise, she is brutally expelled from her home and severely punished for her disobedience. The visual narrative reinforces the status quo of the time.

The Inspire project

Inspire was launched through a series of teacher training sessions led by museum educators and Sheila Ceccarelli from artist-led charity AccessArt. Teachers from local primary schools were taught about the context and meaning of the Cupid and Psyche painting and explored different approaches to discussing the painting and making art with young children (Noble, 2021a). This case study draws on artwork, blog posts, emails, interviews and details from the exhibition submissions to demonstrate some of the different ways in which children and teachers responded to the painting.

Inspire 1: Psyche's Dress

This case study focuses on a group of children from St Peter's Church of England School in Wisbech which is located in a Fenland market town and serves a large number of families facing multiple disadvantages. After Natalie Bailey, class teacher, art lead and special needs coordinator took part in the museum training day, she started working on the project with her class of nine and ten-year-olds by showing them a reproduction of the Cupid and Psyche painting. After careful looking and discussion of the painting, they worked together to re-tell the story and develop their ideas. In this process, Natalie noticed that a small group of children made deep and personal connections to some of the themes in the painting. She realised that they were keen to continue these discussions outside of the time she had allocated to spend on the project, so she then ran a series of workshops for this small group over the summer holidays.

Children taking the lead

As they discussed the story, the children expressed how they were particularly moved by the character, Psyche, and her harsh treatment by the other characters in the story. As they talked, they came up with the idea of designing her a new dress (Figure 7.2). Where the white, delicate fabric of her dress in the painting symbolises her fragility, this new dress would be designed to tell the story of her extraordinary resilience in the face of great adversity. The conversations they had, and decisions they made while making this costume, reveal the benefits of allowing children to express and explore their thinking in three dimensions using a range of different materials and techniques as this quote demonstrates:

> We chose denim fabric to show resilience because your jeans go through a lot. We distressed and deconstructed denim making feathers and tassels. Whatever you do to this fabric, it still looks good. Our parents gave us their old jeans they didn't want anymore. Psyche also felt unwanted.
>
> (boy, aged 9)

The materials they chose – denim, chiffon and string – had different affordances to the paint and pigments used in the original wooden panel painting. Within the interaction of child, story and material new connections, associations and stories are enacted and enabled. These encounters are described by Barad as a process of 'intra-action' transforming our understanding of the potential of the material entanglements within our everyday lives and experiences (2015). The project also demonstrates how children can be supported to draw on their own visual repertoires to challenge dominant narratives within European Art and culture to create new imaginings, which resonate with and are rooted in their own experiences and beliefs.

Figure 7.2 Detail of Psyche's dress designed and made by children from St Peter's School, Wisbech.

21st century psyche: Transforming the visual elements of the design

The children's designs for the dress show them drawing upon many key motifs from the original painting and demonstrate a sophisticated understanding of the visual forms of communication. They discussed the symbolism of Cupid's arrows and were keen to make arrows of their own to incorporate into Psyche's dress (Figure 7.3). They saw these arrows as both representing Cupid's love for Psyche, but also demonstrating that she had a choice to use them for her own defence should she need them. After trying out several different designs including an arrow necklace (Figure 7.4) they decided to put the arrows in Psyche's pockets along with love letters from Cupid to represent how Psyche carried Cupid's love with her as she went through the story.

The children also discussed the use of colour within the painting and made decisions about which colours were appropriate for their own design. This shows them drawing on intertextual knowledge which they had developed while looking at other Italian art of the time as part of the original class exploration of the painting but also drawing on the communicative power of the materials with which they were working. Their explanations demonstrate how they are able to apply this knowledge to make informed and confident choices about how colour, shape and material can be used to symbolise a range of ideas and concepts.

Figure 7.3 Cupid's arrows made from string, wood, denim and buttons.

Figure 7.4 Design for Psyche's dress with idea of arrow necklace.

Thinking and feeling through pictures and making

The children drew on their own life experiences and connected deeply with the theme of love and conflict within the painting as this child's words demonstrate:

> I knew my parents didn't love each other before they did. There was a change… They thought they would keep it secret in case it hurt us… but we already knew. We hear, see and feel everything.
>
> (a girl, aged 9)

This might be difficult to hear as a parent, but art and stories offer a valuable space where children can reflect upon and/or share their feelings in a safe and supportive environment with a trusted facilitator. Natalie describes this process in her blog post for AccessArt on the project:

> As the children's ideas began to develop, I sat back, listened to the natural flow of conversations and made notes. It all became very therapeutic. The children discussed topics which adults would have found tricky to initiate… I soon began to realise that I was experiencing an insight into a new world, one where children feel safe enough to share thoughts, feelings and emotions in an open, honest and carefree environment. There was no judgment here. No one worried about saying the wrong thing. It was easy to talk whilst creative hands were kept busy, directing the gaze away to focus on the task in hand. Over our studio sessions, I became a witness to the deep and meaningful conversations about romantic love and deep moral understandings that I do not think adults give children credit for.
>
> (Bailey 2020)

Although this was a project with a small group of children, some of which took part outside of the busy day-to-day bustle of the classroom, it is worth reflecting on how working with visual narratives in art and picturebooks might support children's emotional as well as their cognitive development. However, it is important to note that although this project might have had a therapeutic effect on the group, this is not the same as art therapy or counselling, which should be led by a trained professional.

Case studies of children responding to visual texts 103

Inspire 2: a whole class approach to multi-sensory and material exploration

This second example is taken from a whole school project at Linton Heights Junior School, Cambridgeshire. After attending a training session at the museum, the Art and Design and Technology leaders, Rosie Komodromos and Anna Campbell, led their own introductory session for colleagues introducing the painting and modelling some creative art activities. The teachers spent time looking at and talking about the painting and brainstorming ideas for cross-curricular exploration and enrichment. The subject and year group leads then planned and led their own activities linked to the painting as part of the school's creative arts week. This painting was introduced to the students by putting up reproductions in classrooms and corridors around the school the week before. Rosie then began the week with a whole class assembly with students acting out to story as she told it.

Class teacher Kirsty Webb decided that her class of nine- and ten-year-olds would work collaboratively in small groups. Each group was given a small section of the painting to explore and was set the challenge of deciding what materials and techniques to use to transform the story through their own artwork. Kirsty describes how she provided opportunities for the children to take ownership of their learning,

> This project gave the children the freedom to explore a range of different materials and ways of working within art. Previous art lessons were generally quite prescriptive, however, here the children were free to go into their surroundings, use unknown items and mediums which they hadn't had the opportunity to use before. They could be as creative as they liked, even using coffee granules, grass and salt to create texture!

The resulting collages were stunning and were displayed in the final exhibition as seen in Figure 7.5 which also shows Rosie, Anna and children from the school giving a

Figure 7.5 Children and teachers from Linton Heights leading a public talk.

lunchtime talk about the project to members of the public in the museum. However, this project also demonstrates the power of making and of materials as demonstrated in this following series of images.

In these images, children work on different sections of the same frieze alongside one another (Figure 7.6), responding through colour, texture and material and making decisions as the story and picture evolve. As they create material, two of the children are entangled, their arms crossing as they work in tandem, adding final details and texture to mixed media collage, absorbed in the act of making (Figure 7.7). Figures 7.8–7.12 show the range of different materials the children have access to. These are both traditional art-making materials (paint, pencil and oil pastel and collage) and found materials such as grasses, seeds, flowers, coffee granules and crushed earth inspired by their research on pigment making in the Renaissance. This freedom of choice gives children the opportunity to explore and experiment with the affordances of each of these different materials to discover their potential for storytelling and meaning-making. Child, artwork and materials all have agency within the 'more-than-human' world (Haynes and Murris 2019). Through dialogue and making, children explore, discuss, experiment, feel, negotiate, move, paint and draw to make important decisions about what goes where and who does what, extending the possibilities of the story and making through multiple retellings and re-imaginings. Child, story, paint, paper, material, pigment, artist and image interact and intra-act to transform and make anew across space and time – fusing storying from the classical world and medieval Italy into the time-space continuum of the contemporary classroom.

Figure 7.6 Collaborative making with paint, leaves and pencil.

Case studies of children responding to visual texts 105

Figure 7.7 Children entangled, arms crossed and working in tandem as they add final details and texture to mixed media collage.

Figure 7.8 Experimenting with materials and story.

Figure 7.9 Detail of doorway from the collaborative frieze showing the use of mixed media including paint, oil pastel, petals and grass seed.

Figure 7.10 Detail from collaborative frieze showing the use of mixed media including paint, oil pastel, paper, seeds, lollipop sticks and cut grass.

Case studies of children responding to visual texts 107

Figure 7.11 Detail from the collaborative frieze showing Psyche meeting Cupid and entering the palace showing the use of mixed media.

Figure 7.12 Mixing palettes, paint brushes, and collage materials.

Case Study 2: *Picnic at the MAMBO* – Marcela Escovar & Luisa Naranjo

Connecting with the Picnics at the Mambo is to feel like a family. To know that we can read any book at any age and have fun. That there are no right or wrong formulas for approaching a story and that even the oldest can be moved by a fictional character. Those stories connect us even if we are far away, separated, taking care of each other, because it happened to someone else and they were able to put part of their story on a piece of paper that reaches me, sometimes between my hands, sometimes between the sounds of my life as well. Belén Báez Moundiroff, Costa Rica.

In March 2020, Colombia was forced into lockdown due to the Coronavirus health crisis, causing cultural and artistic institutions to switch to working virtually. During this difficult time, a new collaboration was born between an initiative called "Picnic de Palabras" (Picnic of Words) and the Museo de Arte Moderno de Bogotá (Museum of Modern Art of Bogota) which resulted in "Picnic en el MAMBO" (Picnic at the MAMBO). The project stemmed from a recognition of the potential that reading and the arts can have in adverse situations, a role that can provide strategies for coping but also the presence of a mediator that accompanies the reader. In what follows, we explain the origins of Picnic de Palabras and how it came to be held in one of the most famous museums in the city of Bogota in Colombia.

Early childhood at MAMBO

The MAMBO is committed to the cultural and social rights of the public of all ages. In accordance with the principle of equality, it aims to serve its early childhood audiences by providing and encouraging experiences with artistic expression through the visual arts but also reading, to add to the holistic development of children. The management of the museum is focused on carrying out a public programme which seeks to demonstrate that art is a process of creation and individual appropriation, capable of raising questions about its place as a transforming, cathartic or communicating axis, all of this within a space for participation and social development. Cultural goods and services for early childhood audiences should facilitate the conditions for supporting children's sensitivity and creativity and they should be able to access and freely use resources such as the visual arts to express their inner worlds.

Picnic de Palabras (Picnic of Words)

The "Picnic of Words" reading initiative has existed for nearly ten years and was created by Marcela Escovar with the aim of inspiring children and families to incorporate reading into their lives by providing reading experiences in public spaces such as parks or squares. In the past nine years, more than 20,000 people have participated in this initiative in different parks and squares in more than ten countries and 20 cities across Latin America, the United States and Europe.

The conviction behind "Picnic of Words" is that shared reading is fundamental to strengthening personal, family and social relationships and that having access to a wide variety of books and genres can develop multiple skills such as empathy, listening, comprehension and analysis. The book sessions offer the opportunity to those who may not have had much exposure to books, to explore them and find out what they are interested in reading more about.

Among the key books offered in the sessions are picturebooks of a high visual and narrative quality which can invite both children and adults to read. For children, the stories in the picturebooks can act as a meeting space where they connect their first experiences of life to the experiences of others through the characters, and where they can engage in conversations with peers, family or mediators. The public, outdoor spaces provide opportunities to form new relationships and bonds as well as consider different perspectives given the reading takes place in a social and community context. The spaces provide the freedom for readers to look at and read books that attract them at their own pace, to reread or move on to new books, to play and to position their bodies in ways that allow for different forms of exploration, for example, lying down or sitting close to someone else.

For the adults who participate in Picnic of Words, this is an opportunity to spend quality time with their own families and with other families and children. It allows them to get to know children's books that they can later look for in public libraries or bookshops. Often these adults have themselves been discouraged from reading by negative experiences and there are others for whom reading is simply not a priority; however, they do want their children to read. In a sense, they are the main target audience because Picnic is keen to offer them a second chance of becoming readers through children's books and perhaps connect with their inner child, a child we all have within us.

Picnic at the MAMBO

The MAMBO has had an interest in using picturebooks to create readers for some time and sees them as children's first 'museums', providing an entrance into this visual space which may inspire them to visit museums and other spaces that participate in cultural and artistic outreach as they grow up. The museum wanted to broaden the scope of its target population and invite families into its space. With these aims in mind, in April 2020, the directors of MAMBO contacted Marcela Escovar to discuss how to create a reading project in this unconventional space. "Picnic at the Mambo" was the result of this conversation. It became both a live and digital project for reading children's picturebooks in which a selection of texts would be curated according to the quality of the stories but also the artistry of their illustrations. The project would make these aesthetic objects available to children and their families which, unlike the paintings on the walls, they could touch and handle for themselves.

The project progressed in three stages. The first involved the design and implementation of the reading sessions including the selection of books. This selection was based on the relevance of their stories and illustrations for life during the pandemic, but the curatorial criteria were focused, above all, on choosing illustrations which could have been exhibited as paintings in a museum. Some of the picturebooks were translations of award-winning illustrators such as Shaun Tan (*The Rabbits*) and Chris Van Allsburg (*The Mysteries of Harris Burdick* and *The Sweetest Fig*); others were in Spanish, by Colombian illustrators such as Claudia Rueda (*El encargo*), Amalia Satizábal (*Río de colores*), Javier Sáez Castán (*La merienda del señor verde*) and Dipacho (*A pesar de todo*). The initial idea was that live reading broadcasts would be done via Facebook, however, due to internet issues they were pre-recorded. Two children, Martín and Santiago, aged eight and six years, participated in the first recording, with Marcela Escovar doing the reading.

The participation of these two children through their voices (they do not appear in the video) allowed for the creation of reading-aloud sessions that could be watched by others and which included interruptions and questions about the details in the illustrations that could have counterpoints with the story.

An average of fifteen participants connected with their families during each of the sixteen sessions and actively participated in the Facebook Live chats, with the mediators responding to them in real time. These videos were posted on the Picnic of Words fan page and on MAMBO's YouTube channel, so they could be circulated more widely after their publication.

The second stage in the project was the opening of a conversation space called "At home with…" where Colombian picturebook authors and illustrators shared their experiences, reflections, readings and sketches. This space allowed readers to connect to authors and their books in a more personal manner. The opportunity to share the stories behind a book not only brings the reader closer to the work and the artist but also allows the readers to ask questions about the artist's history and creative journey, as well as the decisions they took and even the manuscripts that were rejected by publishers. During the interview sessions with the authors and illustrators (which were also pre-recorded) creators showed their sketches and final artwork; they read some of their most recent publications and invited children to draw in response. Alongside the families, several young people who were interested in illustration also participated and this broadened the scope of this project. When the videos were launched, the authors appeared on Facebook Live sessions, answering questions from the audience in real time.

Following these two stages, a third space was created in which the children were invited to participate in sessions where they could draw, inspired by the readings and interviews. The aim was for the participants to share their favourite parts of the picturebooks and create an exhibition of the illustrations, which would result from conversing with the different texts. This was the most difficult stage of the project, because although many children participated, not all of them sent their drawings to the call for entries. On the other hand, virtuality made it possible to broaden the reach and dissemination of these readings and it was also possible to receive drawings from different parts of Colombia outside Bogota.

The original timeframe for this project was three months (between May and July 2020), however, given the interest and the participation, as well as the impact it had on the creation of an audience of families, the MAMBO board of directors decided to extend it for another month and include it in the digital version of one of the most important art festivals in Colombia, ArtBo, which took place online that year during August, and allowed an even greater audience to participate.

Later, in October 2020, an alliance was made with the Colombian Chamber of Books, in charge of organising the Bogotá International Book Fair, and this meant that a presentation about the project and "Picnic at the MAMBO" videos were integrated into the Book Fair programme. Additionally, a budget was allocated to arrange for books to be given to those who had sent in their illustrations to take part in the exhibition. This alliance shows how the scope and impact of articulating cultural projects can add to and strengthen book culture across a whole country. Book fairs throughout Latin America are usually large, inspiring annual events in the calendar of publishers, authors, illustrators and all those who work with books, so for "Picnic at the MAMBO" to have a space in this Colombian book fair was a significant recognition of the project.

Case studies of children responding to visual texts 111

Figure 7.13 "Joaquín loves Picnic, he was happy today (and he even coloured in the drawing, something which he never does)". Zully Pardo, Colombia.

The final event of the year was another Picnic at MAMBO, held in December 2020, but this time in person – although spaces for participation were limited for health and safety. Six families registered for the event, including Zully and Joaquín, a mother with her five-year-old son. While Joaquín was fascinated by the read-aloud of stories for an hour, Zully commented on the relevance of this type of experience for them, as it allowed them to move out of their confinement and routine in the midst of the pandemic. After the reading, the families were given a tour of the MAMBO and the activity ended with time for drawing. Joaquín not only produced a drawing related to the event but also coloured it in (Figure 7.13).

In January 2021, we had the opportunity to host a new reading encounter through an Instagram Live event. On this occasion, we invited the families who participated to tell us about what they were drawing. In real time, about 20 families wrote and shared what the children were creating from their reading. We also invited them to send the drawings by post, some of which included comments from the adults who accompanied the session. All these materials allowed us to glance at what goes on at home behind the electronic screens. It showed it is possible to design reading experiences that link families and encourage encounters between readers and books.

The children's drawings and the adults' comments showed that new links can be forged, beyond the virtual world, with books, stories and illustrations. However, from this experience, we realised that it is not enough to read picturebooks, it is also important to select readings that allow families to connect with their current circumstances and that serve to question, connect and transform their daily lives. We also realised the need to explore the scope of reading beyond a screen. This included facilitating conversations, accepting the interruption of reading through the messages coming through from the participants and finally, the invitation to draw. All of these activities exemplified the potential for connecting with others through spaces for exploration and conversation.

In these exercises, we were faced with live streaming creative processes, triggered by the digital stimulus: this holistic process began with internalising visual and verbal learning; it was followed by the construction of the conversation the reader has with the story, including the cognitive and emotional connections, all of which in turn lead to creative expression evidenced by the drawing activity.

When space and exploration are limited to a screen, it is essential to explore new ways of reading, of presenting images and of sharing them with readers. Reading is not just about telling a story to the camera; even the "framing" of the book needs to be considered. Being able to show details, to zoom in and out (especially in live encounters), to improvise and even to make mistakes, brings us closer to our audience. We realised that while it was harder to keep this audience captive, we are also "flesh and blood" readers who lend our voice, inspiration and heart to welcome others, who we may not be able to see, but who we trust are accompanying us on the other side. The design that these reading encounters required allowed us to consider new ways of accompanying and creating unique spaces that triggered new experiences which took into account current circumstances. In other words, we learned that although it is possible to make virtual experiences of readings, we also had to think and understand that we needed to change the forms of delivery and the timings we were used to.

Reading and museums: Connecting through the visual experience

Spaces and experiences that include images and words can detonate our visual universe, creating resonances and dialogues. We noticed that this happened with the children who participated in the project: inviting them to draw after a read-aloud session that included questions and dialogue, inspired them to make connections to their daily lives, allowed them to express their own voice more fully and explore their inner worlds and perspectives in a graphic manner, without fear of aesthetic judgement. Through their visual experiences, the connection we created with Zully and Joaquín, for example, strengthened the bridges between reality and virtuality. It is probably no coincidence that Joaquín was happy and was encouraged to colour in his drawing after participating in these reading sessions.

The closure of this project as a visual experience was framed by thinking of reading as a place that connects both with our inner world of "words" and with our visual references, in the same way that our experiences connect with a particular illustration in a picturebook or a painting in a museum. Just as reading a book links us to previous readings by the same author or other authors, contemplating illustrations and works of art triggers a series of relationships with other works, books, photographs, film, television, past experiences and people. This space of contemplation requires attention, close looking and the decoding of details as well as reflection on personal experience.

According to Evelio Cabrejo (2001), before children learn to decode words, they intuitively learn to read faces, voices, gestures and images. This development is part of the process of interpreting the reality in which they are immersed. However, stimulation by adults (family and mediators) is fundamental to refine the development of these skills so that when they begin to read, their visual experiences facilitate the process of incorporating meaning and understanding of the images along with textual decoding.

The dialogue that is set up between illustrations and text through children's picturebooks is crucial to nurturing the cognitive development of young readers and their

Case studies of children responding to visual texts 113

aesthetic sensitivity which, through visits to museums, libraries and theatres and other cultural spaces, will in turn allow them to become consumers and producers of other artistic manifestations and expressions.

Writing this text, a year after the beginning of the pandemic, has made us reflect on the fact that we have become accustomed to virtuality but also that we need to continue to create quality content that is meaningful for the families that participate in Picnic and that visit MAMBO. It is essential to reflect on how we can provide an authentic virtual space for reading, keeping in mind the design of the experiences and the relevance of the stories we share, as well as advice for mediators who accompany families in these experiences of reading and art.

Picnic at MAMBO was thus a provocative invitation, in new and unexpected spaces such as a modern art museum, for adults and children to connect with the act of reading and art through books that grow with their readers (Figures 7.14–7.16).

Figure 7.14 Face to face reading in the MAMBO with Joaquín (Dec 2020).

Figure 7.15 Joaquín examines an exhibit inside the MAMBO.

Figure 7.16 Zully and Joaquín looking at an exhibit inside the MAMBO.

Case Study 3: Danny learning more than reading from Polly Dunbar's *Penguin* – Kim Deakin

Kim Deakin's research focused on an eight-year-old autistic boy, Danny,[1] who attended Richmond Hill Special School, where she was his teacher. Danny was a great enthusiast for reading and Kim was surprised one day to find him writing and drawing on a picturebook, behaviour that was unusual for him. When she questioned him gently, his excitement was almost palpable. Here is Kim's account of Danny's encounter with Polly Dunbar's *Penguin*, a delightful picturebook that provides a welcoming space for children to explore their own emotions through the perspective of fictional characters.

As I turned the page, Danny jumped up and down bellowing at the top of his voice, 'SAY SOMETHING!' Laughing and pointing to the page of *Penguin* that he had drawn all over he continued, 'Sorry, Kim, Danny, Kim look, LOOK! EATS, LION EATS BEN/DANNY!' This study examines Danny's exploration of Dunbar's picturebook and how he used the ambiguities and nuances of word and image to give him the time and space to bring his own experiences to the text. The empathy displayed for a fictional character provided a rare glimpse into Danny's altered perspective on the world. Maria Nikolajeva explains how the interplay between illustrations and words in picturebooks can provide a tool for children to glean an understanding of human emotions from fictional characters, but cautions that 'mind-reading normally develops at the age of five and is slower or even totally impeded in autistic children' (2012: 275). Likewise, Nicole Martin suggests that the 'tools of friendship,

---

1 Please note that at the request of Danny Wilkinson, his parents and the school, his real name is given.

Case studies of children responding to visual texts 115

such as reciprocity, sympathy and empathy, are a formidable challenge for a child with autism' (2009: 110).

I began by asking myself some questions to help me unravel some of the possibilities. How does the interplay between word and image in *Penguin* help Danny explore human emotions? How does Danny bring his own experiences to the text? I felt I required a methodology that would provide a way of recording observations that would ensure validity and robustness. I turned, therefore, to research methods used in early years settings, such as child initiated free-play, as they better reflected the cognitive and developmental stage Danny displayed.

Stuart Reifel draws on research by Vivian Paley in which stories, whether through literature or fantasy play, help children to 'interpret and explain [their] feelings about reality' (cited in Reifel 2007: 31). Following Reifel's model, I hoped to capture Danny's engagement with *Penguin* by facilitating three focused but child-led sessions over a two week period, supplemented by observing spontaneous responses that presented themselves during normal classroom activities. Each element of Danny's communication observed throughout the study was recorded to create a 'text' of actions: non-verbal and verbal responses, supplemented by photographs, mark-making and drawings. This enabled me to analyse the effect of the devices Dunbar employed such as space and drama, gaze and perspective, use of language and typography.

The story hinges on Ben's unhappiness with the unresponsive behaviour of Penguin, until one day Penguin does something extraordinary. The lack of a setting or background for *Penguin* offers an uncluttered white space, which Nikolajeva and Scott suggest 'reflect the child's limited experience of the world' (2001: 63). This minimalistic effect means the reader has no distractions from the images of emotional connection (or disconnection) between the characters. As Frank Serafini points out, 'the positioning of objects and characters determines their importance and how viewers react to them' (2009: 21). Hence, a dual perspective is created between the reader and the characters, enabling the former to enter the imaginary situation and exchange places or to watch subjectively the interplay between the characters as they act out the scenario.

Figure 7.17 Penguin and Ben.

116 *Research on children responding to visual texts*

In Figure 7.17, the emotional tension between the characters is demonstrated by their physical distance and gaping white space, while the gutter provides a physical barrier which emphasises how disconnected they are. Ben gets increasingly frustrated by Penguin's lack of response to his friendly overtures. As his fury hits a crescendo, an enormous speech bubble dominates the centre of the spread, signalling a significant turn in the plot as the face of a disgruntled-looking lion creeps in, perhaps a metaphor for an authority figure.

Figure 7.18 Penguin and lion.

However, Penguin becomes the unlikely hero by siding with Ben and biting Lion on the nose (See Figure 7.18). The twist at the end of the story is shown by the images that appear, '*And Penguin said…*' (See Figure 7.19), where a huge pictorial speech bubble projected from Penguin's open beak empowers emergent readers to re-tell the story supported by the sequential illustrations and through the 'voice' of Penguin.

Case studies of children responding to visual texts 117

Figure 7.19 'And Penguin said…'.

As a consequence Ben is finally able to understand that Penguin, although non-verbal, has become the friend he so desperately wanted at the beginning of the story.

Danny's clandestine mark-making in the picturebook suggests that his connection with Dunbar's characters and scenarios was intrinsically linked with his own experience so that he was able to enter a fictional world that explored some of the reality of his own life. Danny retrieved information from both word and image; he memorised words, often repeating the refrain, *Penguin said nothing,* and his mark-making gave indications of how he was feeling. For example, Danny's response to Ben's tantrum sequence can be seen to have triggered a powerful memory of his own. A whirl of looping lines obliterates the words, *Penguin said nothing* (See Figure 7.20).

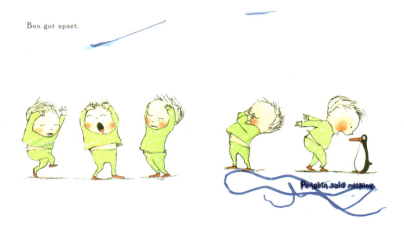

Figure 7.20 Danny's response to Ben's tantrum.

Here we can see the picturebook providing Danny with a vehicle through which he could pause and reflect and show common purpose with the characters – all at his own pace.

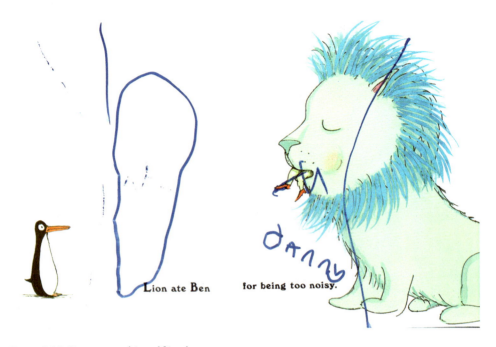

Figure 7.21 Danny puts himself in the story.

Danny also demonstrates self-referentiality, through mark-making (See Figure 7.21). Danny's 'tadpole' which he confirmed as a representation of himself by naming it, is placed in-between the physical gaps of Penguin and the action of Ben being eaten by the Lion – literally positioning himself within the fictional scenario. When asked 'Who's that?' he jumped up and down with excitement, 'IT'S DANNY, IT'S DANNY! LION EATS BEN. EATS DANNY!' Danny felt the need to physically fill the gap. Indeed, I would suggest Danny's altered perspective required him to have a literal reference point through his drawings. The zigzag line across the half-eaten Ben and a strong vertical line across Lion perhaps indicate that Danny reckons he is next in line to be eaten, or even acting as protector of Penguin. On subsequent readings when asked 'Who is that?' his commentary confirms he has adopted Ben's role, but interestingly has also begun to understand Penguin's alternative perspective (Figure 7.22):

Case studies of children responding to visual texts 119

Figure 7.22 Lion licks his lips after eating Danny!

> Picture, blue, Danny.
> Put Ben in the lion.
> Danny in the lion.
> Watch out Penguin!

The impact of Dunbar's drama of being eaten by a lion intrigued Danny, while his signature and comments confirm self-referentiality and suggest closer identification with Ben:

> Lion's eaten.
> Lion he's eaten Ben.
> He's eaten Danny.

Valuable insight into how Danny identified himself with Ben and how he eventually replaced him was revealed further in his blue and orange felt-pen drawing (See Figure 7.23).

Unlike previous marks made across Dunbar's illustrations, where he seemed content to stand beside Ben, this drawing highlights a shift in perspective and for a time Danny appeared to create a double personality, a mix of himself and Ben. Danny began drawing in the middle of the page using blue loops for Penguin's face and body with

Figure 7.23 Danny's drawing of himself and Penguin.

flippers on the left. Unhappy with his first attempt, he placed the toy penguin firmly upside-down and changed to an orange pen. With almost palpable concentration, he drew the feet at the top followed by body, head and features, finally adding flippers.

Deciding on blue, which, interestingly, he had used throughout the picturebook, following Dunbar's choice for depicting an imaginary lion (signifying perhaps his understanding of the difference between real and imaginary worlds), he then produced a much more sophisticated schematic representation of a human body; upside-down, with clearly defined legs but no arms. Remarkably, he then drew two faces, one noticeably smiling, enjoying the fun of being upside-down and the other looking on, more serious. When asked 'Who's that?' he named each face, revealing himself to be the happy boy playing alongside Penguin. This both altered the action in the story, providing an alternative scenario of Penguin joining in and playing, but also clearly showed Danny swapping roles with the unhappy Ben.

Danny confirmed himself firmly within this fictional world later during an ICT lesson (See Figure 7.24).

Figure 7.24 Lion eat Danny.

Here, purely from memory, he added detail to his orange 'tadpole' drawing, representing Lion's mane and beautifully captured the self-satisfied smile as in Dunbar's illustration. Her words, 'Lion ate Ben for being too noisy' were paraphrased below the picture, indicating Danny was now replicating Ben's fate.

Can a picturebook then, as Paley suggests (2005: 15), be the catalyst to provide a vehicle for a child with autism to explore, investigate and reproduce human emotions? Or perhaps, as Kress and Van Leeuwen suggest, the 'emotive immediacy' that visual images provide '… allows the viewer to scrutinize the represented characters as though they were specimens in a display case' (2006: 41). The answer was an overwhelming yes. By instinct, Danny spontaneously demonstrated Paley's assertion (2005: 57) that 'the more complex the thought the greater is the child's need to view its meaning through play', accurately mirroring Ben's facial expressions and gestures as he explored difficult human emotions in a safe environment, giving him the opportunity to enact and understand attempted reciprocal communication. This further enhanced his understanding of both Ben's and his own puzzling attempts at communication. The futility of Ben's efforts at reciprocal communication were evident to Danny through Dunbar's presentation of differing vectors between the characters. As Ben only once looked directly out towards the beholder it offered Danny the opportunity, as Nodelman (2008: 20) suggests, to become more objective and realise that Ben 'is not seeing everything'. Penguin, however, gazes out from the book at least ten times demanding attention, to which Danny responded on one occasion, 'Silly Penguin. Says nothing'.

In subsequent readings, Danny enjoyed emulating Ben's 'dizzy dance' but commented 'Penguin didn't dance'. Although he continued to mimic Ben's actions throughout the tantrum scene, Danny developed a more objective perspective giving him insights into how Penguin may have felt being subjected to that level of anger.

On one memorable occasion, silence descended in the classroom as the adults witnessed Danny suspended in reflection (See Figure 7.25).

Figure 7.25 Danny with Lion.

Hogan reminds us of the ambiguous nature of understanding 'precisely' (2011: 4) what someone is imagining in response to a story but this pivotal moment appeared to nudge Danny into creating a surprise of his own. He had moved from his introspective, autistic perspective, through Ben's egocentric frustrations, then experimented with Penguin's more selfless, altruistic behaviour. Pausing, tracking and commenting on the action, 'Penguin bit lion', he suddenly assumed the heroic role of Penguin, and with great glee, bit Lion's nose (Figure 7.26).

Figure 7.26 Danny bites Lion's nose.

Could it be, as Paley believes, that stories not only allow children to explore complex human emotions within a safe fantasy world but also enable them to transfer that knowledge to the real world? Dunbar certainly invited children to take ownership of her picturebook and Danny demonstrated the capacity to respond by projecting emotions onto inanimate toys. All the more extraordinary as Pamela Wolfberg comments that children with autism 'rarely produce pretend play by... activating dolls as agents' (1999: 3). Many readers enjoy exploring a fantasy world to escape reality but, paradoxically, Danny, with his altered perspective on life, entered a fictional world to explore reality. Dunbar's picturebook serves this function for children who are at the faltering beginnings of trying to fathom how relationships work, to learn that they may yet be able to understand themselves and others. Real life is full of emotionally charged situations and other children's reactions are often fleeting and unpredictable. Picturebook scenarios provide the luxury of space and time to explore, imagine, wonder, think and reflect.

For Danny, the empathetic lessons learnt seem to have become embedded, giving him a promising new perspective when communicating with his peers. Three weeks after my study, Danny, whose normal approach to children new to him often proved unwelcome (such as putting his face too close to the new child, smelling their skin, touching their mouths, eyes, hair, etc.), was observed smiling as he approached a non-verbal child. Paraphrasing *Penguin*, Danny was heard to say:

> Who's that?
> That's Sam.
> Say hello, say hello to Danny.
> No, Sam says nothing.
> Sam doesn't talk.
> Ahhhh poor Sam.

These stirring case studies take us from the narrow focus of a single child's response to a picturebook; to a citywide project based on a single painting in a museum with schools, teachers, artists and art educators; to a countrywide museum initiative 5000 miles across the Atlantic which involved a variety of picturebooks with art educators, authors, illustrators, parents and children. The contexts included art museums, classrooms and community spaces such as parks and squares and mixed virtual scenarios and screens with real-time, face-to-face communication. Timescales ranged from weeks to months to more than a year. However small-scale or wide-ranging in context, time, audience and space, these approaches demonstrate the value of having clear aims, sound planning, imaginative resources and careful observation of young people's responses to visual texts. Two of these projects used art educators, mediators, authors, illustrators and other willing 'creatives' to lend a hand, while the other relied on the skill and empathy of a single teacher. The main purpose of all the projects was to learn from young people and to use that knowledge profitably in the way we approach visual literacy in whichever context we find ourselves. Each project offered wide and deep learning and clearly 'inspired' young readers to read, enjoy and learn in every sense of the word from visual texts.

8 Children reading literary apps

Aline Frederico

Children's literature in digital formats is no longer a novelty. It predates mobile devices like smartphones and tablets, but the emergence of mobile technology has presented new possibilities for digital literary expression. The early 2010s, with the release of the iPad, saw the emergence of a significant number of apps and e-books. One would think that a decade later, considering how most people's lives have changed with and because of technology and its pervasion, that literary apps would now be part of the lives of most children, just as YouTube and other forms of film streaming and digital games have become. However, this has not happened.[1]

Nonetheless, digital technology is not going anywhere and times such as the Covid-19 pandemic, when for some time access to print books was difficult with libraries and schools closed, digital communication became our main source of connection to the external world, highlighting the need for quality digital content for children. Thus, while children's access to literary apps might still be limited, understanding what this form of reading promotes in terms of aesthetic and cognitive experiences is crucial to support children's access to innovative literary and artistic digital texts.

There is a great variety of formats and configurations in which a literary text can appear digitally. The focus of this chapter is on children's digital experiences with texts that make use of the possibilities and the poetics of the digital medium in their literary construction. *Literary apps* – or literary texts available as apps for mobile devices – tend to fall into this category as they often present multimodal and hypermedia literary narratives or poetry whose poetic essence cannot be conveyed in the same way in a print book.

Research on children's responses to digital literature

Empirical research of children reading literary apps is still insipient. Although there have been an increasing number of studies which look at children reading e-books and apps, most of this research has been done in other fields, with most of the work coming from the field of experimental psychology (e.g., Paciga 2015; Sarı et al. 2019; Strouse and Ganea 2017). This research aims to measure children's digital reading experience, their cognitive processing of these texts, and mediation practices, often trying to compare their reading performance in print versus digital reading. These perspectives, however, ignore the literary aspects of these texts and their potential to suggest different kinds of cognitive engagements; they also rarely consider the aesthetic dimension of literary reading.

There has not yet been a major systematic study of children reading digital literature such as those conducted by Arizpe and Styles in this book or Lawrence Sipe's

DOI: 10.4324/9781003106326-11

in *Storytime: Young children's literary understanding in the classroom* (2008). The most encompassing study to date was developed at the Autonomous University of Barcelona, by GRETEL (in English, Research Group in Children's Literature and Literary Education), whose results were published in the book *Digital Reading for Children: Texts, Readers and Educational Practices* (Manresa and Real 2015) as well as in academic and non-academic articles, most of them in Spanish. It involved multiple smaller lines of investigation and discussed digital children's literature from various perspectives, one of which was reader-response. Other researchers, especially from the field of education, have conducted small-scale projects. In this emerging body of work, it is possible to map a few themes that highlight some of the defining features of digital literary reading: the effects of interactivity and reader participation, the highly embodied and performative nature of this experience, the role of adult co-readers and the importance of mediation and the presence of highly commercial apps.

Firstly, most research in this field debates, at least at some level, the definition and impact of interactivity in reading. In most cases, digital texts are considered interactive because digital technology permits the completion of the so-called feedback loop, allowing communicative exchanges from reader to text as well as from text to reader. Aliagas and Margallo (2017) have looked at how interactivity affects the reading experience in their ethnographic study of preschoolers reading apps at home, and have found that they might approach it in three ways: (1) as a challenge or a game, in a stimulus-response mode in which the narrative is left to the background of the reading experience; (2) as a possibility of re-creation of the story – in an app that allowed retelling fairy tales through a digital theatre; (3) as a possibility for reinforcing the experience of the story, leading to the reader's emotional immersion in the fictional universe.

The participatory nature of these texts, promoted by the possibility of interaction, has also led to reflection on the eventful and performative nature of digital literary reading. Nagel (2017) has conducted a phenomenological analysis of the app reading experience and proposes that the study of literary apps must place 'the reading of an app in the centre of the analysis alongside the app itself' (2017: 4). This perspective positions the study of children's responses to literary apps at the centre not only of scholarship in literary education and reception studies but also of more traditional literary studies. The point made by Nagel is underlined in other projects which discuss the aesthetic *experience* of app reading. However, these studies are based on the analysis of the adult researcher's experiences, without involving the actual audience of these apps: children (Hagen 2020; Søyland and Gulliksen 2019). As insightful as these analyses are, they seem to overlook the fact that children's aesthetic experiences with literature can be significantly different from those of the adult researcher.

The interactivity of literary apps also leads to another line of enquiry that is far more prominent in reader-response research with literary apps than with print books: the embodied nature of digital reading and the centrality of interactive gestures. Merchant's (2014) study in a UK nursery resulted in a taxonomy of children's vocabulary of gestures in digital literary reading: *stabilising movements* are used to support the device; *control movements* are used to engage with the text through the interactive features of the touchscreen; *deictic movements* direct the attention of the reader to the text on the screen. Vilela (2019), in a study conducted in a preschool classroom in Brazil, has also highlighted the embodied nature of digital reading through a Benjaminian reading of children's experiences with digital literature. Benjamin (1986) posits that gesture is children's first language and that mimetic behaviours are common in childhood and help children understand the world. Vilela (2019: 148) then proposes that children's embodied engagements with literary apps operate within two realms: 'touching the screen', or this vocabulary of interactive gestures that form a new language and a new culture of reading, and 'the embodied text', or children's aesthetic experience through their bodies.

The topic of mediation also seems to have prominence in this body of empirical research, because the affordances of digital literature and of digital technology more generally seem to affect the relationship between reader and co-readers or mediators. Although the audio features of literary apps such as narration allow even very young, pre-literate children to engage independently with the texts (Aliagas and Margallo 2017; Mackey 2016; Merchant 2015; Real and Correro 2015), new difficulties emerge, especially with regards to interactivity, questioning the myth of children's almost inherent ability to engage with digital technology. Young children might not have the fine motor skills to perform certain interactions (Merchant 2015) or to understand what is expected of them in certain moments where interaction is necessary to move the reading forward (see the case study below). The lack of mediation might lead to extremely fragmented and chaotic reading experiences (Real and Correro 2015) in which the general narrative meaning might be lost. Therefore, adult mediation is highlighted by many researchers, but they also critically analyse the fact that the mediator's role might be reduced in certain cases to the role of technical support rather than that of reading *together* (Aliagas and Margallo 2017; Merchant 2015).

While research in children's responses to picturebooks usually works with a prime selection of literary texts, which emerge from a print publishing market saturated with possibilities, the volume of literary apps published is small and in fact dropping, as developers cannot maintain apps that sell little and require constant updates to keep up with the fast-changing systems and devices. Often, apps that are most popular are associated with media franchises and popular culture, and they tend to appear in studies with a more ethnographic nature. Merchant (2015) mentioned children's preferences for characters they know and love like Peppa Pig; in Aliagas and Margallo's (2017) research, one of the cases involved the child reading a Dora the Explorer app. Similarly, in Real and Correro's study (2015), children's preferences tended towards commercial apps with strong entertainment rather than literary value.

Finally, educational research approaching this phenomenon from a socio-cultural perspective has intersected with some questions and frameworks that are of interest to reader-response research within the field of children's literature.

I highlight the work of Kucirkova, Littleton and Cremin (2016), the first to propose a framework for understanding children's engagements with digital books (e-books and apps) from a reading for pleasure perspective. They propose six facets for this engagement: *affective* (children's feelings and emotions while reading); *creative* (possibility thinking), *interactive* (the child's active contribution while reading), *shared* (the social practice of sharing the reading experience with others), *sustained* (maintain reading engagement through a period of time), and *personalised* (customise and participate in the story with the child's own content). These categories do not refer to children's responses per se, but there is some clear overlap with Sipe's (2008) categories of response, for instance with the affective facet being related to Sipe's 'personal responses', and the creative, to 'performative responses'.

Research designs for the study of children reading digital literature

Literary apps are not yet integrated in school or preschool curricula in most countries, so most of the children's encounters with these texts still tend to happen more frequently in domestic settings. Hence, differently from most studies of children reading picturebooks, which tend to happen in school settings, the design of some projects involved parent-child joint-reading and even ethnographic research looking at children reading at home (Aliagas and Margallo 2014, 2017; Kucirkova and Flewitt 2020). Such choices have, for instance, ethical implications, such as the issues that are involved in entering the intimacy of participants' homes, especially for video recording.[2]

Another implication of researching parent-child shared reading instead of classroom collective readings is that it is only possible to collect the responses from one child at a time (or a few children, in cases involving siblings). This results in a small number of participants and possibly a smaller number of verbal responses, as group formation tends to motivate people to share their thoughts and build meaning together. However, as the case below will exemplify, observing individual readers can lead to the opportunity of looking at other aspects of their responses, some of which only occur in this specific reading configuration.

There are also particular difficulties in developing studies with groups in classrooms: the often one-to-one nature of interactivity with digital texts is a challenge for group reading and multiple devices are not always available in schools, especially in economically deprived contexts.

Furthermore, in terms of methods for data collection, video recording – rather than audio-recording or fieldwork notes – is highly recommended. This is because interactivity makes children's gestures and non-verbal communication extremely prominent, although researchers such as Mackey (2002) have also highlighted their importance when children read picturebooks. Video recording allows the researcher to come back to the reading event multiple times and investigate it in detail. This opportunity signals how much is going on at each reading event that would have been missed through other forms of data collection.

Finally, the study of children's responses to digital literature suggests interdisciplinary theoretical frameworks. The canonical work of Louise Rosenblatt remains relevant, alongside Arizpe and Styles' and Sipe's seminal works in children's responses to picturebooks, but the need to understand digital literary reading in its own right requires a dialogue with other seminal texts in fields such as digital narratology, for instance, the work of Marie-Laure Ryan (2006, 2015) and the study of mainstream digital (also often called electronic) literature, including the works of Katherine Hayles (e.g. 2002, 2008). Multimodal studies, especially the multimodal social semiotics of Gunther Kress and Theo van Leeuwen (Kress 2003, 2010; Kress and van Leeuwen 2020; van Leeuwen 2005), have also been used across some research projects, theoretical and empirical, trying to account for the fact that digital literature goes beyond image-text relationships of picturebooks with the inclusion of the moving image, sound effects, music, narration, gesture and interactivity. This theory also highlights the fact that readers express themselves multimodally.

One of the challenges of studying digital literature is that this is a constantly evolving artform with new possibilities and innovations surfacing with the quick technological changes that take place, requiring a flexibility and speed not always available in academic research. The constant change can present practical consequences for the research, as apps can literally disappear from the app store or stop working after a system update, requiring attention and strategic planning from the researcher.

Case study

Research design

The question of how children read and make meaning with literary apps led me to my PhD research (Frederico 2018), completed at the University of Cambridge. In this project, I conducted case studies with six families of four-year-olds living in England. They read three literary apps in joint-reading situations with a parent. The participant families and I met in a public library, where the child and a parent, in most cases the mother, read together three pre-selected literary apps: *The Monster at the End of This Book* (Stone and Smollin 2011), *Little Red Riding Hood* (Nosy Crow 2013) and *Hat Monkey* (Haughton 2013). The reading of the apps was video recorded with multiple cameras, making sure that both the child's and the parent's responses were captured, including their gestures towards the device, but also that the developments in the narrative were recorded because the digital text depends on the reader's actions to unfold and each reading of a digital interactive narrative can differ. After reading the apps, a process in which I was not involved, I stepped in and requested the children to make a drawing about the story and I engaged in a dialogue about their drawing as they were doing it, trying to unpack the meaning behind their choices of representation. Next, they were given finger puppets, which I created using the images from the apps, and were asked to retell the story to me as an audience. In this case study, I will focus on the main source of data, the video-recordings, but the other methods were also highly relevant in unpacking the layers of meaning from the participant's experiences.

As there is still little research on children's responses to literary apps, it is hardly possible to generalise the findings of any study to indicate how children respond to this art-form. Furthermore, because of such diversity, it might take a great number of studies, considering certain subcategories of literary apps, before we can start to build a real understanding of digital literary reading. That said, an in-depth analysis of the responses of a few participants can highlight many facets of this reading experience.

In this case study, I explore four-and-a-half-year-old Amelia's responses while joint reading the literary app *Hat Monkey* with her mother, Becky. Amelia was a child with little experience of touchscreen mobile technology. She used her father's tablet only a few hours a month. Yet, her mother considered her to be a confident user of digital technology, and my impression during the observations matched her mother's description – even though she had never read a literary app before the study. This specific reading event, however, happened at the third session of the research project, so Amelia had already read the other two apps at this point. When it came to reading print books, she was an avid reader, reading picturebooks almost every day and visiting the library regularly.

The text

Hat Monkey was selected to be part of the study because it had affordances not encountered in the other two apps. While they had traditional narrative arcs, with the setup of a problem, a climax and a resolution, *Hat Monkey*'s narrative is loose and there is no problem to be solved as the narrative progresses. It invites children to live a day in the life of Monkey, accompanying him in his activities. It starts with Monkey coming home; the reader is inside the house to open the door for him. Reader and Monkey then play hide and seek, communicate via text, do high fives, dance, talk on the phone, play music, eat bananas and read a story before going to bed. The end, with Monkey falling asleep in his bed, provides a sense of closure, but there is no cause and effect to connect the scenes in the app. Although it can be problematic to apply categories and genres typical of picturebooks to a different art-form such as the literary app, it is impossible to deny that many literary apps build strongly on the picturebook tradition, and this app has strong resemblance to a concept book. The concept or theme that pervades this app is interaction and communication between people, in their multiple forms.

The app has a very hybrid nature, combining elements typical of picturebooks, others that evoke digital toys and children's imaginative play. It suggests an aesthetic experience that is based on *doing* things within this fictional world, making the reader's actions and the unfolding of the text indistinguishable, highlighting the understanding of digital reading as a performance (Nagel 2017).

Each scene of the app contains two stages, the first is an invitation to the reader in the form of a question: *Can you do something for/with Monkey?* There can be a short contextualisation followed by the question. 'Monkey is hiding. Can you find him?' (2013: n.p.) or 'Monkey is hungry. Can you give him a banana?' (2013: n.p.). Unlike most literary apps, there is no read-aloud option for this text. As the app targets pre-literate children as main audience, the lack of audio narration becomes an implied suggestion for shared reading. The second part of the scene involves the action, and the reader encounters a fully animated Monkey, who moves around a minimalistic setting which is mostly static. Monkey, however, does not speak the reader's language,[3] but expresses himself through gesture, vocalisations and, as will be explored next, speaking his incomprehensible language.

Certain objects, directly involved in the completion of the action, are interactive and sound effects complete the fictional world presented in this app. Although Monkey is interactive in the sense that when readers tap him, there might be a change in his expression, readers cannot control Monkey as they could be an avatar. Through interaction, readers do not act as Monkey, but Monkey is a character they interact *with*. Readers must remain in their position as readers, a partner in Monkey's daily life, which at times assumes the role of a helper or of a more able participant, who can help him.

Next, I will present three vignettes of Amelia and Becky reading one scene of *Hat Monkey* through a multimodal transcription in which I present the most explicit responses they expressed during the event.[4]

In this scene, readers can make a video call with Monkey with a smartphone. They receive the call from Monkey and can either pick it up or turn the call down. If they answer the call, Monkey starts talking to them. After a brief introduction, which can be 'hello' or 'mip', as the responses vary at each reading, he waits for an answer from the reader, who is expected to talk back. The device's microphone captures the sound produced by the readers, but it cannot interpret its content or meaning. As sound is captured, Monkey replies in his own, unintelligible language. If nothing is said, Monkey keeps pointing at the phone and waiting for the reader to speak. They can do a few rounds of 'conversation' before Monkey hangs up. If the reader does not move to the next scene, Monkey automatically makes another call, restarting the exchange (Figure 8.1).

130 *Research on children responding to visual texts*

00-05s [01]
A blue screen with a red text appears. Becky reads it out loud. Amelia makes a confused face.

05-07s [02]
Amelia says:

07-09s [04]
Becky explains the difference by making a gesture of a phone call in the air. (Earlier they had sent text messages to Monkey.)

09-12s [04]
Amelia seems to reflect on such difference while Becky presses the arrow button forward, to the second part of the scene.

Figure 8.1 Vignette 1 — Part 1 of the scene – reading the instructions.

12-15s [05]
The image shows Monkey making a call with the accompanying dialing **sound effect**. Becky anticipates herself and tells Amelia:

15-21s [06]
The screen shows the interface of a phone ringing, with the according **sound effect**. Becky points to show Amelia where to tap to answer. Amelia taps.

21-29s [07]
The screen shows the interface of a phone in a video call. Monkey says hello. Whispering, Becky encourages Amelia to talk. Monkey replies in his own, incomprehensible language.

29-38s [08]
They continue the conversation, and Becky makes a question. Amelia, looking attentive at his mother's responses, repeats the question. Monkey replies in his own language.

37-41s [09]
Becky points to the screen and whispers again, trying to bring Amelia to the interaction. Amelia repeats the question in a low and soft voice.

41-50s [10]
Monkey responds shortly and hangs up the phone making a **sound effect**. Becky asks a question to Amelia, who shakes her head in a negative response.

Figure 8.2 Vignette 2 — First call from Monkey.

Children reading literary apps 131

The second part of the scene is when the actual phone calls between Monkey and the readers happen. Amelia and Becky had three sequential calls with Monkey.

In the first two calls (Figure 8.2), Becky and Amelia seem to be exploring what the scene was about and how to interact with the character. As the phone rings, they have to make a choice which will impact their narrative experience at this scene: they can either pick up the phone or decline the call. To properly express their choice, they need to tap the appropriate button, performing an interactive gesture. In this example, it is evident that Becky takes the forefront of the action, as she decides where they should tap. She does not perform the gesture, however, but explicitly teaches Amelia the 'correct' button to tap. While the decision of where to tap comes from the mother, she refrains from performing the tap herself, waiting for Amelia to do it [06]. The sequence that follows indicates that Amelia struggled at some level to engage in the actual phone call. It is not clear what the issue is, if she did not understand clearly what was happening or simply did not know what to say. At this stage, she seems to be trying to learn what is expected, she observes her mother [08] and repeats what the mother says, but we do not see a participation in which Amelia is at the forefront of the interaction.

This structure of interaction was repeated in the second phone call, with Becky taking the lead, suggesting things for Amelia to say and Amelia repeating them, even though Amelia seems progressively more aware of how the interaction works. Despite Amelia's secondary role in this part of the reading, they seem to take great pleasure from the experience and laugh out loud. At the end of this call, Becky asks Amelia whether she wants to try again or move on to the next scene. Amelia seems suddenly startled by an idea of what to do and wants to try again (Figure 8.3).

This time, Amelia seemed prepared for the interaction. Her response is unexpected: instead of talking in English, as she and Becky did in the previous calls, Amelia starts talking in 'Monkey language', saying incomprehensible things. Monkey replies and then Becky joins Amelia talking Monkey language too, and both laugh loudly. Amelia continues on talking Monkey language, now in a more articulated sentence, with precise syllables and accompanied by animated hand gestures. In this vignette, the lead role changes from the mother to Amelia. Initially, Becky positions herself as a knowledgeable co-reader, who supports Amelia both in terms of interpreting the narrative and in terms of showing her the right way to interact, in light of such interpretation. In this third vignette, however, she appropriates the reading experience, bringing her own take to the action, creatively making use of the interactive framework that is proposed by the app, generating humour. They laugh out loud and as Monkey hangs up, they decide to move to the next scene.

1min30-36s [11]
A seccond, similar call takes place and Becky asks if Amelia wants to move on with the story, but Amelia wants to try again. She taps the phone on Monkey's hand to no effect.

1min36-43s [12]
Becky insists that Amelia does the talking. As the phone rings, she points again which button to press to pick up the call. As Amelia hesitates, Becky grabs her hand and presses it.

1min43-47s [13]
After tapping Monkey to no effect, Amelia moves very close to the screen and starts talking to Monkey in her own version of his language.

1min47-58s [14]
They laugh out loud and after a turn of Monkey talking, it is time for Becky to talk in "Monkey language". They both laugh out loud at the result.

1min58-2min06s [15]
Once again Amelia talks to Monkey in the invented language, this time making enthusiastic hand gestures, adding expression to her "message" to him.

2min06-10s [16]
Becky asks if Amelia wants to go make another call or move on to the next page. Amelia decides to move on, pressing the arrow to go forward with the story.

Figure 8.3 Vignette 3 — Third call from Monkey and the end of the scene.

Considerations about children's responses to literary apps

In this chapter, it is only possible to discuss one participant reading one scene of one app, mostly due to the lengthy nature of the in-depth analysis performed in this study. These vignettes were chosen because they highlight multiple facets that seem typical of children's responses to digital literature in the context of shared reading with a parent. These aspects were seen across the data and also relate to the issues raised above in the literature review.

To start with, these vignettes show one important aspect of digital reading that differs from most traditional book reading: readers are expected to perform meaningful actions when reading digital literature. For such, they must understand the interaction simultaneously at two complementary levels: on the one hand, *how* to interact, the gestures required, the area or hotspot which need to be activated (for touch interaction)[5] but also what the action means in the context of the scene. At first, Amelia struggled to understand what talking to monkey on the phone meant. Such doubt does not seem to depend on a lack of experience of making phone calls but possibly because she did not anticipate the possibility of actually *talking* to the app, as most literary apps do not involve this form of interaction; sending a text message – which in fact was just an emoticon – seems to be as close to 'talking' as she envisioned for a reading event. Even Becky expressed doubt about how the talking on the phone was going to work [04].

These vignettes also capture the dynamics between child and adult co-reader and their central role in meaning-making; the parental style of shared reading shapes children's engagements and responses significantly. In this case, Becky was very active in indicating to Amelia what and how to do things. This avoided frustration for the child reader, something that was seen at some moments with other participants; Becky kept the interaction meaningful even when it seemed not to be working very well and Monkey hung up the phone by suggesting that he did not say goodbye [10]. On the other hand, by initially taking the lead, there seemed to be little space for Amelia to engage in interactions that were meaningful to her. She did seem, though, to need the guidance and modelling as she did not instantaneously engage in the conversation with Monkey. However, the possibility of repeating the interaction gave her the opportunity to make sense of the scene and in the third round, she creatively brought her own twist to the interaction, generating humour. It is important to recognise, though, that there is a learning process taking place during the reading event, one in which the adult co-reader has an important role to play.

Secondly, these vignettes indicate multiple forms of embodied responses present in digital reading, from tapping to navigate the app [04]; tapping to interact with the fictional word, including making choices that shape the fictional experience [06]; forms of interaction – such as talking – that do not use touch but still involve the reader's body [07–09 and 13–15]; expressive embodied responses that are part of the performance of reading but are not captured in any way by the device [15]; deictic gestures that support the shared-reading experience; and embodied expressions that indicate reader's emotions and engagement with the literary text [throughout the scene].

The analysis of these expressions of emotion, in light of the entire event, indicates how very engaged in the app they were and living a very pleasurable, both to child and adult, reading experience, in an affective exchange that is often associated with the shared reading of picturebooks in early childhood. This leads to the conclusion that the pleasures of shared reading can be equally experienced in digital reading, especially when good quality digital literature is present.

The methods of data collection, analysis and also of representation of the data as the vignettes presented above also point to the need of exploring further children's responses (1) beyond the verbal level and (2) *during* the reading event. Most of the research on children's responses to picturebooks have used methods of audio-recording only, and studies such as this one demonstrate that there are other levels of response that can be uncovered through the detailed analysis of video-data and a close look to children's body and facial expressions. Furthermore, these methods allow the capturing of the linear quality of children's responses and the resignification that happens as one scene follows the next, in the process of anticipation and retrospection discussed by Iser (1974). As much as narrative non-linearity is a feature of many digital literary texts, the nature of the reading experience is always linear.

Research on children's responses to digital literature is just starting and there are a plethora of avenues of enquiry to explore for those wishing to. Such areas for future research include, but are not limited to: (1) studies that look at readers of multiple age ranges; (2) the comparison between home and school reading settings; (3) the study of children's responses across media, not only contrasting app and picturebook responses, but, given the hybrid nature of digital literature, also looking at other digital texts, such as animated films and digital games; (4) the consideration of children's responses to specific genres of digital literature, such as wordless apps, non-linear immersive narrative worlds and hypertext fiction.

The research on children's responses to literary apps can also enlighten research on children reading picturebooks and other visual texts by bringing to the fore some under-researched areas, such as the study of the children's responses in shared reading with parents and in contexts such as the home or the library, or the study of the embodied aspects of children's responses to print books, including texts that, like apps, might invite embodied participation, such as pop-ups and other animated books.

Notes

1 Although it is beyond the scope of this study to discuss why literary apps did not become popular, some of the reasons that form the complex equation for their lack of commercial success involve aspects such as: a parents' preference for print literature for their children, especially in the early years (Kucirkova and Flewitt 2020); the high cost of production while the app market imposes very low individual sales prices, from 1.99-3.99 USD; the difficulties in making literary apps know in the mist of millions of apps with other functionalities; the difficulties for users and small producers in keeping the apps functioning when tech companies constantly update operational systems, requiring users to get new devices and producers to release new updated versions of their apps.
2 For the ethical debate regarding studying young children's engagements with technology, check Flewitt (2019) and the Interactive Ethics Tool for Researching Young Children's Digital Literacy Practices, developed by the COST Action DigiLitEY, available at http://digilitey.eu/ethics/.
3 Hat Monkey is a multilingual app. Within the app, readers can choose among 14 languages: English, French, German, Spanish, Dutch, Italian, Portuguese, Swedish, Turkish, Chinese (simplified and traditional), Japanese, Russian and Korean.

4 While traditional transcriptions tend to focus on transcribing verbal utterances and some non-verbal expressions into verbal language, a multimodal transcription transcribes multiple modes of meaning-making in a systematic way. The transcription presented here is a specific form of multimodal transcription used for rhetoric purposes, that is, with the intention of presenting the data for the sake of argumentation in an academic text. Since the aim is to present a complex, multimodal video data in print format, as all forms of transcription, choices are made with regards to what to include and what not to include. In this case, because of the restricted space, the focus is on verbal and gestural utterances and some facial and embodied expressions where suppressed. For more on multimodal transcription, check Bezemer (2014) and Cowan (2014).
5 For further discussion of the structure of touch interaction, see Zhao and Unsworth (2017).

9 Diverse readers, diverse picturebooks, diverse responses

Evelyn Arizpe

When we carried out the original 'Children Reading Pictures' project in 1999, each of the members of the team decided to focus on an aspect of the research that was significant to them and their expertise. Kathy Coulthard, a member of the research team who had been a primary teacher, was at the time an adviser for ethnic minority achievement in the London borough of Enfield. Following Charmian Kenner's research on bilinguality and the cultural dimensions of children's learning, Kathy was concerned with the need to increase teachers' awareness of bilingual children's cultural and text knowledge in order to support their literacy learning. While early important work was being carried out at the time on bilingual learners and literacy by Kenner and Eve Gregory, the field overall was less interested in going beyond the use of functional pedagogic texts and visual clues to engage learners of English. Kathy was quick to understand that asking readers to respond to picturebooks had the potential not only to shed light on different cultural practices around literacy but also to provide ways forward for understanding how they made meaning from challenging visual texts and how they could be used to develop language learning as well as classroom interaction and provides ways towards inclusion.

These ideas were behind Kathy's examination of the data gathered from the schools in which she conducted the interviews for 'Reading Pictures'. These schools both had a high percentage (one up to 70%) of minority ethnic pupils, including both pupils who had recently arrived in the UK and third generation bilinguals (overall, in the sample of the 126 children who participated in the original research project, 'approximately 35% were bilingual with varying linguistic backgrounds' (1st edition, page 7). Kathy's chapter in the first edition, 'Young bilingual learners responding to visual texts', discussed the findings of the interviews and group sessions with five- and six-year-old bilingual learners responding to two picturebooks by Anthony Browne: *Zoo* and *The Tunnel*. Her chapter looked at cultural practices around stories and books and learning to read as well as linguistic development. Kathy found that a few children found both the unfamiliar books more of a challenge and were less comfortable with interpreting the pictures or engaging with the open questions and got no further than labelling the pictures. The majority, however, despite having limited linguistic skills were so engaged by the reading of the picturebook that they were determined to express their thoughts and participate in the conversations.

The result was that readers acquired new vocabulary and learned how language works, growing more confident and becoming less worried about making mistakes when they realised that Kathy was genuinely interested in what they had to say rather than assessing their language skills. The impact of the picturebook sharing, however, went beyond this linguistic development and there were moments of 'profound critical engagement' (166) especially when readers could relate the narrative to their personal histories and understanding of the world. The emotional engagement with a text like *The Tunnel,* which is about conflictive but also loving human relationships, was also evident in the children's responses and in one case it proved transformative in an unexpected and moving way, when a child connected the narrative to a traumatic experience in his past but in a way that seemed to be healing rather than upsetting.

It could be argued that almost 20 years later, the findings from Kathy's chapter continue to be relevant and, in some cases, have provided the building blocks for other studies on response to picturebooks and cultural diversity. The issues that concerned Kathy have proved to be increasingly significant in recent research about culturally situated books and readers as well as in studies on the representation of diversity and inclusion and on the development of empathy. The various strands of research in this area include, among others, studies that have explicitly used picturebooks in English language classrooms for language learning, for literacy development, for intercultural education and for the development of empathy. These studies have involved not only researchers from different parts of the world but also a variety of ethnic groups and other minorities such as refugees and newly arrived pupils. Therefore, in the previous edition of this book, we added a section on new research on response to picturebooks which had to do with language learning, especially English and also with cultural knowledge and understanding of literacy with children from diverse backgrounds. We also included response from mainstream pupils to culturally diverse picturebooks.

However, since 2015, many more studies have explored the relationship between culture, literacy practices, pedagogy and picturebooks. They fully acknowledge "the cultural 'situatedness' of the act of reading" (Arizpe 2017) which implies that personal histories and experiences are inseparably intertwined with cultural backgrounds and these need to be considered when researching the literary and aesthetic transactions that take place during the reading of a picturebook. They also show how a growing familiarity with challenging but meaningful texts, where the images support the context, and where there is a safe space for discussion with a supportive peer community, allows readers to gradually participate in more depth and move from the literal to the inferential, engaging with language, emotions and issues around identity.

With these different perspectives and contexts in mind, for this edition, we realised that a whole new chapter was required to review and discuss the burgeoning interest around diversity and inclusion in response to picturebooks. We also realised we had to extend our overview to a wider range of studies that engage with topics beyond cultural diversity and into response to picturebooks about gender diversity and the differently abled.

Although in what follows we begin by situating picturebooks within the current debates on equity and inclusion, it is important to clarify that this chapter is not about studies on picturebook content and representation but mainly deals with two types of studies: the first, which present readers with picturebooks that attempt to be inclusive of diverse cultures with the explicit aim of developing critical awareness and challenging exclusionary views; the second, which seek to involve readers from a range of groups perceived as minorities within a particular cultural or social context, and examine how they respond to picturebooks with the aim of developing their language, literacy and/or other competences. The chapter will highlight some of the main findings of both groups of studies and include considerations for those teachers and other professionals working with culturally situated readers' responses to picturebooks.

In this way we provide both a synthesis of the chapters that involved diverse readers and/or inclusion from the previous editions as well as other overviews in this area (e.g. Arizpe 2017, 2021; Arizpe and McGilp 2022) but we also consider new research where this focus is reflected either in the selection of books, the methodologies and the participants, or throughout the whole process. It is also important to note that our original database of studies from 2015 was updated through internet searches using a variety of search tools and platforms. Our search terms included "reader-response"; both spellings of "picture books" and "picturebooks"; "culture", "diversity" and "inclusion". However, as in the previous edition, we acknowledge the limits of the present overview in terms of the geographical reach of the studies: with a few exceptions, most are in English.

Diverse readers and inclusion in the context of children reading picturebooks

There are two main perspectives to consider under this section: how the picturebooks reflect the presence (or absence) and lived (or perceived) realities of diverse minority groups and what diverse children say about picturebooks – whether or not the picturebooks they read can be considered as reflecting a diverse world. Other considerations have to do with context and mediation, in other words, where those children are reading (a multicultural school, for example) and who introduces, reads and/or works with those children (teachers, researchers or other mediators). When discussing reader-response research, where the researcher is not the same as the teacher, it is also important to reflect on what group that researcher represents and how they perceive the context in which they are carrying out their study (for example, a monolingual researcher in a multilingual school or a white researcher from the Global North collecting data from a reading promotion charity in the Global South).

If we look beyond the immediate objectives of studies on response to picturebooks that attend to diversity of some kind, the final aim of these studies tends to be some form of inclusion. On the one hand, these forms of inclusion can be aimed at providing more equal access or encouraging a sense of belonging in those excluded or marginalised for some reason, for example, refugee children. On the other hand, their aim could be improving critical skills and/or empathy in order to encourage readers to treat those excluded or marginalised in a fairer and more equal manner, an attitude that entails acceptance and a sense of making them part of the majority group.

The studies mentioned in this chapter thus involve both the 'included' and the 'excluded' and look to improve or develop literacy, language learning, intercultural communication, identity formation and empathy with others. They differ in the ways that they approach the picturebooks involved, with some focusing on them as literary and aesthetic objects and others using them mainly as research and pedagogic tools; yet they are all in some ways revealing about how picturebooks work for readers and how readers make meaning from that special interaction between words and pictures.

Selecting picturebooks for research focused on diverse readers and inclusion

Fundamental changes in the ways in which the terms "diversity" and "inclusion" are being understood in the wider context of education and even beyond means that we must refer to these here, although we do not have the space to engage with them in any depth. These changes have emerged from the social and political climate in the second half of the 2010s which has resulted in more open but at the same time more bitter and divisive discussions about topics such as race and sexuality as well as globalism, migration and postcolonialism, all of which are having an impact on picturebooks and their creators, as well as on parents, educators, and other adults who mediate between texts and children [witness, for example, the way in which the decision of the publisher to withdraw some Dr Seuss books with racist images became highly politicised and used as a weapon in what some people perceive as 'cancel culture' (Nel 2021)]. Ironically, it continues to be the case that the children these books are targeted at are usually the last to be asked about their perspectives – if at all. Now more than ever it is important to both provide children with books that might help to begin to heal some of these divisions and also create spaces where young readers can safely express their thoughts (a topic we will come to in the next section).

In the process of picturebook selection, issues often begin with the existence and availability of books that are genuinely inclusive. In the UK for example, while the Centre for Language in Primary Education (CLPE) reports on cultural diversity in children's books published in this country show there is a positive trend, from 2017 when only 4% of children's books featured a minority ethic main character to 15% in 2020 (in contrast to a UK school population where 33.5% of pupils have minority ethnic origins) (CLPE 2021). The CLPE 2019 report provides useful questions about representation as well as terms for "articulating features of texts that can undermine the quality of representation" (2020: 21). These and other reports and reviews on diversity from around the world highlight the need for texts that promote inclusive discourses especially in the light of current ideological and political movements that uphold exclusive views of ethnic nationalism. In the US and beyond, Rudine Sims Bishop's (1990) "mirrors, windows and doors" metaphor has become the refrain of many who are asking for more literature for children that better reflects the lives of readers; that provides authentic windows into the lives of others and offers ways of moving through the "sliding doors" into those worlds. In order to do this, we now need to go beyond texts that are "multicultural" and "diverse" and join Thomas' call for literature that is also "decolonialized" (2016: 115).

Given the potential impact of the visual representation of characters and settings, picturebooks have become an area of continued scrutiny for any sign that they may perpetuate systems and forms of injustice such as racism, sexism, ableism or classism that exist within society. Picturebook criticism and even censorship is nothing new, but in this heightened climate, the decision of what picturebooks to buy for the classroom has become particularly sensitive, from who writes and/or illustrates them to who reads them, how and why. It is not surprising, therefore, to see emerge from the field of education, not only a plethora of studies that look critically at picturebooks with the aim of decolonising the curriculum but also studies on reader-response, some of which aim to develop critical abilities in readers so that they are aware of and can identify issues around inclusion, exclusion and problematic representations. For example, a study on response to picturebooks in Colombia, showed how the racial prejudice that emerged in the response led to a discussion about this issue (Cuperman 2013). Some scholars are taking this even further, asking questions about how picturebooks can aid in attempts to raise children's awareness about white supremacy and hate (Sciurba 2020).

When thinking about a book selection that would encourage readers to think about representation or to find out how readers view difference, for many researchers the obvious choices are multicultural and/or bilingual picturebooks. Hudelson, Smith and Hawes (2005) and Lohfink and Loya (2010) found bilingual books encouraged Latinx children to attend to the issues of language and bilingualism as well as to made cultural connections and develop their literacy skills. Other research has included multilingual picturebooks, such as McGilp's (2014) study with multilingual children and multicultural fairy tale picturebooks. She aimed to validate the children's first language and culture in the classroom by providing books in their home language(s). Researchers also often use postmodern picturebooks because of the multiple levels of interpretation they offer (Arizpe 2010; Pantaleo 2009a); in Denmark, for example, Møller Daugaard and Blok Johansen looked at multilingual children responding to a Danish postmodern picturebook and especially its metafictional features (2014). Their findings led them to propose that 'multilingual children should be offered postmodern picture books along with other types of books – precisely because of the potential that lies in the apparent difficulty of such books' (2013: 18). Wordless picturebooks are also often used both because of their postmodern features and because they are accessible to speakers of any language, inviting greater co-authoring by the reader (Arizpe 2013; Maine & McCaughran 2021). Wordless picturebooks often raise unexpected but significant topics around diversity and inclusion; for example, when working with a wordless picturebook version of Little Red Riding Hood, Iordanaki (2020) found that the lack of explicit gendered pronouns and other words led 11-year-olds in both England and in Greece to discuss gender identities and roles based on cultural expectations and stereotypes.

Given the above, it is clear that the first crucial step in reader-response research involving picturebooks is to examine them critically, before sharing them with readers. This examination can be supported by a range of theories that can work alongside critical visual approaches (e.g. Kress and van Leeuwen 2006), such as Critical Race Theory, Intersectionality, Disability Studies and Queer Theory. It can also be illuminating to look at ideas that stem from posthumanism, linking materiality and embodiment (García-González and Deszcz-Tryhubczak 2020) which consider the picturebook as a material object in relation to, or even as an extension of the human body. Along with these theories it is recommended that researchers conduct a critical content analysis, following, for example, the work of Botelho and Rudman on critical multicultural analysis (2009); Pérez Huber, Camargo Gonzalez and Solórzano, on their "Critical Race Content Analysis" for books about People of Colour (2020); or Johnson, Mathis and Short (2019) who have extended their framework to critical visual analysis. Finally, a range of articles can also be helpful in examining and recommending picturebooks on themes inclusion related issues and, such as autism (Sigmon, Tackett and Azano 2016) or hope (McAdam et al. 2020). This first step will ensure that teacher and/or researchers select the best books according to their purpose and ensure that the selection will engage children with a range of diverse and authentic voices and contexts.

Context and mediation

The settings for research on response have also been changing in the last two decades, with more non-traditional, non-formal educational where picturebooks are read and shared now being included, as we have seen in the chapters discussing museums and art galleries. Research in schools is usually straightforward because even in highly multicultural, multilingual classrooms there are structures in place, such as curriculum, that guarantee continuity as well as books and spaces for reading them. The reading practices that go on in non-formal spaces can be much more fluid, with variable attendance and sometimes random book choice depending on what is available. In these spaces it is therefore important to consider not only what is read but where, but also who introduces, reads or conducts the research with children or young people in those spaces. Specific contexts will demand specific criteria for selection and also for research methods; for example, when working in multilingual spaces or with groups with low levels of literacy, it helps to include a wider range of arts-based response activities that move away from the hegemony of the written word and which take into account different capacities and forms of cultural and artistic expressions. In some spaces, there may be heightened concern for ethics and safeguarding when participants are vulnerable or marginalised in some way. As Coban, McAdam and Arizpe (2020) argue, involving participants in a more holistic aesthetic process can create more supportive and 'safe' space. When contexts are too sensitive or precarious (for example, refuges for migrants), it can be best to consider working through facilitators or mediators, such as charity workers, librarians or other professionals, rather than directly with the children involved.

It is also important to reflect on the researcher's positionality vis-à-vis the context of the research, in other words, considering what group the researcher represents, how they may be perceived and how they perceive the context in which the study is carried out. Some research projects attempt to redress the power balance between the researchers, teachers and other mediators and the participant children by handing over more agency to the readers and following more critical routes where they participate in designing the study itself (see also Chapter 10). Finally, García-González (2021) provides us with a salutary reminder that the researchers' priorities may be very different from those of the community, for example, in the 'camps' set up in deprived areas near the city of Santiago, in Chile, where the government was setting up libraries in small community schools, researchers found that the mothers who acted as teachers were more concerned with having enough light to open in the winter months and food to provide a small meal to the children that attended rather than with "the potential of picturebooks".

Culturally situated reader-response theories

Along with new approaches in picturebook studies, new ways of looking at readers and their responses to picturebooks have emerged in the first two decades of the 21st century. As we pointed out in the second edition, what has remained a constant in most studies are the basic tenets of reader-response theory, rooted in the importance of the participation of the reader in the act of reading, and usually based on the ideas of Louise Rosenblatt (1978). However, it is also apparent that reader-response theory has become more nuanced regarding the cultural situation of readers and the contexts of their reading practices. Part of this nuance goes back to a questioning of the concepts of "the child" and "childhood", as it is now very clear that theories and pedagogies cannot speak for "all" children. Shirley Brice Heath's (1983) ethnography of literacy practices in different communities in the USA remains relevant nearly 40 years after it was published, highlighting the misalignment that tends to happen between home and school literacies especially when it comes to minority and/or marginalised groups. The twin concepts of 'funds of knowledge' (Gonzales, Moll & Amanti 2005) and 'funds of identity' (Esteban-Guitart & Moll 2014) have helped to recognise and value the cultural knowledge that all students bring to their learning and thus also to their meaning-making. Studies have showed how diverse children use these funds to make sense of picturebooks, share experiences and make intercultural connections (Martínez-Roldán and Newcomer 2011, Arizpe, Colomer and Martínez-Roldán 2014). At the same time, the picturebooks and related activities they are presented within the classroom can impact on the ethnic, racial and readerly identities that minority children construct for themselves (Scherer 2020).

Although his influential framework for examining reader- response did not engage with the ethnic backgrounds of readers in any depth, Lawrence Sipe was aware of the need for further investigation into 'various types of socio-cultural contexts' (Sipe 1990: 120). Brooks and Browne (2012) did extend Sipe's framework in this direction and developed *"culturally situated reader response theory"* that takes into account 'ways literary interpretations are influenced by readers' ethnic backgrounds as well as the cultural milieu embedded in the stories they read' (76). Although they do not refer to picturebooks, these scholars build their theory of response from empirical research and identifying cultural positionings that have to do with 'ethnic group', 'community', 'family' and 'peers', all of which emerge from what they call the reader's 'homeplace'. These positions are fluid and have to do with textual affordances. Their theoretical framework offers those whose research is culturally-oriented a way of moving forward with reader-response theories that considers both how readers culturally position themselves and also personally relate to literature through "cultural access points" so that the text becomes meaningful for them (83).

Finally, it is important to consider literacy theories that encompass an understanding of the influence of diverse literacy practices in the home, for example Cai's work 2008. Both artefactual (Pahl and Rowsell 2011) and visual literacy (Avgerinou & Pettersson 2011) should also be considered here, as different values may be accorded to reading and interpreting text or images. These will also have implications when considering reader response. Although some scholars have raised the issue that reader response could 'invoke students to reproduce dominant discourses' rather than questioning them (Scherer 2020: 6), others have shown that the methods employed when working with response can encourage a critical stance (Callow 2017), and more inclusive one, especially when these methods allow for the expression of the personal, the social and the cultural along with creation of a safe spaces for discussing multiple viewpoints.

Inclusive and inclusion-oriented research design and methodologies

The design of reader-response studies interested in diversity pay attention not only to specific types of books but also to specific types of activities for obtaining response that aims to be inclusive. It must be noted that in some studies it is often not possible -or even desirable- to separate the research data collection method from the pedagogical aim; in other words, the children were learning as they participated in these studies. Not surprisingly, when working with visual texts, methods that include visual responses are employed. However, they are also helpful in overcoming literacy and language barriers and can also be useful for expressing and discussing complex abstract concepts such as "justice".

Studies have shown how artistic responses to culturally relevant picturebooks help minority pupils increase their confidence and literacy skills, for example, bilingual/bicultural Latino children developed their "literate comprehension" in Carger's study (2004) which used painting and clay sculpture. The Visual Journeys project (Arizpe, Colomer and Martínez-Roldán 2014) involved multiple sites in which New Arrival and refugee students used photographs, graphic strips and drawings to respond to wordless picturebooks. Visual responses can also help when dealing with complex issues, as can be seen in Hayik's attempt to develop critical literacy in an English as a Foreign Language (EFL) classroom within a context with profound religious and ethnic tensions, Hayik used picturebooks that revolved around religious diversity and identity and asked her teenage students to "sketch to stretch" (based on Harste, Short & Burke, 1988: 353), to create a sketch symbolising what the story meant to them" Hayik 2011: 99). An analysis of the sketches showed that students were able to consider multiple viewpoints as well as allowing them to actively convey their beliefs about justice and more equal power relations.

Oral methods are also often used, mainly individual or group interviews. The type of questions included in the interviews or group work can help to encourage readers to think more critically about particular issues related to difference, prejudice, social justice and other themes, for example, Callow (2017) asked questions which focused on the choices made by authors and illustrators as well as questions about which characters appeared as more or less powerful in the stories. Oral retellings can also offer insights, such as in the case of Lysaker and Sedberry's study (2015) where two boys with no exposure to culturally diverse peers, were offered picturebooks that allowed them to engage vicariously and empathetically with unfamiliar experiences.

Sherer (2020) examined how minority ethnic pupils constructed their "selves-as-readers" in a multicultural setting. Although she used visual methods and picturebooks, the study only reports on one of the images and there seems to have been no discussion on the visual aesthetics. The illustration to which the children were invited to respond includes diverse characters and Scherer asked the participants a question (borrowed from Patricia Enciso 1996) "If you were in this picture, where would you be?". She also asked

> how they would be feeling were they to be in this picture, in their response. The fact that the chosen illustration included such a wide set of visual representations (old, young, male, female, a character in a wheelchair, Black, White, women wearing hijab) aimed to act as a springboard for discussion about the children's own cultural and social assets and subjectivities.
>
> (2020: 8)

Whether or not the focus of a study is on diverse readers and/or inclusion, reader-response research should always include consideration of issues such as authenticity, representation and power, not only in the picturebooks selected and the questions posed, but also in what readers say (or don't say) and how they say it. Researchers must be aware of which readers tend to dominate the conversation, who struggles to express themselves and who remains silent. When discussing topics such as gender, race or disability, the researcher must also be prepared to deal with comments that reflect and repeat stereotypes and even direct prejudice. A thorough knowledge of the context and the participants, conversations with the teacher or mediator and in-depth reflection on potentially sensitive topics and questions are crucial in this respect.

Current trends in research

In this section we mention selected studies from 2010 to 2021, from as wide a range of contexts as possible, that exemplify current trends. Given the impossibility of including every study we have tried to choose those that also provide a picture of a range of theoretical perspectives and methodologies. We hope that readers will be encouraged to explore these and other studies further. This research adds to our knowledge and understanding of how picturebooks can support teachers and readers, either through picturebooks that represent a diversity of characters and cultural contexts or through working with Black, Asian, Latinx or other minority ethnic readers. Together, the studies also show the fruitful directions in which this type of research is travelling.

Developing as readers in more than one language

Picturebooks are often used for language learning, with most research in this area focused on English language teaching but, while some of these studies touch on diversity and inclusion, given their overarching pedagogical aim, we discuss those studies in Chapter 10. The studies that are of interest for this chapter are those that go beyond simply learning a language. While reading interaction in the home has always been seen as a site for research, considering the multicultural elements in the process of reading picturebooks is now also a focus. Paulick *et al* (2020), for example, observed (without interfering) how one Latinx multilingual family in the US interacted with a wordless picturebook across time. In this case both the mother and the older sister modelled the retelling of the story using Spanish, providing scaffolding for early literacy with the home language as cultural background, while the youngest sister responded by developing her "reading" of the book.

Intercultural connections

Closely linked to language learning is the idea that students must also be able to develop knowledge about other cultures beyond just the words. Picturebooks are the ideal vehicle for learning about different cultures and how these cultures make meaning using non-verbal symbols because the visual elements act as both representation and metalanguage. Young Yeom's study with secondary-school students in South Korea aimed to develop aspects of global awareness while learning English through book club discussions about picturebooks that portrayed "marginalized immigrant youths". Findings suggest that, with the teacher facilitating the process, "the participants were able to make intercultural connections based on empathy and perspective taking" (2019: 15).

Heggernes (2019) describes how students' curiosity was aroused when they read a picturebook/graphic novel in English, *The Wall* by Peter Sis (2007) about growing up in Czechoslovakia, in a secondary English language teaching classroom in Norway. Heggernes concludes that the dialogic space triggered by the multimodal text and the open-ended activities that accompanied the reading facilitated intercultural learning as the students interpreted and discussed the references to a childhood lived under communist regime.

A striking earlier study already mentioned above (Hayik 2011) took place in a middle school in a village in Israel, in an EFL class with Arab minority students from both Christian and Muslim faiths. Hayik used multicultural picturebooks as a 'springboard' for discussing the tensions that often emerged between these two groups and also invited students to respond to them visually. She found "dimensions of critical literacy" in her analysis of some of the drawings, as students were able to move beyond the personal and contemplate multiple viewpoints, a small but important step towards understanding each other.

Migration

The focus on picturebooks about migration has, not surprisingly, increased in the last decade, along with an interest in how children who have experienced forced displacement respond to these and other picturebooks. The Visual Journeys research project (Arizpe, Colomer and Martínez-Roldán 2014) was one of the first to explore the responses of children with an experience of migration to books that represented this experience, and which were read across five international contexts. The children participated through focus groups and visual activities such as drawing and photography. The study found that responses themselves reflected fluid movement across borders: the national and cultural 'borders' of readers and fictional borders. This movement meant that these multiple voices could interact in the same spaces, engaging in shared experiences through the dialogue and pictures and learning from them. The learning included finding common reference points, such as travel experiences as well as intertextual connections to popular culture (e.g. films). The responses also provided insights]for building on the literacy skills they already possessed, and which were less evident in their oral and written expression or assessments. Similar findings emerged in a study by Hope (2017), in which the picturebook about a Somali refugee boy, *The Colour of Home* by Hoffman and Littlewood (2002) was read in a British classroom with few children of White British origin. The researcher noted that a 'simple dichotomy between refugee and non-refugee children in their reactions, was a blunt and unworkable instrument' (161) and that responses varied across year groups, however, with the teacher enabling the children to explore the text in relation to their lived reality, they were able to move towards a better understanding of the refugee experience and demonstrate empathy.

Also drawing on the ideas of Rosenblatt (1978), Brookes and Browne (2012) and Sipe (2008), among others, Vehabovic (2021) looked at translingual children responding to picturebooks because, he argues, 'it is essential to consider the ways in which children from refugee backgrounds interact with and engage in dialogic reading of picturebooks that depict characters who cross borders between nations and states, as well as those that surround physical, cultural, linguistic, racialized, and gendered spaces' (2021: 2). He found that the participants challenged some of the common assumptions and 'unpack myths and distortions' (2021: 19) about migration and refugees, drawing on their own experiences and were able to critically engage with issues around marginalisation, power, justice.

LGBTQ

Möller argues that, following Thomas' (2016) call mentioned above, the "same argument for inclusion and decolonialization can be made for LGBTQ literature—and growing up with the literature means having regular opportunities to actually read and respond to it" (2020: 235). She analysed a group of 23 studies (published between 2002 and 2019) that refer to responses to LGBTQ-inclusive literature. While not all of them used picturebooks, it is evident that they predominated given the settings were either elementary or primary school, and also because their multimodal representations open a range of possibilities for depicting LGBTQ characters, from spotlighting particular visual elements such as clothing to including peripheral references to parental relationships. Möller includes studies that involved pre- and in-service teachers' responses and, as was the case with some students too, some of these responses (ranging from open hostility to silence) expressed a resistance to any LGBTQ related words or depictions. However, other studies -often collaborative and longer term- do show how a careful and reflexive pedagogical approach can build understanding, create welcoming spaces for informed discussion and produce responses that engage more positively and move towards more inclusive attitudes.

Disability

While there are many studies that consider representations of disability in picturebooks and offer useful selection criteria (e.g. Kleekamp and Zapata 2019), in 2014 Adomat pointed out 'the lack of empirical studies which show how children respond to books that feature characters with disabilities' (np online). She researched several classrooms where books selected for "sensitive portrayals of characters with disabilities" were read aloud and discussed. The excerpts show a developing awareness of disability and by the end of the unit, 'the teachers noticed a change in how disabled and non-disabled students interacted in the classroom', with the former recognising and appreciating the representation of children 'like them' (np) and the latter demonstrating more understanding and compassion. In our 2016 edition, we mentioned studies with readers with special needs (see the case study involving autism in chapter 7 this edition), such as deaf children (Williams and McLean 1997) or children with ADHD (Leonard, Lorch, Milich and Hagans 2009), however, apart from Adomat and Bianquin and Sacchi who also used picturebooks to 'address and increase awareness and acceptance of disability among students' (2017:8), there continues to be a dearth of empirical research in this area.

Implications for engaging with diversity in classrooms and other contexts through picturebooks

When it comes to thinking of multicultural education in schools, there has been a call to formulate more 'culturally relevant' (Ladson-Billings 1995) or 'culturally responsive' pedagogies (Souto-Manning 2009) where teachers are alert to the selection of texts and the activities that accompany the reading. Kelly et al (2021) stress the need for detailed knowledge of the setting and population where 'culturally informed literacy instruction' takes place, so that texts really do 'respond' to readers (2021: 91). At the same time, this knowledge can be built up by working with response and art-based activities which offer teachers the opportunity to get know their students and their families and cultures better, leading to those more informed pedagogies that make learning more relevant (Mantei and Kervin 2014; Blakeney-Williams and Daly 2013). For those working in non-traditional contexts, the approaches will be different depending on context and access to books, among other factors, however, the same principle of knowing as much as possible about the books and the readers apply.

When it comes to picturebooks in particular, this means that there should be an awareness of how the images work in order to make the selection; what place visual literacy has in the home culture and what previous experience readers have had with picturebooks. Armed with this awareness, the questions and activities that take place during and after the reading will be more engaging for all who participate, making the experience as inclusive as possible. Classroom projects can then be based on supporting children to understand issues around diversity and inclusion themselves, for example, the issue of migration or racial justice.

Many of the studies and projects that aim to bring experiences that are 'other' to the life of readers refer to the development of awareness and empathy with characters who may be perceived as 'different'. Nikolajeva's (2014) work on building empathy through images is often cited and indeed there is no doubt that this is an important first step for many readers. However, it is also important to go beyond simply stepping into another's shoes or feeling empathy for a while and support readers into engaging with the wider socio-historical contexts as well as reflecting on the ideological drivers behind the picturebook. Studies continue to show that critical literacy should be an essential component of teaching using picturebooks, as it can move students on from a focus on personal and emotional response to a response that engages with cultural, social and even political issues (Hayik 2011). Husband (2019), for example, uses "Critical Reader's Response", where starting with sharing personal experiences and thus creating a safe space to do so, children can begin to see beyond a single perspective and construct multiple meanings (2019: 1076). Callow (2017) adds the notion of developing global literacies where there is a reflection on the potential that both texts and images can manipulate readers; his approach can help to "raise our awareness that other stories and texts may seek to shape our views, sometimes with positive and inclusive views but sometimes with negative or inequitable agendas" (2017: 235).

To conclude let's go back to where we started, with Kathy's chapter, which also reminds us not to lose sight of the individual reader: 'Although children's knowledge, understanding and values are culturally saturated, the extent to which this affects literary interpretation will always be mediated by each child's unique personality as well as the influence of peers' (Coulthard 184). We want to celebrate both uniqueness and diversity, and we want to celebrate our commonalities. This helps to prepare children for living and participating in mutually respectful multilingual and multicultural societies.

Part III

Research and theory for a better future

10 Understanding children's responses to picturebooks through theory and research

Evelyn Arizpe

In this chapter we revisit the most significant theory underpinning our original research as well as noting those that have come to the fore in more recent years and the ways in which they have been used in new research on response to picturebooks. In Chapter 9 we looked at theory and research around diverse picturebooks and diverse readers which have greatly contributed to more inclusive practices. In what follows, we first touch on theories of the semiotic systems – language and image – which have led to useful frameworks for in-depth analysis for understanding how readers make meaning both cognitively and emotionally. We then provide an overview of research which have used these theories in different ways, beginning with pioneering studies and moving on to the most recent critical approaches and methodologies involving readers and picturebooks.

Learning and understanding through language

Lev Vygotsky introduced the seminal idea that language plays an indispensable role in mediating internal thought processes, such as the ability to reason and to reflect, and that social interaction through language is crucial for developing knowledge and thinking. Building on Vygotsky's insights, Jerome Bruner (1986) argued that the development of knowledge and the formation of concepts can be accelerated by 'scaffolding', particularly through the use of mediated language, as the more experienced inducts the less experienced learner into understanding. This is where Vygotsky's influential concept of the 'zone of proximal development' (1978: 86) comes into play. Both ZPD and scaffolding are important in confirming and expanding a child's understanding of a text, particularly a visual one, given that early reading usually happens together with an adult, friend or sibling. Sipe (2008) notes how 'child-centred' scaffolding in the classroom, in which the teacher guides the pupil towards multiple interpretation rather than comprehension, can enable literary understanding, especially when looking at picturebooks. It is not surprising that one of the most significant results from reader-response studies from the last fifteen years is the influential role a mediator can have in encouraging deeper and, eventually, more critical meaning-making.

In our study, the results of co-operatively achieved learning were evident particularly in the semi-structured discussion with a group of children rather than through individual interviews. However, we also discovered that some of the most profound thinking about picturebooks occurred in follow-up interviews some months after the original interviews. Questions were not only working as tools for inquiry, but also as the 'planks' and 'poles' of scaffolding which allowed children to move further into their zones of proximal development. Researchers became facilitators, especially in terms of providing a language through which the children could talk about pictures, modelling concepts, using prompts and leading with questions. More experienced peers unconsciously helped their schoolmates in their understanding as they talked about what they saw and how they made sense of it. This led us to concur with the idea that communal expertise played a more crucial role than individual logical mental operations in determining how far children could make sense of visual texts. We also noted the central role of language in developing thought and that when younger children could not communicate verbally their growing understanding could sometimes be shown in their drawings.

Learning and understanding through image

Consideration of, and literature about, visual literacy has increased, through theoretical and empirical studies as well as practical approaches coming from different disciplines such as neuroscience, cognitive research, cultural and media studies, art history and psychology, as well as various perspectives within the arts, such as painting and film. In particular in this volume, we are giving a focus to the research emanating from the art museum, some of which is in Chapter 6.

Educationalists have explored the potential of images for learning, especially via picturebooks (Farrar, Arizpe and McAdam 2022), graphic novels (Falter 2017) and comics (Ogier and Ghosh 2018) in the classroom. Already in 1996 Kress and van Leeuwen had pointed to the dominance of visual language in many domains and were critical about that fact that this had not been understood by decision makers in education. Given the advances in digital technology in the last two decades one would expect more of an impact of visual studies on official programmes of education but it rarely appears explicitly in the curriculum.

The original edition of this book contributed to bringing the concept of visual literacy to classrooms, judging from the reception the book has had in many countries, and we hope that this revised edition will go further in encouraging policy makers and teachers to include these ideas. It is important to note that we are not saying, nor did we ever say, that visual literacy should become yet another compulsory task in education. However, what we know for certain is that in order to expand or deepen engagement with a picturebook (or graphic novel, comic or any other visual art form, for that matter), some knowledge of terminology, of how visuals work, and of the processes of reading an image can be helpful in order to move readers beyond literal responses, to enrich the reading experience and intensify that initial pleasure. Examples of this abound in accounts of studies and projects involving picturebooks and readers.

This understanding of visual literacy has its roots in structuralism (Saussure, Lévi-Strauss, Barthes, et al.), which suggested that far from coming to texts with an 'innocent eye', the reader is 'a socialised being', a collection of 'subjectivities' responding to the visual world with a body and mind shaped by the realities in which he or she grew up' (Raney 1998: 39). It fits comfortably within the idea of literacy as a set of social practices (Heath 1983; Street 1984) which involve cultural and ideological considerations rather than simply replicating an "autonomous model of literacy" (Street 1984) which, as Raney warns, implies 'that there is a fixed or "single code" to be learnt, that looking at things is a science, or that classifying and dissecting images will uncover their meanings' (1998: 39). This view is particularly important in considering children's responses to multimodal texts, as it clear by now that their previous experiences with reading, viewing art and media, as well as their language, culture and gender, all influence their reactions to a picturebook. Raney therefore still provides, for us, one of the most all-encompassing and convincing definitions of visual literacy:

> [I]t is the history of thinking about what images and objects mean, how they are put together, how we respond to or interpret them, how they might function as modes of thought, and how they are seated within the societies which gave rise to them.
> (1998: 38)

Educationalists and other professionals working with children need to be more aware of visual literacy and the need to develop this along with other forms of literacy. Much of the initial literature on how young children read pictures has come from developmental psychology. The main focus of research in this field examines, usually under test conditions, how children respond to particular, often isolated images, or pictures in textbooks. In fact, a bibliometric overview from 1993 to 2015 of 286 studies carried out by Wu (2018) revealed four 'clusters' were

> formed from the 30 top most-cited articles: joint-reading of a picturebook, verbal and visual literacy for young children's language ability development, young children's cognitive development through picturebook reading, and special education. (432)

Surprisingly, only six out of all the studies mentioned in the bibliography overlap with our bibliography, raising questions about why there seem to be parallel worlds of research on response to picturebooks.

One answer may be that because of its close focus on the cognitive, such research mostly fails to take account of the outstanding artwork in many picturebooks which provokes affective as well as cognitive reactions in young readers, and also ignores the culturally situated nature of response which was discussed in the previous chapter. Because of this lack of understanding of the picturebook as an aesthetic object, as 'total design' to go back to Bader's famously encompassing definition (Bader 1976), we disagree with the premises of some of this type of research. We also question whether a 'developmental' model of response that is valid for all children can be constructed (just as the same is true for developmental models of any other type of children's abilities). However, we do acknowledge that some concepts from theories of cognitive development, while not addressing aesthetics and visual learning directly, are still helpful in understanding how children learn and develop.

Emerging frameworks for exploring visual literacy and picturebooks

Salisbury and Styles note that, 'Today, the boundaries between the book arts, literature and commercial graphic art can be seen to be merging in the children's picturebook' (2012: 50), therefore, new perspectives from a variety of disciplines have contributed to exploring the ways in which readers read the wide range of images they are exposed to and how their visual literacy can be developed to do this in more depth and therefore more critically. In this section we refer briefly to some frameworks that help to analyse how children read images in picturebooks and the seminal ideas behind them.

We previously noted how the question of prior knowledge, understanding and exposure to visual texts came into play as we worked with children with a wide variety of experience of visual literacy, ranging at one extreme from a 5-year-old child recently arrived from another culture who did not yet speak English and who had little exposure to books, to confident, fluent readers of 11 with wide book knowledge who were already familiar with the illustrator's picturebooks. Some children therefore drew on sophisticated repertoires of multimodal reading and were familiar with literacy practices which centred on drawing meaning from texts while other inexperienced readers used what resources they had, making more naive, instinctive responses to the books. Readers tended to be fascinated rather than daunted or confused by the playful postmodern elements of intertextuality, intratextuality and metafiction. For all three books in our original study we observed that the readers became involved with the characters, empathising with their feelings and that they were able to understand what a character thought and felt about others in what was a complex process (such as the mother's allusion in *Zoo* to her son's 'animal-like' behaviour compared to the animals behind the bars). All these observations can be explained and illuminated further by drawing on some of the more recent theories regarding reading and meaning-making.

From the work done on literacy as a social practice (New London Group 1996; Street 1984) we know that we all carry with us 'funds of knowledge' (Moll et al. 2005) which we apply when we learn and also when we read. Visual literacy is not an exception, it is also a set of practices that take place within, and which is determined by, a particular context, and these practices include knowledge and experience of a variety of different media that allow intertextual connections. Sipe was already drawing attention to the place of intertextuality in reader-response in 2000 and Mackey has argued that readers use these 'landmarks' to orient themselves in their reading (2011). Further research on response to picturebooks has confirmed that children's interpretative strategies involve intertextual references derived from their personal experiences, – including popular culture, games and other texts, – which enrich meaning-making (e.g. Flint and Adams 2018; Iordanaki 2020; Scherer 2020) and, as we have seen in the previous chapter, these are inextricably connected to their cultural contexts and identities.

Postmodern literary theory has contributed in a substantial manner to our understanding of the visual, and of picturebooks in particular, by providing terminology and definitions of the features of texts that work in less traditional ways. Although there are many different ways of understanding the 'postmodern', certainly the work on metafiction, intertextuality and non-linearity or fragmentation has helped to illuminate both words and images. While we mentioned the postmodern nature of Kitamura's and Browne's picturebooks in the first edition, these features of picturebooks have subsequently been highlighted and analysed in more depth. Among those who have applied postmodern frameworks are Bull and Anstey (2010) and both Sipe (2008) and Pantaleo (2008). Dresang (1999) took this theory further into what she calls 'radical change theory' while Allan (2012) identified what she calls the 'postmodernesque', which focuses on the way in which picturebooks engage with discourses of postmodernity (141).

The area of semiotics continues to inform our understanding of how texts work in multiple modes. The work of M.A.K. Halliday was used by Kiefer (1995) to categorise response, and the work of Kress, which expands on Halliday's theories, is often used to consider response to texts of the 'new media age', particularly to the elements of design (see also Walsh 2003, 2006). Working with van Leeuwen, Kress developed 'an established theoretical framework within which visual forms of representation can be discussed' (Kress and van Leeuwen 1996: 20). Their work has reclaimed the language of syntax and applied it to visual texts. They argue persuasively that images can be the central medium of communication in any text, also reminding us that ideology is always present, and pointing out that 'visual communication is always coded – it seems transparent only because we know the code already' (32). They show us how we can read images by analysing visual grammar, using a semiotic code of pictures and the vocabulary of design – with terms like vectors representing action verbs, actors and reactors as nouns, colour and focus acting as locative prepositions, and contrasting, for example, rectangular forms as representational of the mechanical, logical, manmade [sic] constructions, with the more organic, natural disposition in curves and circles. The viewer, in turn, responds to the visual address produced by the image, but has some choice about how to respond.

The modes and affordances of texts (Bearne 2009; Kress 2010) have a particular relevance to the picturebook because it is such a versatile medium and can include a variety of features such as pop-ups, tabs, pockets and holes as collage, photography or computer-generated images.[1] Painter, Martin and Unsworth (2013) use systemic-functional theory to extend accounts of the 'grammar' of the visual text and look at what demands it makes on the reader of multimodal texts. Albers (2008: 191) advocates 'critical visual analysis' based on art, cultural studies and other disciplines and uses it to look in depth at the 'representational codes' transmitted to children by Caldecott prize-winning artists across the years. Serafini (2014, 2022) has always emphasised the importance of the semiotic resources in a picturebook which allow interpretation: 'To ignore the perceptual and structural aspects of visual images and multimodal texts in favor of a socio-cultural perspective would limit readers' interpretive repertoire and forego relevant perspectives for making sense of images and multimodal texts' (Youngs and Serafini 2013: 196).

Another direction for research takes account of the functions of the brain in processing symbolic representation in order to explain how visual literacy works, although we would argue that the physical account on its own, ignoring culture, art, language and play, would also limit our understanding of meaning-making and culture. Therefore, we look to the work of Heath who brought together findings from the fields of neuroscience, visual cognition, anthropology, and linguistics (2006), to complement the neurobiological explanation:

> recursive interactions between peripheral images and higher cortical centres that process symbolic representation. Collaborative work through art enables verbal explication and explanation about details, abstractions and process that lead to theory building dependent on propositional, procedural and dispositional knowledge.
> (Heath 2000: 121)

Heath argues that looking and talking about art is a higher brain function that has an effect on our emotions and on how we understand others (Heath 2000; Heath and Wolf 2012). According to Heath (2000), 'art is a particular form of play that ensures ample practice for learning to manage the mental work necessary to bring what is perceived to be disconnected into some kind of whole, however temporary and shifting' (135). She concludes that children's play and involvement in art prepare for this reconciliation and therefore support the 'development of language fluency and empathy for the perspectives of others' (134). Importantly, she highlights that this apparently individual response actually depends on 'communal membership' because 'connections between perceptual and conceptual or linguistic representations [...] always will emerge in socially interactive situations that punctuate, underline, and enlarge individual understanding' (138). Thus, it becomes clear how important mediation and sharing are and establishes the potential for further research in this area.

The emotional aspect of reading has been taken up by other scholars such as Nikolajeva and Kümmerling-Meibauer who have considered the impact of neuroscience through cognitive poetics, in terms of what is expected of the reader, not only on children's literature in general but on picturebooks in particular. Nikolajeva, who uses cognitive literary theory to extend the work on picturebooks that began with Scott (2001) moving from the text to the cognitive effect of reading, emphasising aspects of affective engagement, such as mind-reading and empathy. Drawing on writers such as Wolf (2007), Carr (2010) and Vermeule (2010), as well as research on visual perception, Nikolajeva argues that visual stimuli play a more important part than verbal stimuli in affective interactions because visual knowledge is 'hard-wired in the brain' and therefore 'picturebooks present a whole new dimension of cognitive and affective challenges to novice readers' (2014: 99).

Furthermore, according to Nikolajeva, 'a visual image can evoke a wide range of emotions circumventing the relative precision of words' (2012: 278). She goes on to consider how multimodal literature might convey emotion to the implied reader through vicarious experience by activating long-term emotional memory. This explains why response is so closely linked to life experience and why 'text to life' and 'life to text' elements are – revealed in most of the studies reviewed here – almost always present in response. These and other ideas such as focalisation, 'mind-reading' and *emotion ekphrasis* which Nikolajeva applies to a range of fictional texts are particularly relevant to picturebooks and it is where visual literacy meets emotional literacy.

Kümmerling-Meibauer and Meibauer provide a useful summary of picturebooks and cognitive studies (2018) with frameworks for analysis and examples, including their own work with maps (2015). They have argued that the relationship between cognitive development and picturebooks has not been explored fully, especially the ways in which 'language acquisition and literature acquisition interact, and how these interactions may be related to other cognitive processes, such as vision or emotional development' (2013: 144). Other researchers are now rising to this challenge and examine how specific picturebook features such as visual metaphors encourage decoding skills as well as creative thinking (Purcell 2018).

These new ideas open the field to further studies that bring together visual literacy, picturebook theory, cognitive development and, more recently, materiality. The work of Mackey, for example, has always included concepts of play, performance and tactility (2003, 2011) and drawn on media literacy and gaming theories, including ideas about embodiment and envisionment. Mackey's work demonstrates the "material turn" in literary studies (Nikolajeva 2016), where various perspectives of "new materialism" (García-González and Deszcz-Tryhubczak 2020) are now being applied to picturebooks, through a consideration of the "physical, sensory, and metaphoric qualities of materials" in picturebooks (Veryeri Alaca 2018: 59). Zapata and Kuby sum this up convincingly when they argue that *'we cannot separate languaging and cultures or texts/ text making processes from a broader material, cultural, and emerging material and linguistic ecology'* (emphasis in original 2021: 137), which implies narrowing the theoretical distance between authors, illustrators and readers and considering children as active and embodied partners in the ecologies of reading and viewing.

'Real' children respond to picturebooks

In what follows we look at the ways in which the particular field of studies involving 'real' children responding to picturebooks has advanced in the last 10 years or so. We provide an overview of empirical research on response to picturebooks, most of which has been carried out since the second edition of our book was published, although we also refer to some seminal earlier studies. Current studies continue to build on the work of pioneering and influential scholars in the field and reflect a wide range of perspectives, approaches and methods which reveal the wealth of possibilities for explorations involving readers and picturebooks.

Overall, some studies concentrate on what response tells us about the process of meaning-making; others are more interested in exploring the methods for obtaining response; and finally, the ones with a more educational intention look at how response can develop literary competence and literacy skills. We have tried to organise this review into sections that are related to their main focus; however, in cases where the studies fit into more than one section, they may be referred to more than once.

In 2008, Sipe published an appraisal of both theory and research on response to picturebooks, focused on children from about 4 to 8 years old in classroom situations (Sipe 2008). He noted that these studies tend to be 'qualitative, descriptive and interpretive' (381). Importantly, Sipe called for further research combining 'theoretically informed examinations of the visual features and text-picture relationships in specific picturebooks along with analyses of children's interpretations of those same picturebooks' (387). Our own review from 2008 went back to the 1970s and considered picturebooks within the wider area of multimodal texts and we looked at studies which took into account 'real' readers' responses. We noted how scholars were addressing not only multimodality but also multiliteracies, looking at previous reading experiences, intertextuality and cultural diversity, among others. We also noted the variety of ways in which response data was gathered and the different theories which were used to analyse and make sense of this data. Finally, we observed that much of this research was taking place in the classroom and having an impact on teaching in this context. We concluded that one of the challenges was for researchers to keep up with new technologies and adapt methodologies to work with them, and this was even before the appearance of digital picturebook apps.

Inevitably, the updated review in this chapter has its limitations. In the sections that follow, we have only been able to provide details about some of the major or – in our view – most significant studies since 2000, but we have attempted to at least reference as many others as possible to give an idea of how the field is developing in different directions. Despite our careful search, it is inevitable that we may have missed some publications and, given that new studies are constantly appearing, it is impossible for this review to ever be completely 'up to date'. We have also had to limit this chapter to work that has been published in English, despite the fact much research on response has also been carried out in other countries and languages. Finally, it is worth noting that there are now many studies that examine readers' responses to comics, graphic novels and other types of illustrated books, but this book is perforce limited to research involving picturebooks.

Pioneering and influential scholars in the field

As we mentioned in the Introduction, we built our original study on the pioneering work of Kiefer (1995) and on the few articles and chapters which looked at children's responses to picturebooks, in particular those of Madura, Lewis, Bromley, Watson and Styles. Although we were aware of a couple of Sipe's articles, at the time of our study we did not realise he was conducting similar research to ours on young children's responses to picturebooks and also emphasising the importance of looking at responses to images as well as to words: 'The integration of visual and verbal sign systems is one of the most salient characteristics of picturebooks. Children's learning of illustration codes and conventions deserves more attention by researchers' (2011: 10). His influence in the field of children's literature and education has been widely acknowledged given his aim was to develop, based on the ideas of Rosenblatt, Britton and Bogdan, 'a theory of literary understanding that is specific to contemporary young children, and that is grounded in their responses to literature' (2008: 9). His data was collected from five different studies with young children aged 5–7 and from a range of ethnic and social backgrounds (with a majority of less-privileged children from urban environments). Experienced teachers read aloud from picturebooks by a wide range of internationally renowned author/illustrators such as Maurice Sendak, Eric Carle, Anthony Browne, Chris Van Allsburg, Paul Galdone and David Wiesner. The children were encouraged to talk about the books during and after the readings which were carried out as part of the normal classroom activities and it is their marked engagement with the stories, especially their expressive engagement, that led to the development of his analytical categories.

Sipe focused on children's responses to literature to find evidence of their literary understanding for both hermeneutic and aesthetic purposes, teasing out and identifying different types of responses such as personal, text-to-text and analytical. In two of his articles he describes the intertextual connections made by primary age children when reading versions of traditional tales (*The Gingerbread Boy* (Sipe 2000) and *Rapunzel* (Sipe 2001)). As he notes how images support understanding, he begins to move further towards exploring response to the visual, asking 'How do children use the connections to other visual texts to understand the composition, media, and semiotic significance of illustrations?' (Sipe 2000: 87).

This led to investigating more specific aspects of picturebooks, such as the 'page break', an aspect of the picturebook at the core of the 'drama of the turning page' (Bader 1976) and at the heart of the 'gap-filling' (Iser 1978) experience of reading. Sipe observed a class of second graders read Caldecott Medal and Honour winners talking 'not about the words and pictures in the story, but about what has been omitted from the story' (Sipe and Brightman 2009: 93). Sipe and Brightman show how these discussions can develop with little interference from the teacher and how beneficial they are for 'high-level inference making' (2009: 93). This article includes both implications and acute questions for further research and also for teaching, both of which show just how much potential even this one aspect of a picturebook has for both these areas.

Importantly, Sipe and Brightman also identified categories of resistance or opposition, ranging from not liking a new version of a familiar story to finding characters or events too painful to consider. These categories are significant as they help us realise that children can reject picturebooks as much as they can love them but that this provides an opportunity for discussing, for example, different perspectives or authorial decisions. Sipe (2008) also identifies helpful categories for the 'basic literary impulses' that guide children's responses: the 'hermeneutic impulse' or the desire to 'grasp the meaning of the narrative'; the 'personalising impulse' to forge connections with life experiences; and the 'aesthetic impulse' which involves 'surrendering' to the power of the text (Sipe 2008: 189–192). Finally, always with an eye on the pedagogical side, in his book Sipe also looked at mediation, describing the ways in which the teachers' enabling and scaffolding contributed to the children's understanding. He identifies five conceptual categories for adult talk and highlights the crucial importance of asking inviting questions and encouraging the role of peers as enablers.

Another scholar whose work has run parallel to ours since 2002 is Pantaleo. Like Sipe, with whom she also collaborated, her work is prolific and influential within the field especially in relation to education. Pantaleo has worked with teachers and pupils across primary classrooms using numerous picturebooks and has looked at the creative responses emerging from different forms of activities as well as applying various theories such as Rosenblatt's transactional theory and Dresang's Radical Change Theory (Dresang 1999; Pantaleo 2004a, 2009a). She has focused on young student's understanding of the postmodern aspects of picturebooks such as metafiction (2002, 2004a, 2004b, 2005), intertextuality (2012a), as well as their effect on readers, for example, on their narrative competence (2009b, 2010) and artwork (2012b). Pantaleo has explored collaborative talk (2011), writing (Pantaleo and Bomphray 2011) and creating multimodal texts and artefacts that involve understanding of colour and other visual elements of art and design (2012b, 2012c). She has written about response to particular features of picturebooks and graphic novels such as colour (2012b), typography (2012d) and panelling (2013). Pantaleo's extensive body of work has built up a detailed picture of the transaction between readers and the word-image relationship which has implications not only for literacy and pedagogy but also for advancing our understanding about how picturebooks and graphic novels work. Pantaleo's studies provide solid evidence for the ways in which complex picturebooks and graphic novels can help students develop as readers, writers and imaginative thinkers and therefore, alongside Sipe, provides a leading voice in those calling for the necessity of teaching elements of visual art and design in parallel with using these texts in the classroom.

Both Pantaleo and Sipe's work is behind that of a whole generation of scholars who have produced important research with implications for teaching. Working with Dutch children, Van der Pol built on Sipe's research to examine their implicit knowledge of structures and conventions of picturebooks and what it means to be a competent reader of fiction, arguing for the importance of having literary conversations (rather than simply asking for text to life and life to text connections) in order to deepen children's understanding of features such as character and irony (Van der Pol 2012). Serafini (2002) writes about his discovery, as a young teacher, of picturebooks and of how Sipe's work influenced his thinking about his students' responses; since then, Serafini has also written about response to postmodern picturebooks (2005), to historical fiction picturebooks (Youngs and Serafini 2013) and about developing interpretive responses (Serafini and Ladd 2008).

Other often-cited chapters and articles on response to picturebooks have appeared in three volumes edited by Evans (Evans 1998, 2009a, 2015a), including one which addresses 'challenging and controversial picturebooks'. Evans herself also wrote about the responses of a group of children with whom she had been working for several years; her work consistently shows the potential of picturebooks to draw out children's ideas about challenging topics such as art (2009b) the meaning of life (2011) immigration (2015b).

As for the work by Arizpe and Styles which followed the original study, both of us focused on the postmodern aspect of picturebooks and response (Arizpe 2009, 2010; Arizpe and Styles 2008;). Styles then produced *Children's Picturebooks: The art of visual storytelling* with Salisbury as lead author (2012/2020) that took a historical and thematic approach to picturebooks which focused more on published and developing illustrators than on children's responses to picturebooks, while Arizpe went on to do more empirical work on response with children from diverse backgrounds (in the 'Visual Journeys' project which will be detailed further below) and, more recently, with mediators working with picturebooks in challenging contexts such as shelters for migrants or disaster recovery spaces (Hirsu, Arizpe and McAdam 2020) and around challenging topics such as xenophobia (Coban, McAdam and Arizpe 2020).

Research on response to the specific features of a picturebook

Some studies have concentrated on children's responses to the special features that define picturebooks as a genre. Given that it is the interaction between the words and the pictures that defines a picturebook, most studies consider what children make of this interaction and in particular, whether these semiotic systems are telling the same story (or not). In our original study we found that when the children noticed that words and pictures were not telling the same story, they were fascinated by the differences (Arizpe and Styles 2003). Many other researchers have observed the process that Sipe called 'transmediation' (1998), also referred to in Chapter 9 where the continuous shifts between the meaning from words and images build the readers' understanding.

Research using wordless picturebooks has also served to highlight how children perceive the relationship between words and pictures when the former are 'missing' and also to provide further insights into the process of visual meaning-making (Arizpe et al. 2014; Crawford and Hade 2000). Many studies involve readings and retellings of this type of picturebook to address the wide range of cognitive skills involved in this process, although Arizpe's review of these studies also showed that some of them tend to see the picturebook as a functional medium for collecting data and ignore its aesthetic qualities (2013).

Scholars have explored the way in which the visual features expand understanding of the more traditional elements that normally appear in picturebooks. For example, Sipe and Ghiso (2005) and later Prior, Willson and Martínez (2012) analyse the inferences about characters that children made based on the images. However, most researchers have been excited by the more unusual features that define a picturebook as 'postmodern' and especially those that include a variety of peritextual features and that subvert traditionally written stories where the illustration simply mirrors the text. Arizpe and Styles were among the first to highlight evidence that children can deal with the complexities afforded by contemporary picturebooks and this has also been confirmed through other studies that focus on postmodern features such as Pantaleo, who tends to explore both central and peritextual features in her studies.

Studies that have considered other features in postmodern picturebooks include children responding to endpapers (Sipe and McGuire 2006), page breaks (Sipe and Brightman 2009), frames (Pantaleo 2014; Smith 2009) and typography (Pantaleo 2012d). In a study with a slightly different approach, McClay (2000) compared the responses of adults and children to the non-linear narrative and the ambiguities of David Macaulay's *Black and White* and showed that children tend to have fewer problems than adults when it comes to interpreting postmodern features. However, there is a sense that research has moved on from focusing on these postmodern features and how children make sense of them, to placing the picturebook in a wider context of culturally situated and mediated response. Already Sipe (2008), McGuire, Belfatti and Ghiso (2008) and Swaggerty (2009) were stressing the importance of mediation and discussion to lead to a more critical understanding of picturebooks, postmodern or not, where dialogue with teachers, parents and peers has a crucial role in the complex processes of interpreting and comprehending visual texts. As Farrar shows, the processes of mediation and discussion also applies to adults reading metafictive picturebooks with their children and interacting with the researcher (2020). The way this interaction was set up is an example of the innovative ways of data collection in recent reader-response research: in order to fit in with parents' busy schedules, Farrar's methods included 'bimbling' (183) or walking with parents to and from the school gates or the playground after school (as well as phone conversations in the evening). Farrar found that many parents were "tethered" to "print-centred basics" and lacked "conceptual awareness about visual literacy" (188), however, by sharing in her research, engaging with the books and discussing metafiction with her and their children, they also developed their understanding about picturebooks and multiliteracies.

Research on response to specific genres or themes

An example of a group of studies under this section are those which ask readers to respond to picturebooks based on fairy tales or traditional stories, including versions which may be challenging in some way. Through response to some of the symbolic elements of picturebook versions of Bluebeard, Campagnaro (2015) looked at cognitive and aesthetic development of young readers. Noble (2006) looked at three picturebook retellings of The Frog Prince in her doctoral study to understand how different visual styles and representations were interpreted by young readers of different ages. McGilp (2014) selected fairy tale versions of Cinderella, Snow White and Little Red Riding Hood from different cultures to explore multicultural and language learning with pre-school children. Although not based exclusively on fairy tales, Ghosh (2015) considered response to the portrayal of wolves in 'polysemic' picturebooks and shows how readers bring their knowledge of traditional tales to their reading but also their willingness to engage with irony and ambiguity. In research where children also responded to a wolf character, Mourão's (2015), also about wolves, sums up the general finding from this group of studies which is that young children base their interpretations on cultural expectations and previous knowledge of text.

There are many studies that explore response to difficult or sensitive issues through picturebooks and there is certainly not a shortage of challenging topics, ranging from depression (Pantaleo 2015) to criminal justice (Oslick 2013) and migration (Arizpe et al. 2014; McAdam et al. 2014), but also gender and feminism (Couceiro 2020). While teachers often shy away from discussing some of these topics with children, researchers are often keen to find out how children react to them. This can raise ethical issues and the researcher should have a good justification for selecting topics that may be upsetting, for example, when working with groups of readers who have had particular experience of these issues.

Whether the topics are considered controversial or not, most studies look at ways in which the reading about a particular theme can lead to improving understanding in some way. As seen in Chapter 9, this applies particularly to themes around multiculturalism but also migration and racism, given the intention is to try to increase awareness of diversity, multilinguality and, generally, understanding of the 'Other'. Surprisingly, we were unable to locate reader-response studies on picturebooks with themes around climate change or the environment more generally; surely we will be seeing more of these in the near future.

Research on response with specific groups of readers

Studies usually select a particular group of readers, either with specific special needs or with a common context or background, with the aim of finding out more about their literary understanding, their literacy skills or the personal experience they bring to their reading and in order to develop particular competences. The studies in this section often also include a selection of picturebooks with themes or features that support both the investigation and the development of strategies to support intervention in some form.

Studies with language learners that use picturebooks to teach English as a foreign or additional language (EFL or EAL) are contributing to one of the fastest growing areas of research. We have included these here, rather than in Chapter 9, because their overarching aim is language learning, although some also explore intercultural understanding. Enever and Schmidt-Schonbein (2006) and Bland (2013) have looked at the potential of picturebooks to teach English in Germany as has Mourão in Portugal (e.g. Mourão 2012) and Arizpe and Ryan (2018) asked EAL learners themselves how wordless picturebooks could be used to teach English, with surprisingly creative results. These studies reveal positive findings in the field of language-learning but the researchers also take pains to point out that this learning cannot be separated from the aesthetic and emotional effect of reading.

While we cannot extend this review to research on responses by groups of older readers, it is worth mentioning that there have also been studies involving pre-service teachers and teachers (Anstey 2002; Marshall 2015; McClay 2000; Johnston and Bainbridge 2013; Short 2004; van Renen 2011). There are also a few studies involving adolescent readers responding to picturebooks, although the potential for their literacy and literary learning has been recognised for some time (e.g. Lott 2001; Senokossoff 2013). With the exception of Farrar's study (2020) mentioned above, we are not aware of any research that includes parental perspectives in response to picturebooks.

Looking to the future of this field

There is no doubt that the interest in how readers, and especially young children, respond to picturebooks has increased since we did our original study at the turn of the millennium. With more than 20 years of hindsight, it is now possible to better track the development of reader-response research with picturebooks, noting the influence of different theories and the way the focus has moved away from postmodern features toward social issues and has become more child-centred. The awareness of the importance of listening to children's voices and providing safe spaces for them to express themselves in a variety of contexts, as well as supporting them in terms of agency, has contributed to this interest. It has become even more necessary as a result of the Covid-19 pandemic, during the periods when it was impossible to go into schools or talk to children face to face. This has meant adopting creative methodologies that not only meet the practical challenges of sharing books and technology, but that are also more sensitive to the contexts where participants find themselves (e.g. at home with younger children, anxious parents, etc.).

This is exemplified in Couceiro's reflexive account of having to adapt her methodology in her research on children's responses to collective biographies of women (some of them picturebooks) because she was unable to carry out her interviews and activities face to face (2020). Mindful of what they may have been experiencing, she sent them the books by post and redesigned a range of online activities "with participants' enjoyment and interests at the centre" for them to choose from. These arts-based activities, divided into sections such as "'writing and scribbling'; 'art and performance'; 'building and creating'" also contained vignettes with the participants' suggestions and were presented through an electronic 'reader-response toolkit'. This toolkit allowed readers to respond from a distance but most importantly, provided them with "an opportunity to contribute to analysis of their creations" (2020: 33).

Importantly, participatory research has also meant that children are beginning to be considered as potential co-researchers, such as in the work of Deszcz-Tryhubczak (2016), although this still has not been fully explored in relation to picturebook studies. As the case studies in Chapter 7 have shown, there has also been a move to not only examine picturebooks in different contexts outside the classroom but also to value the material creations which resulted from the interaction with picturebooks and other visual art. There is no doubt we can look forward to new and exciting critical approaches and methodologies which will address the expanding interest in children reading and responding to picturebooks.

Note

1 For useful accounts of what it means to 'read the visual' in terms of multimodality and the multiliteracies that accompany it, see Anstey and Bull (2000), Serafini's (2014) book is an excellent introduction to visual literacy and his recent publication (2022) is an introduction to researching multimodal texts.

11 Epilogue

What children have taught us about reading pictures

Morag Styles, Evelyn Arizpe and Kate Noble

Margaret Meek Spencer once astutely said that we read to find our futures. If she is right, picturebooks can been seen a gift to our children, to the next generation and the people they will become. What does the study of picturebooks with young children tell us about our hopes for the future?

As we began to write the final chapter, the two week COP 26, November 2021, was taking place in Glasgow. Environmental activists from all over the world, including many from the Indigenous communities most affected by climate change, were present, along with Greta Thunberg, David Attenborough and Prince Charles. The essential question was what a fellowship of nations could do, working together, to combat the destruction of the environment, ensuring a future for everything and everyone that lives on Earth. Or not…

We make this point because at the moment in our interlinking worlds of academia, education, art museums and picturebooks we must now make climate change, and all that means, central to our lives and professions. Some picturebook illustrators have been doing that for a long time. Perhaps it could be said to begin most prominently with *Window* (1991) by the English born, Australian author, Jeannie Baker, where the changing environment over time formed the heart of the 'story'. As the publicity for *Window* put it, 'a *wordless picturebook that speaks volumes*' by a publisher whose books '*don't cost the earth.*' Young readers 'became ventriloquists of their picturebooks' as they rose to the challenge of what Meek (1988) called 'playing the texts' (Arizpe and Styles 2008b), orchestrating meaning as a mother and her baby looked out of the same window and, page by page, observed unsustainable growth in the rapidly changing environment. If *Window* was one of the first picturebooks to focus on the threats posed by urbanisation and accelerating change, illustrators and authors have clasped the baton with gusto ever since, raising awareness of the issues of environmental damage for the young and those who read with them.

There is wise fatherly advice in the final pages of Oliver Jeffers', *Here We Are: Notes for Living on Planet Earth,* dedicated to his baby son, Harland. 'There are only three words you want to live by, son: respect, consideration and tolerance' (2017). Jeffers takes young readers on a magical journey through the solar system, before welcoming them to Planet Earth. His quick tour takes in land, city, seascapes, wilderness (not much of that left), the glorious variety of the animal kingdom, and the magnificent diversity of people. 'There are lots of us on here so be kind. *There is enough for everyone.*' Towards the end of the book, he tells readers that 'Things can sometimes move slowly here on Earth. More often, though, they move quickly, so *use your time well. It will be gone before you know it*' (our emphasis). Jeffers concludes with the words, 'Well, that is Planet Earth.

Make sure you look after it, as it's all we've got.' So dangerous is the future of our planet that picturebook authors are warning its youngest inhabitants of the need to care and to rally to the cause as they, and future generations, will be the ones who bear the brunt of climate change. And that if we don't act soon it will be too late.

This volume of *Children Reading Pictures* was also written during the Covid pandemic when the whole world changed, almost overnight. It is certainly interesting to observe that during this time of crisis, sales for picturebooks were extremely buoyant, at least in the UK, but the amount of picturebook sharing on the internet, by the illustrators themselves, as well as by teachers, librarians and other mediators, increased in many regions of the world as a way of reaching children who were unable to leave their homes. In many cases, creative activities were also suggested after the reading, based on simple materials that can generally be found at home, paper, pens, cardboard etc. We feel, therefore, that we cannot ignore these matters in the closing pages of this book.

Picturebooks are natural texts for sharing and the gentle language directed at the young, often combined with a sense of fun and a streak of optimism, were found to be healing during the pandemic. Comfort and inspiration, which often feature in picturebooks for the very young, were also found in the delights of the natural world, offering a welcome escape during the various lockdowns. And the point we have been making about so many picturebooks dealing with the climate crisis in a variety of ways, from gentle allusion to full on straight talking, meant there was critical engagement with these issues and something for everybody.

Another positive outcome of the pandemic was how parents realised how central schools were in their lives once their children were at home all day, understanding better how hard is the job of the teacher and how difficult it can be to motivate children, especially with a dry curriculum.

Also encouraging was the realisation by many of how much they missed the arts, seeing them live, being in an audience – and appreciating how important art and creativity are in our lives. Imaginative alternatives to in person visits to theatres, concert halls, art galleries and museums were devised (such as the experience Escovar and Naranjo describe in the case study in Chapter 7), an unexpected bonus, often with a community thrust. In the same period, many found extended time at home provided opportunities to engage with the arts by making their own art and music, crafting, reading and writing. Mak, Fluharty and Fancourt's (2021) study of arts engagement during the pandemic found evidence that people used art activities positively to help cope with difficult emotions, and to support self-development.

At the start of 2021 when the UK and many other parts of the world went into another lockdown, Kate Noble developed the project described in Chapter 7 by creating 'Inspire Nature' in collaboration with museum educators across the University of Cambridge Museums. The project was delivered through a series of online workshops and was designed to encourage creative connections with nature using museum objects for inspiration and ideas. Despite the challenges they were facing in schools at the time, teachers embraced the project and took enjoyment from the sessions and from the opportunity to look at, think and talk about artworks and objects with others. Feedback collected after the sessions revealed that many found that they had a beneficial impact on their sense of wellbeing at an extremely stressful time. As the examples in this book demonstrate, looking together and sharing ideas and perspectives with others can be a powerful and unifying experience.

New evidence about the educational value of picturebooks based on six years research was published shortly before the start of the pandemic: The Power of Picturebooks: Summary of findings from the research on the CLPE Power of Pictures Project 2013–2019 (CLPE 2019). Charlotte Hacking and colleagues at the Centre for Literacy in Primary Education, collaborating with notable illustrators, such as Alexis Deacon and Mini Grey, worked with 7000 children and 318 schools across the UK. The project demonstrates how picturebooks can 'support the development of sophisticated reading skills, enabling children to develop deep comprehension skills and to learn about narrative structure and character development in an accessible way' (CLPE 2019: 6). They also found that when children were given opportunities to draw as part of the writing process, this both aided their planning and led to richer independent writing (CLPE 2019: 3). Excitingly, the PoP evaluation also revealed pupils' increased confidence and a willingness to 'infer, deduce, think critically, empathise and make personal connections within and across texts and real-life experiences' through working with picture books and illustrators (CLPE, 2021: 6).

The Power of Picturebooks (PoP) was also selected for an evaluation using a randomised control trial by the Royal Society of Arts and Education Endowment Foundation as part of their Learning About Culture programme to investigate the impact of arts-based learning on academic outcomes (Anders et al., 2021). The programme was found to have both a positive impact on writing outcomes but also on pupil's engagement and motivation. This effect was particularly strong for pupils who were seen as non-traditional learners (e.g., pupils who had difficulty engaging with the traditional writing curriculum or did not view their writing skills positively). Teachers also reported that the programme encouraged pupils to add more detail in their descriptions and stories, and that this was caused, 'by the fact that using pictures encouraged students to think more deeply and carefully (Anders et al., 2021:60).' We knew this, as all three editions of our book will testify, but it is reassuring to have such positive recent evidence from further studies and from such a large cohort of children. We are delighted that our original outcomes of more than 20 years ago have stood the test of time in a much larger study.

As bookshops reopened in the Spring of 2021, we learned that children's books enjoyed an 11% boost in sales against the equivalent period in 2019, according to the *Bookseller* (Noble, Carter & Empire, 2021). Picturebooks come into play again here, not just in their role as the literature and art education of early childhood, but in the particularly inventive non-fiction titles which both educate and inspire, as well as the intellectually and aesthetically engaging picturebooks for older readers which cover almost every subject under the sun, including the not insignificant matter of what it means to be human.

Last but not least, the issue that has been at the forefront of many picturebook authors, illustrators and scholars is that of inclusion and exclusion as seen from different sides of the political spectrum. On the one hand, there has been a greater awareness of the racism that Black and minoritised ethnic groups have suffered and continue to suffer, the realisation of white privilege and the legacies of enslavement which are now being brought to light. On the other, censorship which includes picturebooks about the lives of Black people, especially in parts of the USA. Picturebook illustrators like Kadir Nelson present powerful portraits of the history of Black Americans and scholars are conducting in depth examinations of the ingrained racism in some texts but also ways of using picturebooks to create opportunities to discuss power and agency shown by Black characters (e.g. Sciurba 2020). That these books are being banned in some states is a sign of how potent they are seen to be and threatening to those who would rather forget the shameful histories of colonisation and slavery. This is where working with children and picturebooks can come in their own right but also lead to understanding the stories behind artworks and yes, statues. The toppling of statues around the world in response to BLM is also symbolic of the power of images and artwork to control, repress and perpetuate historic inequalities – as educators we must be mindful of this. Hence the need for critical visual literacy and art education.

No matter how many scholarly books we read about picturebooks, or conferences we attend, or projects we set up, and papers we write for academics, museum educators and teachers, the people who have taught us most about how children read pictures and picturebooks are, of course, the children themselves. It is a privilege to talk to children about the picturebooks they are reading, to observe them in the process of reading, to hear their responses to a painting, to discuss with them how they negotiate the act of reading a multimodal text, to invite them to draw in response to a picturebook that has captured their imagination, to hear their views on the author/illustrator's story and how well it has been told. The engagement, insight and dedication to their picturebooks of the many children we, our students, and our teacher partners have witnessed over many years, have been an inspiration to the authors.

We also have to thank so many talented picturebook illustrators and authors for doing such a dazzlingly good job, as their creativity and subject matter knows no bounds. In the background are quiet heroes – the publishers, especially the editors and the designers who have brought the quality of contemporary picturebooks to an ambitious new level. We leave the final word to two previous Children's Laureates. We opened this book with a quotation from Anthony Browne about the sophistication of young readers' interpretation of picturebooks. We close with two quotes from Lauren Child. One is based on her observations on *Power of Picturebooks* report, the other is from her Manifesto for the Children's Laureate:

> There's not enough understanding of how sophisticated picture books can be [...] If we don't understand that, then we don't understand how amazingly sophisticated children are and that they think very deeply and powerfully about things. And we do them a disservice if we don't see this.
>
> (*The Guardian*, September 2021)

> As a child I had favourite artists – Bonnard, Matisse, Braque, Vuillard – just like any adult might. Remembering this reminds me that, whilst of course we need stories and art created specifically for children, they will respond to all forms of artistic expression. Good art is for everyone: adults reading children's literature, watching drama created for children, listening to music with youth at its heart.
>
> (2021: 1)

Child and Browne believe in children and they believe in picturebooks, and so do we. We hope our readers will too.

Afterword

Reading is marvellous anywhere

Jorge Tetl Argueta

A little girl in a market attends a reading session located in an open-air corridor in the market. Everywhere voices are heard selling onions, tomatoes, green chilli, voices loaded with flavours and colours that come and go. Sitting on a mat the girl holds a book in her hands, her eyes travel through pages full of colour illustrations for a story that makes her laugh. In this outdoor environment, this girl can at any time put down the book and play with other children or decide to stop watching or reading the book, she is not being directed by any school method that forces her to continue reading, the decision is hers. Fortunately, the images and the story of the book have been previously selected for the reading programme of an itinerant library and are close to her reality and the girl sees herself reflected in the story.

Another child does not know how to read but knows the book by heart and enjoys it, inventing his story in his own way, that is, the images of the picturebook serve as a guide and take him by the hand. In this same space in the open air, other children do not read, but they have fun with the books, they play with them, they use the books as bricks, when they stand them up they serve as walls and with them they make houses, circles, or trains, according to their imagination. The beautiful thing about this is that at the end of the day, using the book as an object in their play, these children realise that this object can also be opened and when it is opened, the magic begins and the child begins to have fun with the words and the images that make up the story. The child's curiosity is such that they approach the reading mediators or other children who know how to read and ask them: 'Will you read it to me?'

I have had the great satisfaction of working in different outdoor reading programmes: in parks, in markets, on the banks of a river, and other areas where the child comes into contact with a reality outside of school, but where her imagination continues to grow and the child continues to learn while playing. As a cultural worker promoting reading, I have been and continue to be a witness to the marvellous things that happen in these spaces. As a poet and writer, I continue to dream of the wonders that education and reading offer, I am convinced that a child who reads has better chances of succeeding in life, I dream that the children who attend these programmes, who mostly come from humble families, can dream that they can become engineers, architects, doctors, lawyers, teachers. We cannot ensure that our children can achieve these goals, but at least through reading with them we might manage to distance them from violence and take them along paths where sensitivity and creativity are always in their hearts. Just like that child who once told me, referring to a guarumo tree with its big leaves, "that is an umbrella tree…"

Bibliography

Adomat, D. S. (2010) 'Dramatic interpretations: Performative responses of young children to picturebook read-alouds', *Children's Literature in Education*, 41(3): 207–221.
——— (2014) 'Exploring issues of disability in children's literature discussions', *Disability Studies Quarterly*, 34(3), accessed (03/12/2021) at https://dsq-sds.org/article/view/3865/3644
Albers, P. (2008) 'Theorizing visual representation in children's literature', *Journal of Literacy Research*, 40(2): 163–200.
Alexander, R. (2020) *A Dialogic Teaching Companion*, Oxon: Routledge.
Aliagas, C. and Margallo, A. M. (2014) '¿Cómo transforma el ipad las prácticas lectoras literarias? Un estudio etnográfico sobre los efectos del soporte digital en las experiencias de lectura infantil en el contexto familiar', in Moscoso, M. F. (ed.) *Etnografía de la socializacion en las familias*, Madrid: Traficantes de Sueños, 25–31.
———. (2017) 'Children's responses to the interactivity of storybook apps in family shared reading events involving the iPad', *Literacy*, 51(1): 44–52. doi: 10.1111/lit.12089.
Allan, C. (2012) *Playing with Picturebooks: Postmodernism and the Postmodernesque*, New York: Palgrave Macmillan.
Anders, J., Shure, N., Wyse, D., Barnard, M., Abdi, F., Frerchs, J. (2021) Power of Pictures Evaluation Report, Education Endowment Foundation and UCL Institute of Education accessed (21.11.22) at https://d2tic4wvo1iusb.cloudfront.net/documents/pages/projects/Power_of_Pictures_Evaluation_Report_Final.pdf?v=1668765228
Anstey, M. (2002) "It's not all black and white': Postmodern picture books and new literacies', *Journal of Adolescent and Adult Literacy*, 45(6): 444–457.
Anstey, M. and Bull, G. (2000) *Reading the Visual; Written and Illustrated Children's Literature*, Sydney: Harcourt Australia.
——— (eds) (2002) *Crossing the Boundaries*, Sydney: Pearson.
——— (2009) 'Developing new literacies. Responding to picturebooks in multiliterate ways', in Evans, J. (ed.) *Talking Beyond the Page: Reading and Responding to Picturebooks*, London: Routledge, 26–43.
Arizpe, E. (2009) 'Sharing visual experiences of a new culture: Immigrant children in Scotland respond to picturebooks and other visual texts', in Evans, J. (ed.) *Talking Beyond the Page: Reading and Responding to Picture Books*, Abingdon: Routledge, 134–151.
——— (2010) '"It was all about books": Picturebooks, culture and metaliterary awareness', in Colomer, T., Kümmerling-Meibauer, B. and Silva-Díaz, C. (eds) *New Directions in Picturebook Research*, New York: Routledge, 69–82.
——— (2013) 'Meaning-making from wordless (or nearly wordless) picturebooks: What educational research expects and what readers have to say', *Cambridge Journal of Education* 43 (2): 163–176.
——— (2014) 'Wordless picturebooks: Critical and educational perspectives on meaning-making', in Kümmerling-Meibauer, B. (ed.) *Aesthetic and Cognitive Challenges of the Picturebook*, Routledge: London, 91–108.

―― (2017) 'Picturebooks and situated readers: The intersections of text, image, culture and response', in Nikolajeva, M. and Beauvais, C. (eds) *The Edinburgh Companion to Children's Literature*, Edinburgh: Edinburgh University Press.

―― (2021) 'The state of the art in picturebook research from 2010 to 2020', *Language Arts*, 98(5): 260–272.

Arizpe, E., Colomer, T. and Martínez-Roldán, C. with Bagelman, C., Bellorín, B., Farrell, M., Fittipaldi, M., Grilli, G., Manresa, M., Margallo, A.M., McAdam, J., Real, N. and Terrusi, M. (2014) *Visual Journeys through Wordless Narratives: An International Inquiry with Immigrant Children and 'The Arrival'*, London: Bloomsbury Academic.

Arizpe, E. and McGilp, E. (2022) 'Picturebook futures', in Coats, K., Stevenson, D. and Yenika-Agbaw, V. (eds) *A Companion to Children's Literature*, Hobocken, NJ: Wiley-Blackwell, 193–206.

Arizpe, E. and Ryan, S. (2018) 'The Wordless Picturebook: Literacy in Multilingual Contexts and David Wiesner's Worlds', in Bland, J. (ed.) *Using Literature in English Language Education*, London: Bloomsbury Academic, 63–82.

Arizpe, E. and Styles, M. (2003) *Children Reading Pictures: Interpreting Visual Texts*, London: Routledge.

―― (2008a) 'A critical review of research into children's responses to multimodal texts', in Flood, J., Heath, S.B. and Lapp, D. (eds) *Handbook of Research on Teaching Literacy through the Communicative and Visual Arts*, New York: Lawrence Earlbaum Associates, 363–373.

―― (2008b) 'The Voices Behind the Pictures: Children responding to Postmodern Picturebooks', in Sipe. L and Pantaleo, S. (eds.) *Postmodern Picturebooks: Play, Parody and Self-Referentiality*, Oxon: Routledge.

Arnheim, R. (1966) *Towards a Psychology of Art*, Berkeley: University of California Press.

―― (1989) *Thoughts on Art Education*, Santa Monica, CA: Getty Center for Education in the Arts.

Avgerinou, M. and Ericson, J. (1997) 'A review of the concept of visual literacy', *British Journal of Educational Technology*, 28 (4): 280–291.

Avgerinou, M. D. and Pettersson, R. (2011) 'Toward a cohesive theory of visual literacy', *Journal of Visual Literacy*, 30(2): 1–19.

Bader, B. (1976) *American Picture Books: From Noah's Ark to the Beast Within*, New York: Macmillan.

Bailey, N. (2020) Inspired! Psyche's Resilience by The Fitzy Peters blog post for AccessArt accessed 11.12.22 https://www.accessart.org.uk/inspired-psyches-resilience-by-the-fitzy-peters/

Baker, J. (1991) *Window*, London: Random House Children's Books.

Barad, K. (2015) 'TransMaTerialiTies Trans*/matter/realities and queer political imaginings', *A Journal of Lesbian and Gay Studies*, 21(2–3): 387–422. doi: 10.1215/10642684-2843239.

Barbot, B., Randi, J., Tan, M., Levenson, C., Friedlaender, L. and Girgorenko, E. L. (2013) 'From Perception to Creative Writing: A Multi-Method Pilot Study of a Visual Literacy Instructional Approach', *Learning and Individual Differences*, 28: 167–176. doi: 10.1016/j.lindif.2012.09.003.

Bearne, E. (2009) 'Multimodality, Literacy and Texts: Developing a Discourse', *Journal of Early Childhood Literacy*, 9(2): 156–187.

Benjamin, W. (1986) *Reflections: Essays, Aphorisms, Autobiographical Writings*, Demetz, P. (ed.), New York: Schocken.

Benson, C. (1986) 'Art and language in middle childhood: A question of translation', *Word and Image*, 2(2): 123–140.

Bezemer, J. (2014) 'Multimodal transcription: A case study', in Norris, S. and Maier, C.D. (eds), Interactions, images and texts: A reader in multimodality, Berlin: De Gruyter Mouton, 155–170.

Bianquin, N. and Saachi, F. (2017) 'More than just pictures: Using picture books to broaden young learners' disability understanding', *Proceedings*, 1(9): 890, accessed (04/12/2021) at doi:10.3390/proceedings1090890

Bishop, R. S. (1990) 'Mirrors, windows, and sliding glass doors', *Perspectives*, 6: ix–xi.
Björk, C. and Anderson, L. (1987) *Linnea in Monet's garden*, New York: R. & S. Books.
Blakeney-Williams, M. and Daly, N. (2013) 'How do teachers use picture books to draw on the cultural and linguistic diversity in their classrooms?' *SET: Research Information for Teachers*, 2: 44–50.
Bland, J. (2013) *Children's Literature and Learner Empowerment: Children and Teenagers in English Language Education*, London: Bloomsbury Academic.
Botelho, M. and Rudman, M. (2009) *Critical Multicultural Analysis of Children's Literature: Mirrors, Windows and Doors*, New York: Routledge.
Braid, C. and Finch, B. (2015) '"Ah, I know why...": Children developing understandings through engaging with a picture book', *Literacy*, 49(3): 115–122.
Brooks, W. and Browne, S. (2012) 'Towards a culturally situated reader response theory', *Children's Literature in Education*, 43(1): 74–85.
Browne, A. (1979) *Bear Hunt*, London: H. Hamilton.
―――― (1987) *Piggybook*, London: Magnet.
―――― (1989) *The Tunnel*, London: Julia MacRae Books.
―――― (1992) *Changes*, London: Walker.
―――― (1994) *Zoo*, London: Red Fox (first published by Julia MacRae Books, 1992).
―――― (2000) *Willy's Pictures*, London: Walker Books.
―――― (2003) *The Shape Game*, London: Doubleday.
Bruner, J. (1986) *Actual Minds, Possible Worlds*, London: Harvard University Press.
Brunhoff, L. d. (2003) *Babar's Museum of Art*, New York: Harry N. Abrams.
Bull, G. and Anstey, M. (2010) *Evolving Pedagogies: Reading and Writing in a Multimodal World*, Victoria: Curriculum Press.
Burnham, R. and Kai-Kee, E. (2011) *Teaching in the Art Museum*, Los Angeles, CA: The J Paul Getty Museum.
Cabrejo, E. (2021) '*La lectura comienza antes de los textos escritos*', Nuevas Hojas de Lectura, 3: 12–19, accessed (21/01/2021), at https://www.cobdc.net/12JCD/wp-content/materials/SALA_E/CABREJO_lectura_comienza.pdf
Cai, M. (2008) 'Transactional theory and the study of multicultural literature', *Language Arts*, 85(3): 212–220.
Callow, J. (2017) '"Nobody spoke like i did": Picture books, critical literacy, and global contexts', *The Reading Teacher*, 71(2): 231–237.
Campbell, C. (2009) *10 Things You May Want To Know about Cassoni*, London: Courtauld Institute.
Campagnaro, M. (2015) '"These books made me really curious": How visual explorations shape young readers' taste', in Evans. J. (ed.) *Challenging and Controversial Picturebooks: Creative and Critical Responses to Visual Texts*, London: Routledge.
Carger, C. L. (2004) 'Art and literacy with bilingual children', *Language Arts*, 81(4): 283–292.
Carr, N. (2010) *The Shallows: How the Internet Is Changing the Way we Read, Think and Remember*, New York: Atlantic Books.
Chambers, A. (1993) *Tell Me: Children, Reading and Talk*, Exeter: Thimble Press.
Child, L. (2021) *What do You Think about When you Think about Nothing?* [online manifesto], accessed (09/01/2022) at https://foundlingmuseum.org.uk/wp-content/uploads/2021/07/Lauren-Child-CBE-manifesto.pdf
CLPE (2019) *The Power of Picturebooks: Summary of findings from the research on the CLPE Power of Pictures Project 2013–2019*, accessed (19/07/22) at https://clpe.org.uk/research/clpes-power-pictures-research-report-2019
―――― (2020) *Reflecting Realities. Survey of Ethnic Representation within UK Children's Literature 2019*, accessed (03/12/2021) at https://clpe.org.uk/system/files/CLPE%20Reflecting%20Realities%202020.pdf

——— (2021) *Reflecting Realities. Survey of Ethnic Representation within UK Children's Literature 2020*, accessed (03/12/2021) at https://clpe.org.uk/system/files/2021-11/CLPE%20Reflecting%20Realities%20Report%202021.pdf

Coban, O., McAdam, J. E. and Arizpe, E. (2020) 'Hanging out in The Studio to challenge xenophobia: consolidating identities as community writers', *Literacy*, 54(3): 123–131.

Cooper, D. and Noble, K. (2020) '*Schoolchildren, Science and Smartphones Shine New Light on a Florentine Masterpiece.*' Apollo, 6 April 2020 (published online only and not assigned to an issue), accessed (20/11/22) at https://www.apollo-magazine.com/jacopo-del-sellaio-fitzwilliam-museum-cambridge/

Couceiro, L. (2020) 'Disorientation and new directions: Developing the reader response toolkit', in Kara, H. and Khoo, S.-M. (eds.) *Researching in the Age of COVID-19: Volume 1: Response and Reassessment*, Bristol, UK: Policy Press, 30–39.

Coulthard, K. (2003) "The words to say it': Young bilingual learners responding to visual texts', in Arizpe, E. and Styles, M. (eds) *Children Reading Pictures: Interpreting Visual Texts*, London: Routledge, 164–189.

Cowan, K. (2014) 'Multimodal transcription of video: Examining interaction in Early Years classrooms', Classroom Discourse, 5(1): 6–21.

Cox, M. (1992) *Children's Drawings*, London: Penguin.

Crawford, P. A. and Hade, D. (2000) 'Inside the picture, outside the frame: Semiotics and the reading of wordless picture books', *Journal of Research in Childhood Education*, 15(1): 66–80.

Cuperman, R. C. (2013) 'Prejudice and Stereotypes Revealed Through Reader Responses in Pre-School Students', *New Review of Children's Literature and Librarianship*, 19(2): 119–138.

Davis, J. (1993) 'Why Sally can draw. An aesthetic perspective', *Educational Horizons*, 71(2): 86–93.

Deszcz-Tryhubczak, J. (2016) 'Using Literary Criticism for Children's Rights: Toward a Participatory Research Model of Children's Literature Studies', *The Lion and the Unicorn*, 40(2): 215–231.

Dewey, J. (1978) *Art as Experience*, New York: Doubleday.

Dipacho (2020) *A pesar de todo*, Bogota: El Salmón Editores.

Donaldson, J. and Scheffler, A. (1999) *The Gruffalo*, London: Macmillan.

Doonan, J. (1991) 'Satoshi Kitamura: Aesthetic dimensions', *Children's Literature*, 19: 107–137.

———. (1999) manuscript, 'Drawing out ideas: A second decade of Anthony Browne', printed in *The Lion and the Unicorn*, 23: 30–56.

Dresang, E. (1999) *Radical Change: Books for Youth in a Digital Age*, New York: The H.W. Wilson Company.

Dunbar, P. (2008) *Penguin*, London: Walker.

Enciso, P. (1996) 'Why Engagement in Reading Matters to Molly', *Reading & Writing Quarterly*, 12(2): 171–194.

Enever, J. and Schmid-Shonbein, G. (eds) (2006) *Picture Books and Young Learners of English*, Munich: Langenscheidt ELT GmbH.

Erickson, F. (1986) 'Qualitative methods in research on teaching', in Wittrock, M. C. (ed.) *Handbook of research on teaching* (3rd ed.), New York: Macmillan, 119–161.

Esteban-Guitart, M. and Moll, L. C. (2014) 'Funds of identity: A new concept based on the funds of knowledge approach', *Culture and Psychology*, 20(1): 31–48. doi:10.1177/1354067X13515934.

Evans, J. (ed.) (1998) *What's in the Picture? Responding to Illustrations in Picture Books*, London: Sage.

——— (ed.) (2009a) *Talking Beyond the Page: Reading and Responding to Picturebooks*, London: Routledge.

——— (2009b) 'Creative and aesthetic responses to picturebooks and fine art', *Education 3–13: International Journal of Primary, Elementary and Early Years Education*, 37(2): 177–190.

——— (2011) 'Do you live a life of Riley?: Thinking and talking about the purpose of life in picturebook responses', *New Review of Children's Literature and Librarianship*, 17(2): 189–209.

——— (ed.) (2015a) *Challenging and Controversial Picturebooks: Creative and Critical Responses to Visual Texts*. London: Routledge.

―――― (2015b) 'Could this Happen to us?: Responding to issues of migration in picturebooks', in Evans, J. (ed.) *Challenging and Controversial Picturebooks: Creative and Critical Responses to Visual Texts,* London: Routledge, 243–359.

Falter, M. M. (2017) 'The power and potential of graphic novels in the classroom', *Anthropology Now,* 9(3): 144–146.

Farrar, J. (2020) 'Encounters with metafiction: Playing with ideas of what counts when it comes to reading', in Deszcz-Tryhubczak, J. and Kalla, I. B. (eds.) *Rulers of Literary Playgrounds: Politics of Intergenerational Play in Children's Literature,* London: Routledge, 179–190.

Farrar, J., Arizpe, E. and McAdam, J. (2022) 'Challenging picturebooks and literacy studies', in Ommundsen, A.M., Haaland, G. and Kümmerling-Meibauer, B. (eds) *Exploring Challenging Picturebooks in Education,* London: Routledge, 43–56.

Feinstein, L. (2020) 'Beginning of a new era': how culture went viral in the face of a crisis, *The Guardian,* Wednesday 8th April, accessed (18.11.22) at https://www.theguardian.com/culture/2020/apr/08/art-virtual-reality-coronavirus-vr

Flewitt, R. (2019) 'Ethics and researching young children's digital literacy practices', in O. Erstad, O., Flewitt, R., Kümmerling-Meibauer, B., Susana, I. and Pereira, P. (eds), The Routledge Handbook of Digital Literacies in Early Childhood, New York: Routledge, 64–78.

Flint, T. K. and Adams, M. S. (2018) '"It's like playing, but learning": Supporting early literacy development through responsive play with wordless picturebooks', *Language Arts,* 96(1): 21–36.

Frederico, A. (2018) 'Embodiment and agency in digital reading: Preschoolers making meaning with literary apps', University of Cambridge (PhD Thesis), accessed (04/01/2022) at: https://doi.org/10.17863/CAM.31007

Freire, P. (2008) *Education for Critical Consciousness,* London: Continuum.

García-González, M. (2021) *Enseñando a sentir. Repertorios éticos en la ficción infantil,* Santiago de Chile: Ediciones Metales Pesados.

García-González, M. and Deszcz-Tryhubczak, J. (2020) 'New materialist openings to children's literature studies', *International Research in Children's Literature,* 13(1): 45–60.

Gardner, H. (1973) *The Arts and Human Development,* New York: John Wiley & Sons.

―――― (1980) *Artful Scribbles,* London: Jill Norman Limited.

Gee, J. P. (2005) *An Introduction to Discourse Analysis: Theory and Method* (2nd ed.), New York: Routledge.

Ghosh. K. (2015) 'Who's afraid of the big bad wolf: Responses to the portrayal of wolves in picturebooks', in Evans, J. (ed.) *Challenging and Controversial Picturebooks: Creative and Critical Responses to Visual Texts,* London: Routledge, 201–224.

Glaser, B. and Strauss, A. (1967) *The Discovery of Grounded Theory,* Chicago, IL: Aldine Publishing Co.

Gombrich, E. H. (1962) *Art and Illusion,* London: Phaidon Press.

Gonzalez, N., Moll, L. C. and Amanti, C. (eds) (2005) *Funds of Knowledge: Theorizing Practices in Households, Communities, and Classrooms,* Mahwah, NJ: Lawrence Erlbaum.

Gregory, P. (2019) 'Developing competent teachers of art in the primary school', in Hickman, R. (ed.) *The International Encyclopedia of Art and Design Education.* John Wiley & Sons Boston: Wiley Blackwell, 1–20.

Hagen, A. (2020) 'The potential for aesthetic experience in a literary app: An analysis of the fantastic flying books of Mr. Morris Lessmore', *Barnelitterært Forskningstidsskrift,* 11(1): 1–10. doi: 10.18261/issn.2000-7493-2020-01-02

Haughton, C. (2013) *Hat Monkey* [Mobile App, version 1.0.7], Fox and Sheep, accessed (accessed 31/01/2021) at https://itunes.apple.com/

Hayik, R. (2011) 'Critical Visual Analysis of Multicultural Sketches', *English Teaching: Practice and Critique,* 10(1): 95–118.

Hayles, K. (2002) *Writing Machines,* Cambridge, MA; London: The MIT Press. doi: 10.1002/9781405177504.ch27.

——— (2008) *Electronic Literature: New Horizons for the Literary*, Notre Dame, IN: University of Notre Dame Press.
Haynes, J. and Murris, K. (2019) 'Taking age out of play: Children's animistic philosophising through a picturebook', *Oxford Literary Review*, 41(2): 290–309. doi: 10.3366/olr.2019.0284.
Heath, S. B. (1983) *Ways with Words*, Cambridge: Cambridge University Press.
——— (2000) 'Seeing our way into learning', *Cambridge Journal of Education*, 30(1): 121–132.
——— (2006) 'Dynamics of Completion: Gaps, blanks, and improvisation', in Turner, M. (ed.) *The Artful Mind*, New York: Oxford University Press, 133–152.
Heath, S. B. and Wolf, J. L. (2012) 'Brain and behavior: The coherence of teenage response to YA literature', in Hilton, M. and Nikolajeva, M. (eds) *Contemporary Adolescent Literature and Culture: The emergent adult*, Farnham: Ashgate, 139–154.
Heggernes, S. (2019) 'Opening a dialogic space: Intercultural learning through picturebooks', *Children's Literature in English Language Education* CLELE, 7(2): 37–60, accessed (04/12/2021) at https://clelejournal.org/article-2-intercultural-learning/.
Hirsu, L., Arizpe, E. and McAdam, J. E. (2020) 'Cultural interventions through children's literature and arts-based practices in times of disaster: A case study of reading mediators' response to the Mexican earthquakes (September 2017)', *International Journal of Disaster Risk Reduction*, 51, doi: org/10.1016/j.ijdrr.2020.101797.
Hockney, D. and Gayford, M. (2020) *A History of Pictures* (2nd ed.), London: Thames and Hudson.
Hoffman, M. and Littlewood, K. (2002) *The Colour of Home*, London: Frances Lincoln.
Hogan, P. C. (2011) *What Literature Teaches Us about Emotion*, New York: Cambridge University Press.
Hope, J. (2017) *Children's Literature about Refugees: A Catalyst in the Classroom*, London: Trentham.
Housen, A (1999) "Eye of the Beholder: Research, Theory and Practice", Conference paper from "Aesthetic and Art Education: a Transdisciplinary Approach, September 27-29, 1999 Lisbon, Portugal, 1-30 accessed (16/12/2022) http://vtshome.org/wp-content/uploads/2016/08/Eye-of-the-Beholder.pdf
Hudelson, S., Smith, K. and Knudsen Hawes, L. (2005) '"Have you ever used this book with children?": Elementary children's responses to "Bilingual" picture books' in Cohen, J., McAlister, K.T., Rolstad, K. and MacSwan, J. (eds) *ISB4: Proceedings of the 4th International Symposium on Bilingualism*, Somerville, MA: Cascadilla Press, 1053–1061.
Husband, T. (2019) 'Using multicultural picture books to promote racial justice in urban early childhood literacy classrooms', *Urban Education*, 54(8): 1058–1084.
Hutchins, P. (1970) *Rosie's Walk*, London: Bodley Head.
International Society for Education Through Art (2015) *The 2015 LISBON LETTER for Visual Art Education to European Parliamentarians: Committee Education and Culture*, accessed at: https://www.insea.org/docs/2014.17/regions/VAE_Lisbon_Letter_InSEA2015.pdf.
Iordanaki, L. (2020) 'Older children's responses to wordless picturebooks: Making connections', *Children's Literature in Education*, 52: 493–510, accessed (05/01/2022) at: https://doi-org.ezproxy.lib.gla.ac.uk/10.1007/s10583-020-09424-7.
Iser, W. (1974) *The Implied Reader: Patterns of Communication in Prose Fiction from Bunyan to Beckett*, Baltimore, MD; London: The Johns Hopkins University Press.
——— (1978) *The Act of Reading: A Theory of Aesthetic Response*, London: Johns Hopkins University Press.
Jeffers, O. (2017) *Here We Are: Notes for Planet Earth*, London: HarperCollins.
Johnson, H., Mathis, J. and Short, K.G. (eds) (2019) *Critical Content Analysis of Visual Images in Books for Young People*, London: Routledge.
Johnston, I. and Bainbridge, J. (eds) (2013) *Reading Diversity through Canadian Picture Books: Preservice Teachers Explore Identity, Ideology and Pedagogy*, Toronto: University of Toronto Press.
Kellog, R. (1979) *Children's Drawings, Children's Minds*, New York: Avon.

Kelly, L. B., Wakefield, W., Caires-Hurley, J., Kganetso, L. W., Moses, L. and Baca, E. (2021) 'What is culturally informed literacy instruction? A review of research in P–5 contexts', *Journal of Literacy Research*, 53(1): 75–99.

Kenner, C. (2000) *Home Pages: Literacy Links for Bilingual Children*. Stoke-on-Trent: Trentham Books.

Kiefer, B. (1993) 'Children's responses to picture books: A developmental perspective', in K. Holland (ed.) *Journeying. Children Responding to Literature*, London: Heinemann, 267–283.

────── (1995). *The Potential of icturebooks: From Visual Literacy to Aesthetic Understanding*, Hoboken, NJ: Prentice-Hall.

Kitamura, S. (1992) (with H. Oram) *A Boy Wants a Dinosaur*, London: Red Fox.

────── (1997) *Lily Takes a Walk*, London: Happy Cat Books.

Kleekamp, M.C. and Zapata, A. (2019) 'Interrogating depictions of disability in children's picturebooks', *The Reading Teacher*, 72(5): 589–597.

Kosaka, K. (2020) 'Satoshi Kitamura's key to children's literature? Making complex ideas simple', *The Japan Times*, accessed (27/12/2021) at: https://www.japantimes.co.jp/culture/2020/04/18/books/satoshi-kitamura-children-literature/.

Kress, G. (1997) *Before Writing: Rethinking Paths to Literacy*, London: Routledge.

────── (2003) *Literacy in the New Media Age*, London: Routledge.

────── (2010) *Multimodality: A Social Semiotic Approach to Contemporary Communication*, London: Routledge.

Kress, G. and van Leeuwen, T. (1996) *Reading Images: The Grammar of Visual Design*, London: Routledge.

Kress, G. and van Leeuwen, T. (2006) Reading Images: The Grammar of Visual Design (2nd ed.), London: Routledge.

────── (2020) *Reading Images: The Grammar of Visual Design* (3rd ed.), Abingdon, Oxon; New York: Routledge.

Kucirkova, N. and Flewitt, R. (2020) 'Understanding parents' conflicting beliefs about children's digital book reading', *Journal of Early Childhood Literacy*, June, doi: 10.1177/1468798420930361

Kucirkova, N., Littleton, K., and Cremin, T. (2016) 'Young children's reading for pleasure with digital books: Six key facets of engagement', *Cambridge Journal of Education*, 3577(April): 1–18. doi: 10.1080/0305764X.2015.1118441

Kümmerling-Meibauer, B. (1999) 'Metalinguistic awareness and the child's developing concept of irony: The relationship between pictures and text in ironic picture books', *The Lion and the Unicorn*, 23(2): 157–183.

Kümmerling-Meibauer, B. and Meibauer, J. (2013) 'Towards a towards a cognitive theory of picturebooks', *International Research in Children's Literature*, 6(2): 143–160.

────── (2015) 'Maps in picturebooks: cognitive status and narrative functions', *BFLT Nordic Journal of Childlit Aesthetics*, accessed (24/04/15) at: http://www.childlitaesthetics.net/index.php/blft/article/view/26970%20-%20article

────── (2018) 'Picturebooks and cognitive studies', in B. Kümmerling-Meibauer (ed.) *The Routledge Companion to Picturebooks*, London: Routledge, 391–400.

Ladson-Billings, G. (1995) 'Toward a theory of culturally relevant pedagogy', *American Educational Research Journal*, 32(3): 465–491.

Lambert, M (2015) Reading Picturebooks with Children: How to Shake Up Storytime and get Kids Talking about What they See, Waterton MA: Charlesbridge.

Lefroy, R. (2018) 'Creating links across the arts: How an art museum experience can be used to teach about the construction of meaning in texts', *English in Education*, 52(2): 147–159. doi: 10.1080/04250494.2018.1438120.

Leonard, M. A., Lorch, E. P., Milich, R. and Hagans, N. (2009) 'Parent-child joint picture-book reading among children with ADHD', *Journal of Attention Disorders*, 12(4): 361–371.

Lewis, D. (1996) 'Going along with Mr Gumpy: Polysystemy and play in the modern picture book', *Signal*, 80: 105–119.

Lewis, D. and Greene, J. (1983) *Your Children's Drawings – Their Hidden Meanings*, London: Hutchinson.

Lohfink, G. and Loya, J. (2010) 'The nature of mexican american third graders' engagement with culturally relevant picture books', *Bilingual Research Journal*, 33(3): 346–363.

Lott, C. (2001) 'Picture books in the high school English classroom', in Ericson, B. (ed.), *Teaching Reading in High School English Classes*, Urbana, IL: National Council of Teachers of English, 139–154.

Lysaker, J. T. (2019) *Before Words*, New York: Teachers College Press.

Lysaker, J. and Sedberry, T. (2015) 'Reading difference: Picture book retellings as contexts for exploring personal meanings of race and culture', *Literacy*, 49(2): 105–111.

Mackey, M. (2002) *Literacies across Media: Playing the Text*, New York; London: Routledge. doi: 10.4324/9780203218976.

——— (2003) '"The most thinking book": Attention, performance and the Picturebook', in Styles, M. and Bearne, E. (eds) *Art, Narrative and Childhood*, Stoke on Trent: Trentham Books.

——— (2011), *Narrative Pleasures in Young Adult Novels, Films, and Video Games*, Basingstoke: Palgrave Macmillan.

——— (2016) 'Digital picturebooks', in Arizpe, E. and Styles, M. (eds), *Children Reading Picturebooks: Interpreting Visual Texts* (2nd ed.), London; New York: Routledge, 169–179.

Macaulay, D. (1990) *Black and White*, Boston: Houghton Mifflin.

Madura, S. (1998) 'An artistic element: Four transitional readers and writers respond to the picture books of Patricia Polacco and Gerald McDermott', *National Reading Conference Yearbook*, 47: 366–376.

Maine, F. and McCaughran, B. (2021) 'Using wordless picturebooks as stimuli for dialogic engagement', in Maine, F. and Vrikki, M. (eds) *Dialogue for Intercultural Understanding*, Cham: Springer, doi: 10.1007/978-3-030-71778-0_5

Mak, H.W. and Fancourt, D. (2021) 'Do socio-demographic factors predict children's engagement in arts and culture? Comparisons of in-school and out-of-school participation in the Taking Part Survey', *PLoS One* 16(2): e0246936. doi: 10.1371/journal.pone.0246936

Manguel, A. (1997) *A History of Reading*, London: Flamingo.

Manresa, M., and Real, N. (2015) *Digital Literature for Children: Texts, Readers and Educational Practices*, Brussels: Peter Lang.

Mantei, J. and Kervin, L. (2014) 'Interpreting the images in a picture book: Students make connections to themselves, their lives and experiences', *English Teaching: Practice and Critique*, 13(2): 76–92.

Marsden, J. and Tan, S. (1998) *The Rabbits*, Port Melbourne: Lothian Children's Books.

Marshall, E. (2015) 'Fear and strangeness in picturebooks: Fractured fairy tales, graphic knowledge and teachers concerns', in Evans, J. (ed.) *Challenging and Controversial Picturebooks: Creative and Critical Responses to Visual Texts*, London: Routledge, 160–177.

Martin, N. (2009) *Art as an Early Intervention Tool for Children with Autism*, London: Jessica Kingsley Pub.

Martínez-Roldán, C. M., and Newcomer, S. (2011) 'Reading between the pictures: Immigrant students' interpretations of the arrival', *Language Arts* 88 (3): 188–197.

Matarasso, F. (2019) *A Restless Art*. Lisbon and London: Calouste Gulbenkian Foundation, accessed (01/02/2021) at: https://arestlessart.files.wordpress.com/2019/03/2019-a-restless-art.pdf

McAdam, J., Abou Ghaida, S., Arizpe, E., Hirsu, L. and Motawy, Y. (2020) 'Children's literature in critical contexts of displacement: Exploring the value of hope', *Education Sciences*, 10(12): 383, accessed (31/12/2021) at: doi: 10.3390/educsci10120383.

McAdam, J. E., Arizpe, E., Devlin, A. M., Farrell, M., and Farrar, J. (2014) 'Journeys from images to words', Project Report: Esmée Fairbairn Foundation.

McClay, J. (2000) '"Wait a second...": Negotiating complex narratives in *Black and White*', *Children's Literature in Education*, 31 (2): 91–106.

McGilp, E. (2014) 'From picturebook to multilingual collage: Bringing learners' first language and culture into the pre-school classroom', *Children's Literature in English Language Education*, 2(2): 31–49.

McGuire, C., Belfatti, M. and Ghiso, M. (2008) '"It doesn't Say How?": Third graders' collaborative sense-making from postmodern picturebooks', in Sipe, L. R. and Pantaleo, S. (eds) *Postmodern Picturebooks: Play, Parody and Self-Referentiality,* London: Routledge, 193–206.

McLellan, R. et al. (2012) *The Impact of Creative Partnerships on the Wellbeing of Children and Young People*, Newcastle, accessed (02/01/2022) at: https://www.creativitycultureeducation.org/publication/the-impact-of-creative-partnerships-on-the-wellbeing-of-children-and-young-people/.

McLeod, N. et al. (2017) 'Visual Rhythms: Facilitating Young Children's Creative Engagement at Tate Liverpool', *European Early Childhood Education Research Journal*, 25 (6): 930–944.

Meek, M. (1988) *How Texts Teach what Readers Learn,* Stroud: The Thimble Press.

Merchant, G. (2014) 'Young children and interactive story-apps', in Burnett, C., Davies, J., Merchant, G. and Rowsell, J. (eds) *New Literacies Around the Globe*, Abingdon, Oxon: Routledge, 120–139.

——— (2015) 'Keep taking the tablets: iPads, story apps and early literacy', *The Australian Journal of Language and Literacy*, 38(1): 3–11.

Meyer, T. (2017) 'Next art education: Eight theses future art educators should think about', *International Journal of Education through Art*, 13(3), doi: 10.1386/eta.13.3.369_1.

Moll, L.C., Amanti, C., Neff, D. & Gonzalez, N. (2005) 'Funds of knowledge for teaching: Using a qualitative approach to connect homes and classrooms', in González, N., Moll, L. C. and Amanti, C. (eds) *Funds of Knowledge: Theorizing Practices in Households, Communities, and Classrooms,* Mahwah, NJ: Lawrence Erlbaum, 71–87.

Möller, K. J. (2020) 'Reading and responding to LGBTQ-inclusive children's literature in school settings: Considering the state of research on inclusion', *Language Arts*, 97(4): 235–251.

Møller Daugaard, L. and Blok Johansen, M. (2014) 'Multilingual children's interaction with metafiction in a postmodern picture book', *Language and Education*, 28(2): 120–140.

Mourão, S. (2012), 'Response to the lost thing: Notes from a secondary classroom', *Children's Literature in English Language Education*, 1(1): 81–105.

——— (2015) 'What's real and what's not: Playing with the mind in wordless picturebooks', in Evans. J. (ed.) *Challenging and Controversial Picturebooks: Creative and Critical Responses to Visual Texts,* London: Routledge.

Moya Guijarro, A. J. (2014) *A Multimodal Analysis of Picture Books for Children*, London: Equinox.

Nagel, L. (2017) 'The Picturebook App as Event: Interactivity and Immersion in Wuwu and Co.', *Journal of Children's Literature Research*, 40: 1–17. doi: 10.14811/clr.v40i0.290.

National Society for Education in Art and Design (2016) 'The National Society for Education in Art and Design Survey Report 2015–16', 1–46.

Nel, P. (2021) 'Breaking up with your favorite racist childhood classic books', accessed (03/12/2021) at https://www.washingtonpost.com/education/2021/05/16/breaking-up-with-racist-childrens-books/.

New London Group (1996) 'A pedagogy of multiliteracies: Designing social futures,' *Harvard Educational Review*, 66(1): 60–92.

Nikolajeva, M. and Scott, C. (2000) 'The dynamics of picturebook communication', *Children's Literature in Education*, 31: 225–239.

Nikolajeva, M. and Scott, C. (2001) *How Picturebooks Work*, London: Garland.

Nikolajeva, M. (2012) 'Reading other people's minds through word and image', *Children's Literature in Education*, 43(3): 273–291.

——— (2014) *Reading for Learning. Cognitive Approaches to Children's Literature*, Amsterdam: John Benjamins.

——— (2016) 'Recent Trends in Children's Literature Research: Return to the Body', *International Research in Children's Literature*, 9(2): 132–145.

Noble, F., Carter, I., Empire, K. (2021) 'The Best children's books of 2021' The Guardian, Sunday 12th December, accessed (21.11.22) at https://www.theguardian.com/books/2021/dec/12/the-best-childrens-books-of-2021

Noble, K. (2006) *Picture Thinking: The Development of Visual Literacy in young children*, (PhD Thesis), The University of Cambridge.

——— (2021a) '"Getting hands on with other creative minds": Establishing a community of practice around primary art and design in the art museum', *International Journal of Art and Design Education*, 40(3): 615–629. https://doi.org/10.1111/jade.12371

——— (2021b) 'Challenges and Opportunities: Creative Approaches to Museum and Gallery Learning during the Pandemic', *International Journal of Art and Design Education*, 40(4): 676–689. https://doi.org/10.1111/jade.12380

Nodelman, P. (1988) *Words about Pictures. The Narrative Art of Children's Picture Books*, London: University of Georgia Press.

——— (2008) *The Hidden Adult: Defining Children's Literature*, Baltimore, MD: John Hopkins University Press.

——— (2010) 'On the border between implication and actuality: Children inside and outside of picture books', *Journal of Children's Literature Studies*, 7(2): 1–21.

——— (2018) 'Touching art: The art museum as a picture book, and the picture book as art', *Journal of Literacy Education* (1). doi: 10.7203/JLE.1.12085.

Nosy Crow. (2013) *Little Red Riding Hood* [Mobile App, version 1.0.4], Nosy Crow (app no longer available).

Ogier, S. and Ghosh, K. (2018) 'Exploring student teachers' capacity for creativity through the interdisciplinary use of comics in the primary classroom', *Journal of Graphic Novels and Comics*, 9(4): 293–309.

Orben, A. (2020) 'Teenagers, screens and social media: A narrative review of reviews and key studies', *Social Psychiatry and Psychiatric Epidemiology*, Springer, 55(4): 407–414. doi: 10.1007/s00127-019-01825-4.

Oslick, M. E. (2013) 'Children's voices: Reactions to a criminal justice issue picture book', *The Reading Teacher*, 66 (7): 543–552.

Paciga, K. A. (2015) 'Their teacher can't be an app: Preschoolers' listening comprehension of digital storybooks', *Journal of Early Childhood Literacy*, 15(4): 473–509. doi: 10.1177/1468798414552510.

Pahl, K. and Rowsell, J. (2011) 'Artifactual Critical Literacy: A New Perspective for Literacy Education Berkeley', *Review of Education*, 2(2). doi: 10.5070/B82110050.

Painter, C., Martin, J. R. and Unsworth, L. (2013) *Reading Visual Narratives*, Sheffield: Equinox.

Paley, V. G. (2005) *A Child's Work: The Importance of Fantasy Play*, Chicago, IL: University of Chicago Press.

Pantaleo, S. (2002) 'Grade 1 children meet David Wiesner's three pigs', *Journal of Children's Literature*, 28(2): 72–84.

——— (2004a) 'Young children and radical change characteristics in picturebooks', *The Reading Teacher*, 58(2): 178–187.

——— (2004b) 'Young children interpret the metafictive in Anthony Browne's', *Voices in the Park*', *Journal of Early Childhood Literacy*, 4(2): 211–233.

——— (2005) 'Young children engage with the metafictive in picture books', *Australian Journal of Language and Literacy*, 28(1): 19–37.

——— (2008) *Exploring Student Response to Contemporary Picturebooks*, Toronto: University of Toronto Press.

——— (2009a) 'Exploring children's responses to the postmodern picturebook', in *Who's Afraid of the Big Bad Book?*' in Evans, J. (ed.), *Talking Beyond the Page: Reading and Responding to Picturebooks*, London: Routledge, 44–61.

——— (2009b) 'The influence of postmodern picturebooks on three boys' narrative competence', *Australian Journal of Language and Literacy*, 32(3): 191–210.

——— (2010) 'Developing narrative competence through reading and writing metafictive texts', *Literacy Research and Instruction*, 49(3): 264–281.

——— (2011) 'Middle years students' collaborative talk about 'The Red Tree': "A book that really works your mind"', *Australian Journal of Language and Literacy*, 34(3): 260–278.

——— (2012a) 'Exploring the intertextualities in a grade 7 student's graphic narrative', *L1-Educational Studies in Education and Literature*, 12(1): 23–55.

——— (2012b) 'Meaning-making with colour in multimodal texts: One 11-year-old student's purposeful "doing"', *Literacy*, 46(3): 147–155.

——— (2012c) 'Middle-school students reading and creating multimodal texts: A case study', *Education 3–13: International Journal of Primary, Elementary and Early Years Education*, 40 (3): 295–314.

——— (2012d) 'Middle years students thinking with and about typography in multimodal texts', *Literacy Learning: the Middle Years*, 20(1): 37–50.

——— (2013) 'Paneling "matters" in elementary students' graphic narratives', *Literacy Research and Instruction*, 52 (2): 150–171.

——— (2014) 'Reading images in graphic novels: Taking students to a "greater thinking level"', *English in Australia*, 49(1): 38–51.

——— (2015) 'Filling the gaps: Exploring the writerly metaphors in Shaun Tan's *The Red Tree*' in Evans, J. (ed.) *Challenging and Controversial Picturebooks: Creative and Critical Responses to Visual Texts*, London: Routledge.

——— (2020) 'Slow looking: "reading picturebooks takes time"', *Literacy*, 54(1): 40–48. doi: 10.1111/lit.12190.

Pantaleo, S. and Bomphray, A. (2011) 'Exploring grade 7 students' written responses to Shaun Tan's *The Arrival*', *Changing English: Studies in Culture and Education*, 18(2): 173–185.

Paris, A. H. and Paris, S. G. (2001) 'Children's Comprehension of Narrative Picture Books: CIERA Report 3–012.', accessed (24/04/2015) at: http://www.ciera.org/library/reports/inquiry-3/3-012/3-012.html.

Parsons, M. J. (1987) *How We Understand Art*, Cambridge: Cambridge University Press.

Paulick, J., Miller Quinn, A., Kibler, A. K., Palacios, N. and Hill, T. (2020) 'Lessons for teachers: A wordless picturebook in the hands of one Mexican immigrant family', *TESOL Journal*, 11: e513. doi: 10.1002/tesj.513

Pavlou, V. (2020) 'Art technology integration: Digital storytellying as a transformative pedagogy in primary education', *International Journal of Art and Design Education*, 39(1): 195–210, doi: 10.1111/jade.12254.

Pérez Huber, L., Camargo Gonzalez, L. and Solórzano, D.G. (2020) 'Theorizing a critical race content analysis for children's literature about people of color', *Urban Education*. doi: 10.1177/0042085920963713

Perkins, D. (1989) 'Art as understanding', in Gardner, H. and Perkins, D. (eds) *Art, Mind and Education: Research from Project Zero*. Urbana, IL: University of Illinois, 111–131.

——— (1994) *The Intelligent Eye: Learning to Think by Looking at Art*, Cambridge, MA: Harvard Graduate School of Education.

Prensky, M. (2001) 'Digital natives, digital immigrants Part 1', *On the Horizon*, 9(5): 1–6, doi: 10.1108/10748120110424816.

Prior, L., Willson, A. and Martínez, M. (2012) 'Picture this: visual literacy as a pathway to character understanding', *The Reading Teacher*, 66(3): 195–206.

Purcell, J. M. (2018) '"Seeing the light": A cognitive approach to the metaphorical in picture books', *Children's Literature in Education*, 49(3): 356–375.

Raney, K. (1998) 'A matter of survival. On being visually literate', *The English and Media Magazine*, 39: 37–42.

Real, N., and Correro, C. (2015) 'Digital literature in early childhood: Reading experiences in family and school contexts', in Manresa, M. and Real, N. (eds), *Digital Literature for Children: Texts, Readers and Educational Practices*, Brussels: Peter Lang, 173–189.

Reifel, S. (2007) 'Hermeneutic text analysis of play: Exploring meaningful early childhood classroom events', in Amos Hatch, J. (ed.) *Early Childhood Qualitative Research*, London: Routledge, 25–42.

Ritchhart, R. (2011) *Making Thinking Visible: How to Promote Engagement*. San Francisco, CA: Jossey-Bass.

Rosenblatt, L. M. (1978) *The Reader, The Text, The Poem: The Transactional Theory of the Literary Work*, Carbondale: Southern Illinois University Press.

────── (1982) 'The literary transaction: Evocation and response', *Theory Into Practice*, 21: 268–277.

Royal Society of Arts/Education Endowment Foundation, *Using Picture Books and Illustration to Improve Pupils' Literacy*, accessed (19/07/22) at https://educationendowmentfoundation.org.uk/projects-and-evaluation/projects/power-of-pictures.

Rueda, C. (2020) *El encargo*, Mexico City: Oceano Travesia.

Ryan, M.-L. (2006) *Avatars of Story*, Minneapolis, London: University of Minnesota Press. doi: 9780816646869.

────── (2015) *Narrative as Virtual Reality 2: Revisiting Immersion and Interactivity in Literature and Electronic Media*, Baltimore, MD: Johns Hopkins University Press.

Sáez Castán, J. (2007) *La merienda del señor verde*, Barcelona: Ediciones Ekaré.

Salisbury, M. and Styles, M. (2012) *Children's Picturebooks: The Art of Visual Storytelling*, London: Laurence King.

Sarı, B., Başal, H. A., Takacs, Z. K., and Bus, A. G. (2019) 'A randomized controlled trial to test efficacy of digital enhancements of storybooks in support of narrative comprehension and word learning', *Journal of Experimental Child Psychology*, 179: 212–226. doi: 10.1016/j.jecp.2018.11.006.

Satizábal, A. (2020) *Río de colores*, Bogota: Editorial Monigote.

Scherer, L. (2020) '"Where would you be in the picture': Using reader-response with children in the primary school', *Journal of Early Childhood Literacy*, accessed (06/01/2022) at: doi: 10.1177/1468798420913991.

Scieszka, J. and Smith, L. (1995) *Seen Art?* New York: Viking Press.

Sciurba, K. (2020) 'Depicting hate: Picture books and the realities of white supremacist crime and violence', *Teachers College Record*, 122(8), accessed (03/12/2021) at https://doi.org/10.1177/016146812012200813

Sedgwick, D. and Sedgwick, F. (1993) *Drawing to Learn*, London: Hodder & Stoughton.

Sendak, M. (1994). Preface. *I Dream of Peace.Images of War by Children of Former Yugoslavia*: New York: UNICEF HarperCollins.

Senokossoff, G. W. (2013) 'Picture books are for little kids, aren't they? Using picture books with adolescent readers to enhance literacy instruction', *Reading Horizons: A Journal of Literacy and Language Arts*, 52 (3), accessed (03/12/2021) at https://scholarworks.wmich.edu/reading_horizons/vol52/iss3/2.

Serafini, F. (2002) 'A journey with the wild things: A reader response perspective in practice', *Journal of Children's Literature*, 28(1): 73–79.

────── (2005) 'Voices in the park, voices in the classroom: Readers responding to postmodern picture books', *Literacy Research and Instruction*, 44(3): 47–64.

────── (2009) 'Understanding visual images in picturebooks 'in Evans, J. (ed.) *Talking Beyond the Page: Reading and Responding to Picturebooks*, Oxon: Routledge, 10–25.

────── (2014) *Reading the Visual: An Introduction to Teaching Multimodal Literacy*, New York: Teachers College Press.

────── (2015) 'The appropriation of fine art into contemporary narrative picturebooks', *Children's Literature in Education*, 46(4): 438–453. doi: 10.1007/s10583-015-9246-2.

────── (2022) *Beyond the Visual: An Introduction to Researching Multimodal Phenomena*, New York: Teachers College Press.

Serafini, F. and Ladd, S.M. (2008) 'The challenge of moving beyond the literal in literature discussions', *Journal of Language and Literacy Education*, 4(2): 6–20.

Short, K. (2004) 'Building teachers' understandings of art as meaning-making in picture books', *International Reading Association Journal of Children's Literature and Reading: The Dragon Lode*, 22(2): 12–18.

Sigmon, M. L., Tackett, M. E. and Azano, A. P. (2016) 'Using children's picture books about autism as resources in inclusive classrooms', *The Reading Teacher*, 70(1): 111–117.
Sipe, L. R. (1998) 'How picture books work: A semiotically framed theory of text–picture relationships', *Children's Literature in Education*, 29(2): 97–108.
——— (2000) '"Those 2 gingerbread boys could be brothers': How children use intertextual connections during storybook readalouds', *Children's Literature in Education*, 31(2): 73–88.
——— (2001) 'A palimpsest of stories: Young children's construction of intertextual links among fairytale variants', *Reading Research and Instruction*, 40(4): 335–352.
——— (2008) *Storytime: Young Children's Literary Understanding in the Classroom*, New York: Teachers College Press.
——— (2011) *Young Children's Responses to Picture Storybooks: Five Types of Literary Understanding*, Seminar: Universitat Autònoma Barcelona, accessed (18/04/2015) at: http://literatura.gretel.cat/sites/default/files/barcelona_lecture.pdf.
Sipe, L. R. and Brightman, A. (2009) 'Young Children's Interpretations of Page Breaks in Contemporary Picture Storybooks', *Journal of Literacy Research*, 41(1):68–103.
Sipe, L. R. and Ghiso, M. P. (2005) 'Looking closely at characters: How illustrations support children's understandings of character through picturebook illustrations', in Roser, N. and Martinez, M.E. (eds) *What a Characters! Character Study as a Guide to Literary Meaning Making in Grades K-8*, Newark, NJ: International Reading Association, 134–153.
Sipe, L. R. and McGuire, C. E. (2006) 'Picturebook endpapers: Resources for literary and aesthetic preparation', *Children's Literature in Education*, 37 (4): 291–304.
Sis, P. (2007) *The Wall: Growing Up Behind the Iron Curtain*, New York: Farrar, Straus and Giroux.
Smith, V. (2009) 'Making and breaking frames: Crossing the borders of expectation in picturebooks', in Evans, J. (ed.) *Talking Beyond the Page: Reading and Responding to Picturebooks*, Routledge: London, 81–97.
Smith, L. F., Smith, J. K. and Tinio, P. P. L. (2017) 'Time spent viewing art and reading labels', *Psychology of Aesthetics, Creativity, and the Arts*, 11(1): 77–85. doi: 10.1037/aca0000049.
Søyland, L. and Gulliksen, M. S. (2019) 'Sense-making through touch interaction with a picturebook app', *Barnelitterært Forskningstidsskrift*, 10(1): 1–12. doi: 10.18261/issn.2000-7493-2019-01-02.
Strauss, A. J. (1987) *Qualitative Analysis for Social Scientists*, Cambridge: Cambridge University Press.
Strauss, A. and Corbin, J. (1998) *Basics of Qualitative Research: Techniques and Procedures for Developing Grounded Theory* (2nd ed.), Thousand Oaks, CA: Sage.
Street, B. (1984) *Literacy in Theory and Practice*, Cambridge: Cambridge University Press.
Stone, J., and Smollin, M. (2011) *The Monster at the End of this Book* [Mobile App, version 5.1], Sesame Workshop, available from https://itunes.apple.com (accessed 31/01/2021).
Strouse, G. A. and Ganea, P. A. (2017) 'Toddlers' word learning and transfer from electronic and print books', *Journal of Experimental Child Psychology*, 156: 129–142. doi: 10.1016/j.jecp.2016.12.001.
Styles, M. (1996) 'Inside the tunnel: a radical kind of reading – Picture books, pupils and post-modernism', in Watson, V. and Styles, M. (eds) *Talking Pictures*, London: Hodder & Stoughton.
Styles, M. and Bearne, E. (eds) (2003) *Art, Narrative and Childhood*, Stoke-on-Trent: Trentham Books.
Swaggerty, E. (2009) '"That just really knocks me out": Fourth grade students navigate postmodern picture books', *Journal of Language and Literacy Education*, 5(1): 9–31.
The Guardian (2021) 'Charlie and Lola author Lauren Child says children's books should be taken seriously', accessed (19/07/22) at https://www.theguardian.com/books/2021/sep/21/charlie-and-lola-author-lauren-child-says-childrens-books-should-be-taken-seriously
Thomas, E. E. (2016) 'Stories still matter: Rethinking the role of diverse children's literature today', *Language Arts*, 94(2): 112–119.
Thomson, J. (1987) *Understanding Teenagers' Reading*, Melbourne: Methuen.

Tishman, S. (2018) *Slow Looking: The Art and Practice of Learning through Observation*, London: Routledge.

Van Allsburg, C. (1984) *The Mysteries of Harris Burdick*, Boston, MA: Houghton Mifflin.

——— (1993) *The Sweetest Fig*, Boston, MA: Houghton Mifflin.

van der Pol, C. (2012) 'Reading picturebooks as literature: four-to-six-year-old children and the development of literary competence', *Children's Literature in Education*, 43(1): 93–106.

van Leeuwen, T. (2005), *Introducing Social Semiotics*, London: Routledge.

van Renen, C. (2011) 'Having their say: Engaging with contemporary picture books at work and at play', *Journal of Literary Studies*, 27(2): 1–25.

Vehabovic, N. (2021) 'Picturebooks as critical literacy: Experiences and perspectives of translingual children from refugee backgrounds', *Journal of Literacy Research*, 53(3): 382–405. doi: 10.1177/1086296X211030469

Vermeule, B. (2010) *Why do We Care about Literary Characters?* Baltimore, MD: The Johns Hopkins University Press.

Veryeri Alaca, I. (2018) 'Materiality in picturebooks', in B. Kümmerling-Meibauer (ed.) *The Routledge Companion to Picturebooks*, London: Routledge, 59–68.

Vilela, R.L.S. (2019), 'Literatura infantil digital: Arte, Infância e Tecnologia Na Escola', Federal University of Rio de Janeiro (PhD Thesis), accessed (04/01/2022) at: https://ppge.educacao.ufrj.br/teses2019/tRafaela Louise Silva Vilela.pdf

Vygotsky, L. (1978) *Mind in Society*, Cole, M., John-Steiner, V., Scribner, S. and Suberman, E. (eds) Cambridge, MA: Harvard University Press.

——— (1986) *Thought and Language*, A. Kozulin (ed.) Cambridge: MIT Press.

Wallis, N. & Noble, K. (2022) 'Leave only footprints: how children communicate a sense of ownership and belonging in an art gallery', *European Early Childhood Education Research Journal*, 30(3). doi.org/10.1080/1350293X.2022.2055100

Walsh, M. (2003) 'Reading' pictures: What do they reveal? Young children's reading of visual texts', *Reading Literacy and Language*, 37 (3): 123–130.

Webb, K. (2020) Inspired! Re-Creating Cupid and Psyche in Mixed Media by Year Fives at Linton Heights blog post for AccessArt accessed 11.12.22 https://www.accessart.org.uk/inspired-re-creating-cupid-psyche-mixed-media-by-year-fives-linton-heights/

——— (2006) 'The "textual shift": Examining the reading process with print, visual and multimodal texts', *Australian Journal of Language and Literacy*, 29 (1): 24–37.

Williams, C. and McLean, M. (1997) 'Young deaf children's responses to picturebook reading in a pre-school setting', *Research in the Teaching of English*, 31(3): 337–366.

Wolf, M. (2007) *Proust and the Squid: The Story of Science and the Reading Brain*, New York: HarperCollins.

Wolfberg, P. J. (1999) *Play and Imagination in Children with Autism*, New York: Teachers' College Press.

Wu, J. (2018) 'A bibliometric analysis of picture book research between 1993 and 2015', *Reading Psychology*, 39(5): 413–441.

Young Yeom, E. (2019) 'Disturbing the still water: Korean English language students' visual journeys for global awareness', *CLELE*, 7(1): 1–20, accessed (04/12/2021) at https://clelejournal.org/article-1-disturbing-still-water/.

Youngs, S. and Serafini, F. (2013) 'Discussing picturebooks across perceptual, structural and ideological perspectives', *Journal of Language and Literacy Education*, 9(1): 185–200.

Zapata, A. and Kuby, C. R. (2021) '(Re)making the past/present/future: Experiencing the picturebook making of Duncan Tonatiuh and Yuyi Morales', in R. Kuby, C. Porter and R. Griffo (eds) *The Matter of Practice*, Charlotte, NC: Information Age Publishing, 119–142.

Zhao, S. and Unsworth, L. (2017) 'Touch design and narrative interpretation: A social semiotic approach to picture book apps', in N. Kucirkova and G. Falloon (eds), *Apps, Technology and Younger Learners: International Evidence for Teaching*, Abingdon, Oxon; New York: Routledge, 89–101.

Index

Note: *Italic* page numbers refer to figures and page numbers followed by "n" denote endnotes.

Adomat, D. S. 20, 146
adult mediation of digital texts 126
aesthetic response to art: autonomy, judgement and dialogue 89, 91; beauty and realism 89–90; expressiveness 89, 90; favouritism 89; medium, style and form 89, 90
affective/cognitive reactions of young readers 153
affective response 16, 80
Alemagna, B. 90
Alexander, R. 93
Aliagas, C. 125, 126
Allan, C. 154
Anstey, M. 33, 154, 163
Argueta, J. T. 5
Arizpe, E. 1, 3, 90, 124, 127, 141, 159, 160, 162
Arnheim, R. 56, 59
art making 93–95, 104
art materials 27, 95
art museum: aesthetic response to art, stages 89–91; developmental theories 88–89; linking looking and thinking 87–88; pedagogy 97; from picturebook to 96–97; pictures in response 95–96; slow looking together in 86–87; using image-based thinking routines 91–92
arts: based activities 163; based learning 166; based responses 141; creative 103; education 87; engagement 165; painting and film 152; visual 108
art teaching: decline 96; training 96
artworks 159; comic-style 43; elicited responses 20; experience for children 97; group work 93; in picturebooks 153
Attenborough, D. 164
autism/autistic 5, 11, 32, 33, 114, 115, 121–122, 140, 146
autonomy 89, 91

Baker, J. 164; *Window* 164
Barbot, B. 93
Bear Hunt (Browne) 41
Bearne, E. 58
beauty 89–90
Belfatti, M. 161
Benjamin, W. 125
Benson, C. 68
bilingual books 140
bilingual children 136
Bishop, R. S. 139
Black Americans 166
Black characters 166
Black Lives Matter (BLM) 167
Bromley, H. 1, 158
Brooks, W. 142
Browne, A. 1–3, 10, 12, 13, 18, 19, 37–40, 42–48, 52, 55, 56, 57, 62, 64, 69, 72–74, 78, 89, 136, 142, 145, 154, 158, 167; *Bear Hunt* 41; *Changes* 90; *Piggybook* 38; *The Shape Game* 3; *The Tunnel* (see *The Tunnel* (Browne)); *Willy's Pictures* 3; *Zoo* (see *Zoo* (Browne))
Browne, S. 142
Brueghel, P. the Younger 86
Bruner, J. 151
Bull, G. 33, 154
Burnham, R. 92

Cabrejo, E. 112
Caldecott Medal and Honour winners 158
Callow, J. 143, 147
Camargo Gonzalez, L. 140
Cambridge 3, 5, 10
Campagnaro, M. 161
Carger, C. L. 20, 142
Carle, E. 89, 91, 158

Index

Carr, N. 156
cartoonish style 23, 26, 29, 30
Ceccarelli, S. 99
challenging picturebooks 1, 4, 13, 21
Chambers, A. 20
Changes (Browne) 90
child-adult interaction on digital texts 125
Child, L. 167
child-led research 115
children drawing: analysing the drawings 60; and communication 65, 68; developmental differences 67–68, *68*; humanities project 69–70, *70, 71,* 72; internal structure *64,* 64–65, *65, 66,* 67; literal responses 60, *61*; and metacognition 50–52, 55, 58, 59, 67, 80; in museum 3, 86; overall effect *62,* 62–64, *63*; and pleasure 15, 59, 80, 126; responses to picturebooks 13, 80–81; in response to picturebooks 21n6, 81n3; and thinking 3, 9, 12, 13, 55, 67, 68, 76, 81; vignette: Yu (4) 76–80, *77, 79*; visual literacy 81; and writing 93, 163; *Zoo* project 72
children responses: illustrator's use of body language/colour/line/light/pattern/perspective 11, 15, 18, 29, 39, 44, 52, 76; illustrator's use of visual metaphors 1, 44; moral, ethical, environmental issues 1, 14, 31; plot, sequence, characters 32, 93; religious iconography 45
children's engagements with digital books 126; affective 126; creative 126; interactive 126; personalised 126; shared 126; sustained 126
classrooms: activities 115, 158; art museum in 86, 91–92, 96, 97; British 145; 'child-centred' scaffolding 151; comics 152; diversity in 146–147; graphic novels 152; for language learning 136–137; multicultural 140; multilingual 140; parent-child shared reading 127; picturebooks in contexts outside 5, 16, 146–147, 152, 159, 163; preschool 125; teachers 15–16, 20, 85; using image-based thinking routines 91–92; working on *Zoo* 60, 78
climate change 4, 162, 164–165
close looking: at paintings 93, 112; at picturebooks 91, 93, 97
CLPE Power of Pictures Project 5, 166
Coban, O. 141
cognitive criticism 21
cognitive literary theory 156
cognitive poetics 156
collaborative looking 81, 92–93
collaborative making 104

collaborative reading 159
Coulthard, K. 1, 5, 136
Covid pandemic 124, 162, 165
Cox, M. 77
creative methods 162
Cremin, T. 126
critical visual analysis 140, 155
cultural diversity 137, 139, 157
Cupid and Psyche (del Sellaio, Jacopo, Fitzwilliam Museum) *98,* 99, 100
Czerki, P. 96

data analysis 13, 21n6
Davis, J. 13, 60, 67, 68
Deakin, K. 5, 114
Deszcz-Tryhubczak, J. 163
dialogue 89, 91
digital games 124, 134
digital literary reading: control movements 125; deictic movements 125; stabilising movements 125
digital literature 124–128, 133–134
digital technology 124–126, 127, 128, 129, 152
disability 32, 140, 143, 146
diversity: in classrooms 146–147; in context of children reading picturebooks 138; selecting picturebooks for research focused on 138–140
Donaldson, J. 94
Doonan, J. 27, 37, 43
Dresang, E. 154, 159
Dunbar, P. 2, 114, 115, 117, 119–122

e-books 124, 126
embodied responses 134
emotional aspect of reading 156
emotional engagement 4, 137
emotional memory 156
empathy 5, 19, 24, 41–42, 46, 73, 90, 108, 114–115, 123, 137, 138, 145, 147, 155–156
English as a foreign or additional language (EFL or EAL) 143–144, 162
environment 37, 43, 47, 70, 91, 96–97, 102, 121, 158, 162, 164, 168
Escovar, M. 108, 109
experiential intelligence 88
expressiveness 89, 90
eye movements by children when reading pictures 51–52

Fancourt, D. 165
feedback loop 125

Fitzwilliam Museum 3, 5, *86,* 92, 94, 98, *98*
focus painting 99
form 89, 90
Frederico, A. 3, 5
funds: of identity 141; of knowledge 141, 154

Galdone, P. 158
García-González, M. 141
Gardner, H. 59, 67, 68, 70, 72, 73, 87
Gayford, M. 95
gender 87, 140, 143, 145, 153, 161
Ghiso, M. 160, 161
Ghosh. K. 161
Gombrich, E. H. 9, 73
graphic novels 144, 152, 157, 159
Gravett, E. 89
Greene, J. 60
Grey, M. 89, 166
Grounded Theory 13, 20–21
group discussions 12

Hacking, C. 166
Hat Monkey app 128–129, 135n3
Hayles, K. 127
Haynes, J. 95
Heath, S. B. 141, 155
Heggernes, S. 144
Here We Are: Notes for Living on Planet Earth (Jeffers) 64
Hockney, D. 95
Hoffman, M. 145
hope 4, 115, 140, 144–145, 152, 164, 167
Hope, J. 145
Housen, A. 91
How Texts Teach What Readers Learn (Meek) 1, 2
Hudelson, S. 140
Husband, T. 147
Hutchins, P.: *Rosie's Walk* 22, 28

identity 99, 137, 138, 141, 143
images: based thinking routines 91–92; learning and understanding 152–153; metaliteracy 53–55; reading 51; and word, interplay between 115
implied author 55
inclusion: in context of children reading picturebooks 138; oriented research design and methodologies 142–143; selecting picturebooks for research focused on 138–140
Inspire project 99–100; Psyche's Dress 100–102; whole class approach to multi-sensory and material exploration *103,* 103–107, *104, 105, 106, 107*
Instagram Live event 96, 111
The Intelligent Eye: Learning to Think by Looking at Art (Perkins) 87
interactive reading of digital texts 125–126, 128
interactivity 125–127
intercultural 137–138, 142, 144, 162
Iordanaki, L. 140
Iser, W. 19, 134

Jeffers, O. 164; *Here We Are: Notes for Living on Planet Earth* 164
Johnson, H. 140
judgement 89, 91

Kai-Kee, E. 92
Kellog, R. 59, 76
Kelly, L. B. 146
Kiefer, B. 13, 18, 21, 52, 154, 157
Kitamura, S. 2, 10, 12, 23–25, *26,* 27, *27,* 29–35, 55–57, 62–64, 89, 90, 154
Knudsen Hawes, L. 140
Kress, G. 58, 73, 121, 127, 152, 154
Kucirkova, N. 126
Kümmerling-Meibauer, B. 38–40, 43, 156

language: learning and understanding 151–152; of syntax applied to visual texts 155
Leeuwen, T. van 58, 121, 127, 152, 154
Lefroy, R. 93
levels of interpretation 14, 140
Lewis, D. 22, 60, 158
LGBTQ 145–146
Lily Takes a Walk (Kitamura) 10, *26, 27*; children drawing 27, *27,* 60; children's own reading/viewing processes 30–31; different perspectives 22–23; humour 22, 23; the implied reader 30–31; intertextuality 27, 29; lack of observation or imagination 24; linking words and pictures 28–29; perspectival counterpoint 23, 53; significance of book as a whole 31–32; vignette: Charlie (9) 33–35, *34;* visual features and artistic intentions 29–30
linguistics 20, 155
literal translation 13
literary apps for children: children's responses to 133–134; digital literary reading 125; empirical research 124; *Hat Monkey* 128–131, *130, 131, 132,* 133; interactivity of 125; *Little Red Riding Hood* 128; *The*

Monster at the End of This Book 128; research design 128; responses to picturebooks 126
Little Red Riding Hood app 128
Littleton, K. 126
Littlewood, K. 145
live-streaming picturebook readings 112
Lohfink, G. 140
looking *vs.* seeing 86
Loya, J. 140
Lysaker, J. 143

Macaulay, D. 160
Mackey, M. 2, 20, 127, 154, 156
Madura, S. 13, 158
Mak, H. W. 165
MAMBO (Museum of Modern Art Bogota): early childhood at 108; picnic at 109–112, *111,* 113, *113, 114;* Picnic de Palabras (Picnic of Words) 108–109
Manguel, A. 50
Margallo, A. M. 125, 126
marginalization 138, 141, 144, 145
Martínez, M. 160
Martin, J. R. 155
Martin, N. 114
Matarasso, F. 92
materiality 140, 156
material turn (Mackey) 156
Mathis, J. 140
Mayhew, J. 3
McAdam, J. E. 16, 141
McClay, J. 160
McGilp, E. 140, 161
McGuire, C. 161
McLeod, N. 93
mediation 20, 124–126, 138, 140, 156, 159–161
medium 89, 90
Meek, M. 1, 2, 23, 164
Merchant, G. 125, 126
metacognitive 59, 67, 80; awareness 40; skills 50–52, 55, 58
metaliteracy: artistic process 55–57; deductions 52–53; how to read a picturebook 51–52; image/text relationship 53–55; thinking, reading, looking, learning 57–58
methodology 14–15, 19–21, 86, 115, 138, 142, 144, 157, 162–163
migration 139, 145–146, 159, 161
The Monster at the End of This Book app 128
moral dimensions 41, 70
Moundiroff, B. B. 108

Mourão, S. 161, 162
multicultural: classrooms 140; education 146; elements 144; picturebooks 140, 144
multilingual: children 140; classrooms 140; picturebooks 140; school 138
multiliteracies/multimodality 157, 161, 163n1
multimodal texts 9, 15, 144, 152, 155, 157, 159, 163n1, 167
Murris, K. 95

Nagel, L. 125
natural world 4, 165
neuroscience 152, 155–156
Nikolajeva, M. 23, 24, 39, 53, 54, 114, 115, 147, 156
Noble, K. 1–3, 20, 35, 91, 92, 98–99, 161, 165
Nodelman, P. 16, 28, 38, 39, 85, 121
non-linear narratives 160

original study: aims of 9; children 10–11; children drawing 13; data analysis 13–14; eliciting response 17–19; group discussions 12; implications for research and pedagogy 14; interviews 11; methodologies 19–21; picturebooks 10, 16–17; research design 9–10; revisiting 12–13; schools 10; well-crafted study 15–16

Pacovska, K. 97
Paley, V. G. 115, 121, 122
Pantaleo, S. 21, 92, 96, 154, 159, 160
paratextual clues 39, 43
parent-child joint reading of digital texts 127
Parsons, M. J. 60, 81, 88, 89, 90, 91
participatory research 163
Paulick, J. 144
Pavlou, V. 95
Penguin (Dunbar): alternative perspective *117,* 118–119, *119;* autistic perspective 122; drawings 115, 118–121, *120;* emotional tension between characters *115,* 116; empathetic lessons 122–123; engagement with 115; interplay between word and image in 115; lack of a setting or background for 115; mark-making *117,* 117–118, *118;* pictorial speech *116,* 116–117, *117*
Pérez Huber, L. 140
performance 20, 52, 80, 91–92, 124, 129, 134, 156, 163
peritextual features of picturebooks 160
Perkins, D. 87, 88, 96: *The Intelligent Eye: Learning to Think by Looking at Art* 87

personal engagement 88
Picnic at the MAMBO, Picnic of Words *see* MAMBO (Museum of Modern Art Bogota)
picturebooks: in the art museum 5, 95; in contexts outside the classroom or home 5, 16, 146–147, 159, 163; disability 146; and EFL/EAL 143–144, 162; future field 162–163; intercultural connections 144; for language learning 144; LGBTQ literature 145–146; migration 145; pioneering and influential scholars in field 157–160; 'real' children respond to picturebooks 157; research on response to specific features 160–161; research on response to specific genres or themes 161–162; research on response with specific groups of readers 162; responding creatively to 94, *95*, 95–96; through making and materials 95–96; visual literacy and 153–156
Piggybook (Browne) 38
play: children's imaginative 129; dramatic 98; media 9; music 129; picturebooks 1, 97
'playing the texts' 164
pop-ups 134, 155
posthumanism 140
postmodernesque 154
postmodern picturebooks 22, 140, 159, 160
Power of Picturebooks 5, 167
Prior, L. 160

race 139–140, 143
Radical Change Theory 154
reader-response theories 141–142
reading together 126
realism 89–90
reflective intelligence 88
refugee 4–5, 138, 142, 145
Reifel, S. 115
representational codes 155
research design 5n1, 9–10, 15, 17, 127, 128, 142–143
research studies 15
Rosenblatt, L. M. 2, 19, 127, 141, 145, 158, 159
Rosie's Walk (Hutchins) 22, 28
Rueda, C. 109
Ryan, M.-L. 127, 162

Sáez Castán, J. 109
Salisbury, M. 90, 153, 160
Satizábal, A. 109
scaffolding 144, 151, 159

Scheffler, A. 94
Scherer, L. 143
schools 10, 96–100, 103, 127
Scieszka, J. 3
Scott, C. 23, 24, 39, 53, 54, 115, 156
Sedberry, T. 143
Sedgwick, D. 59
Sedgwick, F. 59
del Sellaio, J. 98
semiotics 20, 127, 154
Sendak, M. 89, 158
Serafini, F. 85, 115, 155, 159
The Shape Game (Browne) 3
Shelley, D. 4
Short, K.G. 140
Sipe, L. R. 21, 142, 145, 151, 154, 157–161
Sis, P. 144
slow looking: as a learnable practice 92, 97; together in art museum 86–87
Slow Looking: The Art and Practice of Learning Through Observation (Tishman) 87
Smith, K. 140
Smith, L. 3
Snap Chat 96
social interaction, through language 151
Solórzano, D.G. 140
special needs 33, 100, 146, 162
structuralism 152
style 89, 90
Styles, M. 1, 3, 124, 127, 153, 158, 159, 160
surrealism 37, 39, 89
Swaggerty, E. 161
systemic-functional theory 155

tactility 156
Tan, S. 89, 109
teaching close looking 97
teaching drawing 68
teaching visual literacy 80
textual markers 43
Thomas, E. E. 139, 145
Thunberg, G. 164
TikTok 96
Tishman, S.: *Slow Looking: The Art and Practice of Learning Through Observation* 87
transmediation 160
The Tunnel (Browne) 10; artistic process 57; children drawing 60, 65, *65*; children's response to 1, 59, 136; emotional reactions to 90, 137; perspectival counterpoint 53, 54; readers' deductive processes 52; reading images 51; realism 89

Unsworth, L. 155

Van Allsburg, C. 109, 158
Vehabovic, N. 145
Vermeule, B. 156
vignettes: of Amelia and Becky, *Hat Monkey* 129, 130, *130, 131,* 133; Charlie (9), *Lily* 33–35, *34*; Lara (10), *Zoo* 47–49; Yu (4), *Zoo* 76–80, *77, 79*
Vilela, R.L.S. 125, 126
A village festival in Honour of St Hubert and St Anthony (Brueghel, Pieter the Younger, Fitzwilliam Museum) *86,* 87
visual and verbal narrative 32, 96, 99, 102
visual cognition 155
visual literacy: development of 92–93; education 95–96; and picturebooks 153–156
visual metaphors 1, 18, 44, 48, 156
Visual Thinking Strategies (VTS) 91; accountative viewers 91; classifying viewers 91; constructive viewers 91; interpretative viewers 91; re-creative viewers 91
Vygotsky, L. 41, 92, 151

Watson, V. 158
well-crafted study 15–16
wide-spectrum cognition 88
Wiesner, D. 158
Wilkinson, D. 2

Willson, A. 160
Willy's Pictures (Browne) 3
Window (Baker) 164
Wolfberg, P. J. 122
Wolf, M. 156
wordless picturebooks 20, 140, 143, 144, 160, 162, 164
word/picture dynamics 53
words and pictures telling different stories 34
written and pictorial narrative 31
Wu, J. 153

YouTube 110, 124

zone of proximal development (ZPD) 151
Zoo (Browne) 10; affective and moral dimensions 41–43; analysing visual imagery 43–45; artistic process 56, 57, 62; children drawing 60, *61, 62,* 63, *63, 64,* 64–65, 69–70, *70, 71,* 72–74, *74, 75,* 76–80, *77, 79*; children's response to 1, 136; emotional reactions to 90; empathy and personal analogy 46–47; the gorilla 45–46; group discussions 40, 46; ironic picturebooks 38–39; perplexing features 40–41; perspectival counterpoint 53, 54; reading images 51; realism 89; seeing and thinking 39–40; vignette: Lara (10) 47–49; vignette: Yu (4) 76–80, *77, 79*; visual analysis of 37–38